297
K53i

D0796990

Islam Uncensored

14 Leaders:

Liberals, Conservatives, Muslims,

Jews, Atheists,

Christians

And

A Former CIA Director

Reveal:

What Government and Media

Won't Tell You About Islam

Jeff King

San Diego Christian Colle
Library
Santee, CA

"Islam Uncensored–14 Leaders: Liberals, Conservatives, Muslims, Jews, Atheists, Christians, and A Former CIA Director

Reveal: What Government and Media Won't Tell You About Islam"

Copyright © 2011, 2012 by Jeff King

All rights reserved. No part of this book may be reproduced or transmitted in any form or by any means without written permission of the author.

ISBN 10: 0578082799
ISBN 13: 9780578082790

ACKNOWLEDGMENTS

This book represents thousands of hours of work from many sources who wish to remain anonymous. I would like to acknowledge D.G., A.D., D.H., Tracy T. and Shari C. for their incredible investment of time and effort that went into the creation of this book.

TABLE OF CONTENTS

Anjem Choudary is a radical Islamist in the UK who founded "Islam4UK" which was shut down by the British government. One expert reported that one in six people in prison on terror charges in the UK are connected with Choudary. Choudary explains that Islam is not "a religion of peace."

Robert Spencer, an author of nine books on Islam, gives a broad overview of Islam.

Ayaan Hirsi Ali was born the Muslim daughter of a Somali warlord. She emigrated to Holland where she became a member of Parliament and an outspoken feminist/atheist critic of Islam, especially in regards to Islam's treatment of women. Due to death threats and the assassination of a friend and collaborator, she was forced to flee to the US. She is the author of several books.

Nonie Darwish grew up as the Muslim daughter of a high-ranking Egyptian military officer tasked with guerilla warfare operations against Israel. After emigrating to the US, she left Islam and became a Christian and author of two books on Islam.

Mosab Hassan Yousef grew up as the son of one of the founders of Hamas. He was Palestinian royalty! Captured by Israel, he spent time in Israeli jails for terrorism. He spied for Israel, alerting them to approaching suicide bombers, and eventually left Islam and converted to Christianity. His perspective on Islam and the Middle East is fascinating.

Wafa Sultan, a psychiatrist, is a former Muslim (now an atheist) who has written two books about Islam. She exploded onto the world scene after and Al Jazeera-televised debate with a bullying Muslim cleric. In the middle of his rant, she shouted five famous words: "Shut up, it's my turn!" She then went on to list the problems with radical Islam. The video of the debate went viral and swept around the world. She lives under constant threat of death and has to move every six months.

Dr. Ahmed Mansur, an Islamic reformer and a former professor at the world's premier Islamic university discusses the Muslim Brotherhood, the role of Saudi Arabia in radicalizing Islam, and his efforts to reform Islam.

Stephen Suleyman Schwartz is a convert to Islam. He exposes the Saudi role in radicalizing the world's Muslims.

R. James Woolsey, a Democrat and a former director of the CIA under President Clinton, talks about Saudi Arabia and how to defeat radical Islam.

Bat Yeor discusses dhimmitude: Islamic laws and restrictions designed to slowly strangle and kill other faiths in Islamic cultures.

Douglas Murray is the head of the Centre for Social Cohesion, the first British think tank to specialize in the study of radicalization and extremism within Britain. Murray talks about dealing with radical Islam within a democracy, Islam and Europe, and social cohesion.

Steven Emerson twice testified to the US Congress prior to 9/11, warning of a coming attack from radical Islam that would include massive deaths of Americans. He is a known expert on American jihad.

Andrew Bostom, a Brown University professor and an atheist, talks about Islamic history and says "no other civilization has enslaved as many people as has Islam."

Introduction

The intersection of Islam and the West is a highly contentious space. Some people speak of the struggle between Christians and Jews on one side, and Muslims on the other as a "war of civilizations." Critics of Islam point to September 11, and other acts of terrorism to say that Islam is violent, while Muslims and their defenders call Islam a "religion of peace."

The average person in the midst of their busy life has little time or inclination to do research, get to the bottom of this puzzle and answer the question, "What is Islam?"

Westerners desperately need answers to this vital question. As I set out to write a book to answer this question, I came to the humbling realization that in the end, it didn't matter what I had to say. The issue has become so politicized and polarized that readers that are aligned with me in terms of politics, religion, or worldview would accept my views, while those on the other side of the philosophical fence would reject my views, seeing them as hopelessly biased due to whatever factors that separate us ideologically.

It was at that point that I set out to create a book about Islam that didn't exist. I decided to interview a broad cross spectrum of experts on Islam that reflected our fractured and discordant culture: leftists, right wingers, atheists, Muslims, Jews, Christians, feminists, etc. I decided to interview experts from all ends of the spectrum(s) to discuss Islam and discover any common threads of truth.

I started by interviewing a radical Islamist that is known for his candor. From there, I interviewed a popular, established author and critic of Islam. I went on to interview four ex-Muslims whose views span the political spectrum; two are atheists and two have converted to Christianity. One was a feminist and another was the son of one of the founders of the terrorist group Hamas. I then interviewed two Muslim reformers, a historian who grew up as a Muslim, an expert on Islam and Western culture, an expert on *dhimmitude* (Islam's laws on dealing with sub-cultures within Islamic nations), and finally an ex-director of the CIA.

Though I'm certain war would break out if these experts were ever locked in a room together and told to define Islam, the aspects of Islam on which they agree are stunning. Out of their incredible diversity of worldview, political orientation, and religious views, there are very clear, recurring, and disturbing points of agreement.

Obviously, I won't give those away at the beginning of the book, and ultimately they are yours to discover. For now, I will simply remind you that this is ***Islam: Uncensored***!

A RADICAL
ISLAMIST
SPEAKS CANDIDLY

Chapter One:

The Islamist

Anjem Choudary was challenged to condemn Islam's targeting of innocent victims, specifically speaking of the victims of the London tube bombings.

"Look, at the end of the day, when we say 'innocent people' we mean Muslims—as far as non-Muslims are concerned, they have not accepted Islam and that is a crime against God…. If you are a Muslim then you're innocent in the eyes of God. If you're a non-Muslim then you're guilty of not believing in God."

(See Author's Notes p. 21)

Anjem Choudary

Anjem Choudary is a British Islamist. What makes him so fascinating is that he is completely open about his extremist views and the sources of those views (the Qur'an, Hadith, and Sira[1]). He is a fundamentalist and will tell you quite plainly that all non-Muslims are legitimate targets and that converts that depart from Islam should be killed (as Muhammad decreed). He will also cite chapter and verse from the Qur'an/Hadith on any extreme view he has. This is what makes him a fly in the ointment for governments and media elites that are pushing the "Islam is a religion of peace" angle. The truth is that Muhammad was very violent and his actions and views were encoded into the holy books of Islam. Because Choudary is not only outspoken, but clearly a fundamentalist (adhering to the core teachings of Muhammad), he must be silenced. That is why the press labels him as a buffoon and a laughing stock, etc.

He was a spokesman for a now banned Islamist group known as Islam4UK. He makes frequent appearances on CNN, BBC, and other major mainstream media. One expert on terrorism in the UK told ICC that one in six people imprisoned on terrorism charges in the UK were associated with Choudary.

Prepare to be fascinated.

---

[1]See pg. 340.

JEFF KING: Mr. Choudary, I want to start off by saying how much I respect you. Many would think I'm crazy to say that, but you are refreshing because you are honest. You tell the truth. You know we don't always run into that with Islamic leaders. We study the Qur'an. We understand the Qur'an, the Hadith, and Muhammad and so we know what you're saying about Islam is correct. I just want to say upfront that I respect your honesty and it's refreshing. (See author's note #1, pg. 21).

What would you say is the Qur'anic definition of *Taqiyya*?

Taqiyya[2] is associated with the Shiite branch or sect in Islam. Taqiyya is to say something but not really to believe it in the heart. It is tantamount to lying. There is no concept of Taqiyya in Islam as far as we are concerned. We (Sunni Islam) have *Tauria*.[3]

Tauria is to say something which could have two meanings in order to defend your life or your honor or your property. Otherwise lying is completely prohibited in Islam.

The only time when lying is allowed is in three situations:

First, for example, at war in the battlefield if the enemy is asking you where the supplies were, then I have an obligation not to tell him. (Secondly) if you want to reconcile two people I can say to one, "Look, he really likes you," that may incline their hearts together. The third is on the issue of the husband and wife (white lies such as: "Do I look good in this dress?").

JEFF KING: So then, you're a fundamentalist. You're trying to live your life by the commands of the Qur'an, the Hadith and Muhammad's life, and that's why you're honest. Because you

---

[2] See pg. 346.

[3] See pg. 346.

say wait a minute, it's not correct for me to deceive or lie except under these circumstances.

You know, honesty is something which every Muslim should have. I mean the Prophet once said that a Muslim could fall into sin, but when asked about lying, he said a Muslim never lies. Therefore truth and the soundness of the truth is something which is part and parcel of our belief, part of our character.

JEFF KING: So many other fundamentalist Muslim leaders will not tell the truth as you do on any number of subjects, whether it's in regards to jihad, women, or terrorism. They'll have one message in the West and have one message at home. Is this because they have a misunderstanding of Taqiyya? What's going on there?

I do believe that we live in strange times. When you talk about basic concepts of Islam, when you talk about Sharia, and the role of women, et cetera, Muslims are being brought up in a non-Islamic environment where they don't teach about Islam. We live in an environment where it's very difficult for Muslims who don't even know the basics of Islam. And we even have people who are Imams and scholars who just study about, if you like, ritual acts and they don't have the knowledge about the transactions, about the foreign policy, about jihad and things like that. But they're put in a position where they're forced to answer questions. And you have so many so-called representative bodies really made up of businessmen and others who never really have a deep understanding of Islam and therefore we get this range of obfuscation, really, about the real issue and the meaning of concepts like jihad, the Sharia, khilafah (Caliphate),[4] and so on. So that's why it's quite refreshing when you meet people like Sheik Omar Bakri Muhammad, Sheikh Abu Qatada, Sheikh Ayman al-Zahrawi (See author's note #2, pg. 21), Sheikh Abu

---

[4] See pg. 339.

Muhammad al-Maqdasi (See author's note #3, pg. 21), and so on. These are the real scholars. When you meet them, they won't compromise and they have good knowledge about the other areas as well.

JEFF KING: And yet I would say even those Muslims who have a solid understanding of Islam will say the right [radical] things at home, but when they're in a democracy or in the West, they'll feel pressure, and they'll hide what they truly believe.

One of the problems that we have is that many of the people who would say the kind of things that I'm saying, or people like Sheikh Omar Bakri Muhammad, they're behind bars. I do believe there are three types of Muslims nowadays: those who are in prison, those who are on their way to prison, and those people who are not really practicing.

JEFF KING: Which points to the idea that if a Muslim has a worldview that they are at war with the West, he could employ Taqiyya to lie in interviews with the Western world in order to protect himself?

Yes, but from purely a Sharia perspective, it would not be allowed.

JEFF KING: Many paint you as radical or fringe Muslim in terms of your views. But, you tell me, are your views extreme from a Muslim perspective?

For those who believe in liberal democracy, I know it's extreme. But as far as the Sharia [adhering to fundamental Islam] is concerned, I don't believe that my views are extreme at all. And I believe this categorization of people who are extreme and radical and moderate, and so on, is deliberately orchestrated by the media to isolate certain individuals so they can be picked on, vilified, and arrested. So I don't subscribe to this classification at all.

JEFF KING: I would even say it's coming from somewhere deeper than the media. I would say the media is being directed.

They've been given a handbook, so to speak, and they've been given marching orders to play a chess game. It's a chess game that will try to divide the so-called moderate and the so-called radical and to shame the radical into silence. Do you agree with that?

Yeah. I agree with it, and I think the media do not work in isolation. Certainly, they are the right hand of the government.

JEFF KING: Many people say Islam is a religion of peace, but in reality the Qur'an is full of references to violent acts. What is your take on this? Is Islam a religion of peace?

Well, the word Islam is not derived from *salam,* as people say, which is like peace. Rather, it means submission, *istislaam.* So the Muslim is the one who submits. Islam is submission, the Muslim is the submitter. We submit to the Sharia and the Sharia is encapsulated with many, many duties and responsibilities, one of which is jihad. *So nobody can say that Islam is a religion of peace.*

We can live peacefully together. We lived for 800 years in peace with Jews and Christians [in Spain/Andalusia]. But certainly where the land is occupied and where Muslim life or property is being attacked, then we will respond to that. And that is not peaceful.

JEFF KING: But in living in peace, you're saying under dhimmitude. If they're living in a Qur'anic state, and if Jews and Christians are obeying the laws of dhimmitude, we can live at peace. Is that what you're saying?

Well, what I'm saying to you is, if we live together in a society where the life, the honor, and the property of all the citizens is protected, they are given free food, clothing and shelter; where they are given resources like electricity, gas, water, et cetera, free of charge, which are all guaranteed under Islam [to provide]; and where they are allowed to practice their own religious beliefs in terms of the ritual aspects of [their beliefs]. But as far as the society is concerned, they are governed by certain laws, which you know, for me, must be the divine laws, then we can live together and you know societies have proven that they can survive like that.

Spain is a good example of where the Jews, Christians and Muslims lived together. When the inquisition started with Queen Isabella and King Ferdinand, the Jews ran to the Islamic State in Africa for sanctuary. So they found themselves protected and looked after and it was a very flourishing time for Christians and Jews in terms of their texts and translations into different languages, and so on.

JEFF KING: But again, what you're saying is we can live at peace if we're all living under the divine laws, living under Sharia, and Christians or Jews are living within the rules of Sharia (dhimmitude)?

That's correct. You've got it. What I would say to you is that this issue of you all being a *dhimmi* (see author's note #4, p. 22). You know I agree with you that they would be dhimmi, but the dhimmi is not required to be part of the army. They are protected by the Muslim army. Their life and honor and dignity are protected. The churches and synagogues which have been around for over a thousand years in places like Syria and Lebanon are testimony to the fact that we don't have this concept of ethnic cleansing. I mean they can survive there. They've got the same cross [on the church] in Damascus that they had one thousand years ago.

You know it was not our policy to do what happened in Sarajevo and what happened for example in India, and Gaza and other places. We don't have this concept of wanting people out. They can practice their own religion. They can have their own places of worship. But of course there's law and order publicly. I think this is the debate: Does sovereignty belong to man or does it belong to God? I believe it belongs to God.

JEFF KING: There are many verses (in the Qur'an and Hadith) that make it clear that part of dhimmitude is for the Muslims to humiliate the *dhimmi*, to make it difficult to live in their religion. And when you're taking *jizya*,[5] you slap him across the face. That's Hadith, I think. What was created was a system to make it difficult to live under another religion. So it's not a happy state to live as a Christian or Jew within an Islamic state.

Well, you know, I think you got to be careful from where you're taking your information. There's nothing authentic to say that when people pay jizya you slap them across the face (see author's notes #5-6, pp. 23-24).

JEFF KING: But you understand the reference that I am quoting?

I have studied this topic in detail and there is no reference like that which is authentic. And I think there are people, we call them Orientalists, who study Islam from a Western perspective. If you have the objective of worshipping Allah and you really want to authenticate and verify every text of the Hadith narration, then I think you would agree that this particular narration that you're talking about doesn't exist and has been fabricated. There's no instance or example where people are slapped in paying the jizya.

JEFF KING: So-called moderate Muslims would argue that Islam is hijacked by terrorists. They would say you're a terrorist, whether by act or by your views. Again, do you agree with that? Are you hijacking Islam?

Well, no, I believe there is a place for terrorism in Islam. Note terrorizing enemies is mentioned in Sura 8:60. Allah said, "Prepare as much as you can in skills of war in order to terrorize the enemy."

---

[5] See pg. 344.

Now, we are not talking about the propagation of Islam, but when you're fighting someone in the battlefield, obviously you'll kill each other. You terrorize each other trying to win the battle. So, in the context of fighting in jihad, then, terrorism is certainly part and parcel of jihad.

JEFF KING: The fighting, though, doesn't have to be defensive. I would say that history has shown that Islam was expansionist by design. What did Muhammad say? What was he sent to do? Until the whole world understood that there is one God and it is submitted to Him? So the attacks don't have to be defensive, they can be offensive. Is that correct?

It is correct that there are two types of jihad. There's jihad *daft'*, which is defensive jihad, to defend life or property. And there's something called jihad *mubada'ah* which is offensive jihad. And this particular one is carried out by the Islamic state as a foreign policy, to remove obstacles in the way of implementing the Sharia outside of its boundaries. So certainly there would never be a year which goes by without at least one expedition to conquer other lands and to put them under the Sharia. And we believe that the Sharia is a mercy for mankind.

We believe the divine law will take people out of the shackles and the oppression of man-made law into the beauty and justice of Islam. In an ironic way, that's really what the British and the Americans were doing in Iraq. They said, "Look, these people are being oppressed. Let's go over there forcibly and remove the regime and implement democracy." On the other hand, Muslims obviously don't believe in that kind of oppressive regime, and we don't believe in democracy and freedom. But when we say, "Look, under an Islamic state, we will have a foreign policy to do justice and remove oppression," people will suddenly ask how they are expected to accept that. Well, the Americans have been doing that for the last one hundreed years, even the British.

JEFF KING: Agreed. But the point is that Islam is by nature expansionist. So it's not just designed to free people from oppression, but it's to bring the world under Islam. It's God's way. It's God's law. That's legitimate?

But let me make one distinction. [The Qur'an says] *"Do not compel people to become Muslim."* Nobody will ever be compelled to become a Muslim. However, the Sharia, the divine law, must be implemented as a law and order in the public arena. So, the ruling system, the judiciary, the economic system, et cetera, will be according to the law of the land. But what they do in private, what they do in their own homes, what they do in their own churches, in their synagogues, is really their business. Nobody's going to be spying upon them.

JEFF KING: But within the idea that Islam is expansionist, as a Muslim you don't have to compel anybody. They are free to live, under dhimmitude, that is, if they're people of the book—Jews or Christians. But Islam is expansionist. It is supposed to take territory and bring the world under submission to God. Islam is submission.

That's true. It is correct because Allah said in the Qur'an, I believe in 9:33, he said, "The Prophet was sent by God with all the guidance and ideology of truth for it to be dominant upon all other beliefs and ideologies no matter what the polytheistic people think."

So, certainly, you know, we do believe in the concept of the domination of the world by Islam. We have many prophecies that, in fact, one day the whole world will be under the authority of Muslims.

JEFF KING: That's why it's refreshing to talk to you, because you will just come out and say the truth. What should happen to a Muslim who converts to Christianity under Sharia?

Well, the messenger Muhammad said "whoever changes his religion, kill him." So there is a capital punishment.

It's a one-way conversion. Once you become a Muslim, there's no going back. It's part of the Sharia law. You cannot go back to any other belief. But the Muslim is given a certain amount of time to study about his religion. And, obviously, when you're living under the Sharia, there will be Islamic education. There will not be this public propagation of any other religion and ideology. So, this kind of thing will be very rare but, certainly, there is capital punishment. It will be assessed by a judge and you will be given a certain amount of time, maybe, to...

JEFF KING: To repent.

You're given time. It could be three days, three weeks, three months. It could even be up to one year. And then, after that, if they're not convinced and they don't realize their mistake, then there's capital punishment.

JEFF KING: Now what about Christians and Jews? What restrictions would they live under within a Sharia state in the UK?

Well, they will have many rights. The Jews and Christians will have many rights living under the Sharia. As I said, what they do in their own homes is their own business. In the meantime, they will have free food, clothing and shelter. And they do not need to be part of the army. They are protected by the army and they can travel freely within the Islamic state, apart from certain areas, but they can pass through. They cannot live in certain places like Mecca and Medina.[6] But they can travel and they can trade freely. So, there will be a lot

---

[6] See pg. 344.

of divine rights which are given, but they're divine rights, they're not man-made.

JEFF KING: You are speaking of rights but I'm asking about the restrictions. What are the restrictions?

Well, non-Muslims will not be able to propagate their own religion publicly or openly, although we can have debates on television and things like that. They will not be able to propagate their own religion in the streets and convert people or try to convert the people away from Islam. And they will not be allowed to create any kind of hardships for Muslims by trying to put doubt in their minds about Islam, about the Qur'an, about the Prophet, and so on. Obviously, they will not be allowed to insult the Prophet in any way.

They will have respect for the Muslims. And the non-Muslims, as well, must be respected. On his death bed, one of the last things that the Prophet said was, "I will be a plaintiff against the one who oppressed the dhimmi on the Day of Judgment." So (he said) I will be against him in the court and I will be against him in favor of the *dhimmi*. So to harm them in any way is not allowed...

JEFF KING: That is, if they're obeying the laws of dhimmitude, they should not be harmed. Is that correct?

That's true.

JEFF KING: Are they going to pay a tax?

The *zakat*[7] is 2.5% in terms of wealth and different in terms of cattle, crops and so on.

---

[7] See pg. 346.

It's quite small, though, because the actual jiyza, even if we take the upper limit among scholars, is about four dinars.[8] The middle limit is two dinars, and for those people who only have the basics, is one dinar. And the women and the children and the elderly, those people who are ill, they would never need to pay. It's only taken from the young man. And, in return, he is protected.

If you think about it, one dinar is 4.25 grams of gold and I believe 1 gram of gold is about 25 pounds. So that amounts, let's say, to 150 pounds. Four dinar, let's say, is about 600 pounds. You will never pay anything more than that as a dhimmi. Six hundred pounds a year is all you will pay, but the zakat is a lot more than that. If you are a Muslim and have money, you pay a lot more.

JEFF KING: So, they're treated differently. The Christian and Jews will have to pay a tax that Muslims don't have to pay. You're saying it's small...

They will be treated differently.

JEFF KING: Do you consider yourself to be a British citizen, primarily a British citizen?

Well, it depends on what you see. I see the citizenship as merely, you know, kind of classification by the non-Muslims and I see my passport as a mere travel document. I'm a Muslim first and last. If I'm American, I [would see myself] as a Muslim living in America.

JEFF KING: Is the goal of Islam to dominate and take over Europe?

Europe, the whole world. That is the reason why Allah sent Muhammad. For the domination of the world by Islam.

---

[8] See pg. 340.

JEFF KING: What is the strategy to take over Europe, to bring Europe under subjection?

There's only four ways in which any nation will come under the Sharia. One of them is that the people themselves will embrace Islam. That could happen. It happened in quite a few places. Or alternatively, a certain section of the community might decide that they want to overthrow their regime and come under the Sharia. Thirdly, it could happen by the kind of war scenarios that we have nowadays. For example, in Afghanistan, Iraq, and Somalia. Once the war finishes, the Muslims could find themselves in authority. And then, four, it could happen via a foreign policy.

JEFF KING: On your website you showed how Buckingham Palace would be converted to a mosque one day. What are you trying to say? What's your message there?

Well, you know, a lot of publicity is for generating debate and discussion. I mean Buckingham may not be a mosque, but what we're saying is—look, under the Sharia there'll be no monarchy and obviously there'll be no palaces for monarchs. So we need to make use of those buildings, one of the possibilities is it could be a mosque. A mosque is not just for prayer. A mosque is a hospital. It's a refuge. It's a place where people study. It's just one of the options, but it did generate a big discussion and that is why we have discussions like we're having now, so that we can get to the truth.

JEFF KING: Theo van Gogh, a Dutch filmmaker, was killed (after he made a movie critical of Islam). Do you think people who criticize Islam or defame Muhammad should be killed, if they're not Muslim?

Not people who criticize Islam, but certainly anyone who attacks the honor of the Prophet has a capital punishment. The Prophet said that very clearly. Now, somebody would argue, is that the job of an individual or is it the job of the state? Ultimately, we don't go around just killing people. There is a law and order. Usually, this would come before a Sharia judge to assess the situation. He will see if in fact a crime has been committed, and he will implement the capital punishment. In the absence of the Sharia as a law and order, there is no judge nowadays and people say, "Look, the honor of the Prophet belongs to each one of us. It does not belong only to the state to decide to defend." And, therefore, under that guise, people will take into their own hands. So they have a legitimate argument, but ultimately I would say it is something that should be assessed by a Sharia judge.

JEFF KING: Many people are familiar with the demonstrators in London with the radical signs saying to kill those who defame Islam, et cetera. Was it your group that was holding up the signs and marching?

We organized that demonstration. What you need to understand is that at demonstrations people hold placards and those placards are going to be provocative and you don't want to take them literally. I mean if something said, "Bomb, bomb Denmark," nobody is really going to bomb their homeland. So I think you want to look at the placards in context and the context of any group that holds a demonstration.

JEFF KING: But, at the same, time many of those placards were in line with the Qur'an, with the Hadith. It says behead those who insult Islam.

You cannot take that literally and just apply that everywhere. That's not correct, and if you said something disparaging about Islam to me, you know I'm not going to behead you. But the rules under the Islamic state are different. Certainly, under an Islamic state, if someone insulted Islam or insulted the Prophet then, obviously, he would lose his covenant of security and, therefore, that would be quite serious for him; you know, the implications of that. Therefore, it's different when living under the Sharia. But, nowadays, I don't think anyone is doing that if you just insulted Islam, unless you obviously attacked the honor of the Prophet.

JEFF KING: But if they attacked the honor of the Prophet, they should be killed. Again, under Sharia, there's one way to do it, but we don't have Sharia, so they're subject to people taking it into their own hands.

People do take it in their own hands.

JEFF KING: Muhammad was married to Aisha when she was only six. He consummated the marriage when she turned nine. Do you think this example should be followed?

Well, one has to have criteria on when someone becomes mature, and when they are allowed, for example, to get married and so on. And ultimately, there are some things in the life of a Prophet which you are not allowed to imitate. For example, in the social area in the marriage, he can marry more than four wives and he had various things that we are not allowed to do, but he needed that role as a Prophet. But, in terms of when someone becomes mature and you are allowed to marry them, maturity in Islam begins when the woman begins her menses.

So the menses, for the lower limit, might be nine. And, obviously, by the time of fifteen, everyone usually reaches their menses. So, it is when the woman reaches her menses that she becomes mature, and, therefore, she's subject to get married and consummate the marriage.

JEFF KING: So, just to clarify, under Islamic law, nine will be the lower limit and it is legitimate to marry her as long as she has started her menstruation.

If she begins her menses, yeah.

JEFF KING: You called for the destruction of democracy and the concept of human rights. Why?

Well, I think democracy and human rights are man-made and, therefore, fallible and oppressive. Allah said in the Qur'an, "Those who rule and judge by other than what Allah has unveiled they are the disbelievers. They are the oppressors. They are the people who are sinful." So I believe it is oppression. Democracy is oppression. And I don't believe that the majority of the people should decide what is good for mankind. I don't think they can decide. We have to have criteria, and I believe that there's man-made law and divine law, sovereignty of man or sovereignty of God. I believe sovereignty belongs to God.

So I do believe in the superiority of Islam and I believe in the injustice and the oppression of man-made law as manifested in freedom, democracy, human rights, and so on. But it's not because we don't have an alternative. I mean we have a better alternative. The Prophet said, "Islam is superior and will never be surpassed."

JEFF KING: There's no church within Saudi Arabia, and yet Muslims are allowed to construct mosques all over the world. What's the double standard?

It's not a question of double standards. It's a question of what the divine law says. If you believe in freedom and democracy and you believe that mosques can be built anywhere, then that's your own ideology and that's your own way of life. You should abide by that. But we don't believe in that, and the fact that we could take advantage of the freedom and the liberalism that you may have does not mean that we give any credence to that. I think it's not a question of double standards. It's a question of abiding by what you believe.

AUTHOR'S NOTES:

#1: Choudary is a Syrian-born Islamist who lived in the UK. In 2005, he left the UK and the British officials refused to allow him to return, arguing his return is "not conducive to the public good." During his stay in the UK he successfully developed a radical Islamic group, Hizb ut-Tahrir, into a major Islamic organization. He later left the group and headed al-Muhajiroun, a UK-based Islamic extremist group which was disbanded in 2005. He currently lives in Lebanon.

Among his statements is included: "*We don't make a distinction between civilians and non-civilians, innocents and non-innocents. Only between Muslims and unbelievers. And the life of an unbeliever has no value. It has no sanctity.*" In a statement to the *Daily Mail* he said, "*When I first heard about [the September 11, 2001, attacks], there was some initial delight about such an attack. I received a phone call and said, 'Oh, wow, the United States has come under attack.' It was exciting.*"

#2: Egyptian-born medical doctor and founder of the Egyptian Islamic Jihad. He is currently believed to be the second-in-command within al-Qaeda. He has been referred to as the "real brains" of al-Qaeda and has emerged as al-Qaeda's operational and strategic commander.

#3: Maqdisi is an infamous Islamist who is known for being the spiritual mentor for Jordanian terrorist Abu Musab al-Zarqawi, the initial leader of al-Qaeda in Iraq. According to the *New York Times*, Maqdisi even influenced Osman bin Laden through his speech and writings.

According to a study by the Combating Terrorism Center of the United States Military Academy (USMA), Maqdisi "is the most influential living Jihadi Theorist," and that, "by all measures, Maqdisi is the key contemporary ideologue in the jihadi intellectual universe." He currently lives under house arrest in Jordan.

#4: *Dhimmitude* comes from the Arabic word dhimmi, which literally means "protected." In an Islamic state, dhimmis are Jews, Christians and other non-Muslims. They are subjected to discrimination, humiliation and subjugation. They are also forced to pay special tax called *jizya*.

#5: Jizya: From leading dhimmitude historian Bat Ye'or's book *Islam and Dhimmitude: Where Civilizations Collide*:

> The numerous sources consulted seem to confirm that measures to ensure humiliation were applied to Jewish and Christian dhimmis at all times over the whole *dar al-Islam*.

> Verse 9:29 of the Qur'an links the obligation of jihad to the exaction of the jizya. In theory, women, the poor, the sick, and the infirm were exempt from the poll tax; however, Armenian, Syrian, Serbian, and Jewish sources offer abundant proof that the jizya was demanded from children, widows, orphans, and even the dead.

> Anyone who left their homes without their receipt for the jizya or who had lost it incurred the greatest danger. In the Ottoman Empire, the receipt had to be produced on pain of immediate imprisonment, at the demand of the tax collectors who stopped dhimmis–recognizable by their distinctive dress–in the street.

> According to the Shafi'i rite, as described by an-Nawawi in the thirteenth century: "The infidel who wishes to pay his poll tax must be treated with disdain by the collector: the collector remains seated and the infidel remains standing in front of him, his head bowed and his back bent. The infidel personally must place the money on the scales, *while the collector holds him by his beard and strikes him on both cheeks*" (emphasis added).

According to the Moroccan jurist al-Maghili (d. 1504), whose preachings incited pillage of Jews and their slaughter in the Gurara and Tuat oases in the fifteenth century: "On the day of payment they [the dhimmis] shall be assembled in a public place ... They should be standing there waiting in the lowest and dirtiest place. The acting officials representing the Law shall be placed above them and shall adopt a threatening attitude so that it seems to them, as well as to the others, that our object is to degrade them by pretending to take their possessions. They will realize we are doing them a favor (again) in accepting from them the jizya and letting them (thus) go free. Then they shall be dragged one by one (to the official responsible) for the exacting of payment. When paying, the dhimmi will receive a blow and will be thrust aside so that he will think that he has escaped the sword through this (insult). *This is the way that the friends of the Lord, of the first and last generations will act toward their infidel enemies, for might belongs to Allah, to His Apostle, and to the Believer*" [emphasis added].

(Ye'or, Bat. *Islam and Dhimmitude: Where Civilizations Collide*. Cranbury: Associated University Presses, 2002. 69-70, 90.)

Historically, a dhimmi could not ride a horse, but he could ride an ass or a donkey. If they were caught on a horse, they could be pulled off and beaten. When a dhimmi met a Muslim on the sidewalk, he had to step out into the street and let the Muslim pass. The dhimmi also had to wear special clothing or, if not special clothing, a belt or a patch on the clothing to immediately identify a person as a dhimmi. The only protection that a Christian or a Jew had would be to make Muslim friends because many times the Muslim friend could keep the weight of dhimmi laws off of his Christian or Jewish friend.

The persecution of the dhimmis was unrelenting. It went on for generation after generation. Finally, the dhimmi would give up and become a Muslim. All of a sudden, he had more money because he didn't have to pay the jizya tax.

#6: The amount of money paid as jizya tax varied from time to time and place to place. There were instances in which the payments were so onerous that the dhimmis converted to Islam in order to stop paying it (Muslims are not required to pay the tax.) Interestingly, some Muslims rulers prohibited conversion to Islam in order to continue getting the lucrative jizya tax. For detail on this, please see:

http://wikiislam.net/wiki/Jizyah#cite_note-0.

An Overview of

Islam

Chapter Two:

The Watchman

In Islam, there is no recognized orthodox mainstream sect of Islam or school of Islamic jurisprudence that does not teach warfare against unbelievers and the necessity to subjugate them violently under the rule of Islamic law. In Islam, the traditional authorities all teach warfare against unbelievers, and you don't find any that don't. So this is not a matter of a few extremists in a corner; it is a mainstream teaching.

Robert Spencer

Robert Spencer is the director of Jihad Watch, a program of the David Horowitz Freedom Center. He is also the author of ten books, including the *New York Times* bestsellers *The Truth About Muhammad* and *The Politically Incorrect Guide to Islam (and the Crusades)*. He is a weekly columnist for *Human Events* and *FrontPage Magazine*, and also leads seminars on Islam and jihad.

He is outspoken about Islam and when I asked him if he was in danger, he had this to say:

> *"I receive a great many death threats—lately, on a daily basis. I'm on the al-Qaeda hit list. Adam Gadahn, the first American to be tried with treason since World War II, is somebody who has named me specifically in a video. He is high up in al-Qaeda, and so I think that (my) assassination is a very real possibility. But if Americans are not willing to stand up and defend their society, laws and customs, then we will lose them. We have to be willing to take some risks."*

Books by Robert Spencer:
- *The Complete Infidel's Guide to the Qur'an*
- *Stealth Jihad*
- *Religion of Peace?*

- *The Truth about Muhammad*
- *The Politically Incorrect Guide to Islam (and the Crusades)*
- *The Myth of Islamic Tolerance*
- *Onward Muslim Soldiers*
- *Islam Unveiled*
- *Inside Islam*
- *The PostAmerican Presidency by Pamela Geller with Robert Spencer*

JEFF KING: Robert, tell us how you became involved in your current work.

I grew up in a household listening to my grandparents tell me stories about their childhood and youth in the Ottoman Empire. They were exiled for refusing to convert to Islam. Their experiences drove me to study the religion to understand what had happened to them. As time went on, I began to consult, initially on an informal basis, with some people who were interested in getting information about the motives and goals of the jihad terrorists. When it all exploded on the world stage on September 11, 2001, suddenly Islam and jihad were of immense national interest. That, in itself, led to my doing this work.

I'm a Christian and a believer, but I don't make my faith a forefront of my work because I'm trying to build a coalition of people—Jews, Christians, Hindus, Buddhists, atheists, etc.—who share the potential to be victimized by Islamic Jihad. I want to build bridges with those people to form a united front against jihad.

JEFF KING: You keep a pretty high profile and you are very outspoken in regard to Islam. Are you in danger? How often do you receive death threats?

I receive a great many death threats—lately on a daily basis—and I'm on the al-Qaeda hit list. Adam Gadahn, the first American to be tried with treason since World War II, is somebody who has named me specifically in a video. He is high up in al-Qaeda, and so I take the threats seriously. But if Americans are not willing to stand up and defend their society, laws and customs, then we will lose them. We have to be willing to take some risks.

JEFF KING: Robert, what are some things the average person might not know about Muhammad and Islam?

Muhammad is the founding prophet of Islam. He was born in 570 and died in 632. In the year 610, he said that he had received a vision from a heavenly being [whom he later identified as the angel Gabriel] who gave him a series of messages which were supposedly the perfect word of God.

After Muhammad's death, the messages were compiled to form the Qur'an, which is the holy book of Islam and is considered to be a perfect book, the supreme guide to human behavior.

The average person might think that Muhammad was a teacher of peace. Most people assume that if somebody is the founder of a great religion, then he must be a peaceful figure. In the popular mind, religions have figures like Jesus Christ or Buddha—somebody in a white robe teaching brotherhood, peace, or the Fatherhood of God. Yet, Muhammad is, in fact, hardly somebody that you would ordinarily think of in the mold of a great religious leader. People are very surprised when they find out that the early Islamic sources say that Muhammad was a warlord, a polygamist, and a man with a nine-year-old wife. He was somebody who fought numerous battles in order to bring people under his political rule.

JEFF KING: You say he fought battles in order to bring people under the sway of his group. Where did this idea that came to be known as "jihad" originate?

As Muhammad moved from Mecca to Medina in the twelfth year of his prophetic career, there was a great development in the doctrine of jihad warfare. Before that, when Muhammad's following was a tiny band in Mecca, he did not counsel warfare. He counseled tolerance. That tolerance, although it is much trumpeted today, was not actually a call for Muslims to tolerate non-Muslims. It was actually a call for non-Muslims to tolerate Muslims because the non-Muslims had all the advantages, had all the numbers, had all the power. But when Muhammad moved to Medina, he began to "receive" what he represented as revelations from God telling him that the Muslims were to defend themselves and to fight in order to extend the sway of the rule of Islamic law over the world.

JEFF KING: How did Islam expand after the death of Muhammad?

Islamic apologists tend to get very indignant when people say that Islam was spread by the sword in the early days, but that is precisely what happened. The armies, energized by the jihad ideology, conquered over half of what had been the Christian world up to that point in the seventh century, as well as Persia. They also conquered portions of India.

Forced conversion is against Islamic law, although that was often honored in the breach. The conquering Muslim armies forced conquered nations to abide by Islamic law.

Islamic law mandates a second class status for non-Muslims, so that they are made always to feel the consequences of their rejection of Islam and Muhammad. Those who are conquered are made to suffer in this world, as the Qur'an directs, as well as in the next, as the Muslims see it, for their rebellion against God.

The only thing that would relieve this institutionalized discrimination and harassment was conversion to Islam. So, that is exactly what happened.

This is what made Egypt, Syria, and North Africa Islamic. The heart of the Islamic world today wasn't made by large numbers of people compelled by the beauty or truth of Islam to become Muslims. They were just suffering from so many material depravations and so much discrimination, difficulty, and harassment that, ultimately, they converted to Islam to be relieved of all those difficulties.

JEFF KING: There have been some people who have described three waves of historical jihad. What's your take on that?

That's generally so. These waves of jihad corresponded to periods in which the Islamic world was powerful.

First, was the initial wave coming out of Arabia right after Muhammad's death. Within a hundred years, the Muslims had conquered huge expanses of land. But then, as time went on, the Islamic rulers began to weaken. There was no reform, no rejection of the jihad ideology, and no rejection of the law of Islam that counseled jihad, just the inability to carry them out.

In the second wave, the great medieval Islamic empires once again extended the scope and reach of Islam.

When Islam weakened again, jihad subsided with it until the advent of modern Saudi oil money provided a new impetus for jihad.

A lot of people think that the latest manifestation of jihad in the West is some new thing in Islam and is a manifestation of some development of new doctrine that makes Islam different from what it had been. This is not the case. The Islamic doctrine on jihad is essentially constant and has been the same throughout Islamic history. What has changed is the ability of Muslims to carry that doctrine through in practice, and that corresponds to periods in which the Islamic world simply has the economic and military power to make it happen. That's happening now, even if nowadays most of the military power is in an unconventional form.

JEFF KING: What about the Golden Age of Islam that so many writers write about?

The Golden Age of Islam is a historical myth that is politically motivated and designed to make people less concerned about the Islamization that's going on in the West today. It's an idea that there was a multi-cultural paradise of peace and harmony among Jews, Christians, and Muslims in Islamic Spain and in the Ottoman Empire in the days of the Middle Ages. Supposedly, under Islamic rule,

Jews, Christians and Muslims in these places lived together in peace and harmony and mutual respect. When you actually look at the record, that's not the case. There was some peace and harmony, but it was the kind of peace and harmony that you would find in the South during the time of slavery. When the slaves accepted their place as slaves, sure, there was plenty of peace and harmony.

This wasn't the peace and harmony of people who are legally equal to one another. It was the peace and harmony of the conqueror and the subjugated.

JEFF KING: Now none of this seems to line up with the widely-held or widely-pushed idea that jihad is actually only an inner struggle.

Well, everybody who reads the Qur'an with any attentiveness is not going to see jihad as an interior struggle. Jihad is taken for granted as meaning warfare in Islam and in the Qur'an. The idea of jihad as inner struggle is based on a weak Hadith, which is a tradition of Muhammad. A Hadith is classified as "weak" by Islamic scholars if it is considered inauthentic and not actually spoken by Muhammad or containing an accurate depiction of something he did. There is a great thirst within Islamic theology (al-Ghazali) for traditions about what Muhammad said and did because they are normative for Islamic practice. The Hadiths explain what Muhammad said and did in virtually any conceivable situation. The ones that are considered authentic in Islamic theology are considered normative for Islamic law.

There is no authentic Hadith, that is considered by Muslims to be reliable, that says that jihad is the inner spiritual struggle. This idea is based on a later tradition that is of doubtful reliability, whereas the traditions which are much earlier and more numerous have Muhammad saying that jihad is warfare against unbelievers and behaving in that way by waging that warfare.

JEFF KING: On the subject of the Qur'an—how was it compiled? Are there alternative versions?

The Qur'an was compiled on the fly. There are some alternates available in various parts of the world, although most of them have been destroyed. When Muhammad died rather suddenly, he had made no provisions to compile the Qur'an. There are people who had memorized various parts of it, people who had even written down various parts of it, but it had not been collected together in one place. Eventually, several people did that, and there were differing versions.

Ultimately, there was one version that was chosen as canonical and became the basis for the Qur'an as we know it today. All other versions were collected and destroyed. That was about twenty years after Muhammad's death.

There are some very intriguing traditions in Islamic literature about alternate versions and about large sections of the Qur'an that have been lost. One of the main reasons why it started to be collected in the first place was because several of the people who had memorized parts of it had been killed off in a battle during the wars of apostasy right after Muhammad's death. Some of the Islamic leaders started to realize that if they didn't act, they were going to lose the Qur'an altogether. So they compiled it, but there were some pieces [evidently that had been considered part of the Qur'an] that were lost with the death of the people who had memorized those parts.

JEFF KING: Muslims would have us believe that the Qur'an was delivered from heaven in pristine form. For discerning minds, are there clues that this is not true—that there are actually other sources for the Qur'an?

For one thing, the Qur'an obviously relies upon various Jewish and Christian traditions, both Biblical and extra-Biblical. The Qur'an also contradicts itself, but that is explained away in Islamic teaching by the doctrine of abrogation[9] (*an-naskh wal mansukh*). But really, the idea that Allah, the perfect, supreme God, would change His mind is difficult to imagine. There is also the fact that there are changes in the Qur'anic text itself, although Muslims deny their existence.

JEFF KING: Robert, would you say the Qur'an & Hadith are books of peace? Why is it so easy for non-Muslim readers to miss the violent passages?

For one thing, the Qur'an is not easy to read. It's not arranged in any chronological order. It's arranged roughly from the longest chapter to the shortest, and it's a series of various hectoring sermons by Muhammad that are essentially complaining or rebuking the unbelievers for their rejection of his message. They are mixed into various Bible stories or versions of Bible stories.

Reading the Qur'an is kind of like walking into a conversation between two people that you don't know, and they don't bother to fill in the details of what they're talking about. In the Qur'an, Allah speaks to Muhammad. He refers to incidents in Muhammad's life, but he usually doesn't explain them or spell them out. It's assumed that all the hearers will know what it's all about and what's going on. It becomes very difficult to follow.

Muhammad was not writing for posterity. He was writing for the people right around him at that time, even though what he purported to be giving them were the eternal words of God. It all had to do with particular situations in their lives [those in Muhammad's time] that he doesn't bother to fill in the details about.

So, if an American in the twenty-first century picks the Qur'an up, it's very difficult to understand. It's very difficult to figure out

---

[9] See pg. 339.

what's going on, what's being said, or what the significance of what's being said is. These things are by no means clear.

That's one of the reasons why I wrote *The Complete Infidel's Guide to the Qur'an*, because you can only really understand the Qur'an by going to the commentaries of the Qur'an written by Muslims, and the authoritative Hadith [the traditions of Muhammad] which fill in the circumstances of the revelation.

JEFF KING: What passages would you cite to say that these books (the Qur'an and the Hadith) counsel violence? Are you cherry-picking?

The primary passage that counsels violence against unbelievers is chapter nine. It is not cherry-picking to pick the ninth chapter, because the ninth chapter of the Qur'an is chronologically the last one to have been revealed that includes doctrinal content. That's very significant because in Islamic doctrine, the passages that come later supersede those that come earlier if there's any contradiction between the two. So to say that a particular passage comes late in Muhammad's career is to say that it has an authoritative status over earlier passages.

The difficulty for unbelievers is that the later passages are generally violent and counsel violence against unbelievers, whereas, the earlier passages are generally peaceful or at least teach tolerance. Tolerance for Muslims, if anything, but there are at least statements that there should be tolerance between people of different religions.

It's universal among the sects and schools of Islam that the later teachings supersede the earlier, and thus, the doctrines of warfare supersede the doctrines of tolerance.

JEFF KING: Robert, give me some specific verses that preached tolerance. What's actually in there?

Chapter 109 of the Qur'an tells Muhammad to say to the unbelievers that they have their religion and he has his. He's not going to believe in theirs and they're not going to believe in his. Essentially, he is saying something like, "Let's leave each other alone."

That's really as generous as the Qur'an gets toward the unbelievers. There are others who point to passages that say that the Jews and Christians will be saved, but those are universally interpreted by Islamic theologians as referring to the Jews and Christians who convert to Islam or who accept the true teachings of the Muslim Moses and Muslim Jesus who were, in fact, Islamic prophets who taught Islam, according to Islamic theology in the Qur'an.

JEFF KING: Give me some specific passages on violence. Specific verses.

The famous one is the birth of the sword, which is 9:5. "Slay the unbelievers wherever you find them," which is a phrase that also appears in 4:89, and 2:191. It is generally understood as meaning that pagans, or polytheists, are to be given the choice of conversion or death and that's it.

Non-Muslims are in two groups. There are the People of the Book and the pagans. The People of the Book are given the choice of conversion or subjugation as inferiors under the rule of Islamic law or death. Whereas, for the pagans, it's just to convert or die. No subjugation is offered.

JEFF KING: What does the Qur'an say about women?

The Qur'an essentially treats women as commodities, or as possessions of men. They are decidedly second-class, inferior human beings. A man can beat his disobedient wife [4:34]. A woman's testimony is valued lower than that of a man's, and her inheritance rights are devalued [2:282, and 4:11]. Polygamy is allowed, which objectifies women and treats them as commodities [4:3].

JEFF KING: Do these ideas come from Muhammad? When you look at his life, and his interactions with women?

Muhammad is really the key to all of this, because he is considered to be the supreme model for conduct. Islamic law, based on the Qur'an [33:21], says that Muhammad is an exemplary model of conduct. Essentially, if Muhammad did something, then it's good, then it's right. So the idea that women are commodities and that polygamy is allowed and that child marriage is allowed, all these things come from Muhammad's example.

JEFF KING: When they were in battles and they captured and subjugated people, what was allowed for the female captives?

Even in Islamic law to this day, if a woman is captured on a battlefield her marriage is immediately annulled. Rape and captivity is legal within Islamic law. Women are, again, essentially regarded as commodities that can be seized just like spoils of war.

JEFF KING: You are saying rape is not only tolerated, but it was modeled in Muhammad's life and actions?

Yes. After one battle, Muhammad seized a wife of one of the men that he had killed and took her for himself right there. This is again considered to be an exemplary example of behavior (since it came from Muhammad).

JEFF KING: Is it true that the Qur'an says that there is only one sure way that the Muslims can get to heaven. Will you comment on that?

The Qur'an has no guarantee of paradise. Chapter twenty-one, verse forty-seven, says that your deeds will be weighed on a great scale, and if your good deeds outweigh your bad deeds, then you will go to paradise. But if your bad deeds outweigh your good deeds, then you'll go to hell. So the problem that presents for the Muslim is that you can never know how much a deed weighs. How do you know how much your good deeds weigh versus your bad deeds? Even though there's some tradition saying that any good deed weighs five times more than any bad deed, do you even know how many good deeds or bad deeds you've committed? We do so many things in life and they have consequences that we've never foreseen and consequences that we'll never realize until after death.

The only guarantee that the Qur'an has is that the person who slays and is slain for Allah is guaranteed paradise. Chapter 9, verse 111, of the Qur'an does say that Allah guarantees paradise once you've killed and are killed for Allah. This is the theological basis for suicide bombings. If you kill the infidels and are killed in the process, then you'll go to paradise.

JEFF KING: Let's compare the Qur'an to other religious texts. The Old Testament contains a lot of violent episodes and even mandates from God that some would say are genocidal. What's the difference? Is there a difference?

Yes, several differences.

One is that the Old Testament is descriptive rather than prescriptive. It says that God told particular people to do these things and they did it, but there are no universal commands to behave in the same way. In the Qur'an, there are commands for all believers to wage war against unbelievers to subjugate them. That's one difference.

Another difference is that neither the Bible nor the Qur'an exists in a vacuum. They both existed as part of interpretative traditions that are ongoing. Christians and Jews spiritualize those passages of the Old Testament so that they are not considered to be mandates for believers to brutalize unbelievers, but are rather considered to be spiritual parable mandates to fight against sin and to make war against it and to bring one's life in conformity with the will of God.

In the Islamic tradition, by contrast, the violent passages are universally interpreted as counseling warfare against unbelievers on an ongoing basis. They are not spiritualized at all. There is no spiritualizing the passages counseling warfare in the Islamic tradition.

JEFF KING: Many people believe that radical Islam represents only two to three percent of Muslims. The "crazies" you would find in any religion. What do you say to that?

Well, you don't find the "crazies" in every religion, for one thing. We've seen recently a lot of headlines about this allegedly Christian militia group, "Hutari," that had planned to explode some bombs and kill some people. Now, this group, if it is in any sense Christian, is following a theology that's rejected by the overwhelming majority of Christians, by every major Christian group, every major Christian church, every Christian domination, and every Christian sect. They represent no Christian traditions. They represent no Christian teachings.

In contrast, in Islam, there is no recognized orthodox mainstream sect of Islam or school of Islamic jurisprudence that does not teach warfare against unbelievers and the necessity to subjugate them violently under the rule of Islamic law. So this is a night-and-day kind of situation. In Islam, the traditional authorities all teach warfare against unbelievers, and you don't find any that don't. In Christianity, it's just the opposite. So this is not a matter of a few extremists in a corner, it is a mainstream teaching. Now, with that said, why is it that you only have a small group that is waging violence?

There are a number of reasons for that. One is that most people don't want to get involved in that sort of thing. They want to live their lives, have a family, have a job, take care of the people around them and that's it. They're not interested in going out and killing themselves for Islam or jihad or Allah. That's true, really, in every religious tradition. You find people who are very committed to it and people who are less fanatically committed to it, and that will make a difference in how they act even if both groups identify themselves by the label of the religious group.

You also have in Islam the fact that the Islamic ceremonial religious observances are all in Arabic, and yet most Muslims are not Arabic speakers. There is, actually, as odd as it may seem, a large number of Muslims around the world today who actually don't know what they're saying. They will recite the prayers and they are observant in Islam, but unless somebody teaches them about the doctrines of jihad warfare, they're actually not fully aware of them. That can make a big difference in terms of how they're going to live them out if they don't even know that they're there.

While you don't find a large number of Muslims committing acts of violence, you certainly don't find them rejecting acts of violence.

You'll find them agreeing generally in polls and you'll find them generally not standing up against jihad. You would expect to find large numbers of Muslims standing up and actively opposing the Islamic jihad that is being carried out in their name, and yet you have instead only vague and general condemnation of terrorism by Islamic groups. Muslim groups have condemned attacks of innocent people, which sounds great until you realize that in Islamic theology, non-Muslims are not innocent. So it's not really saying anything. It's just something that fools people.

JEFF KING: You wrote in one of your books *A Politically Incorrect Guide to The Islamic Crusades* that Muslims can seem hypersensitive about the Crusades. Can you give us your perspective on the Crusades?

The Crusades are considered to be the cause of all our troubles. Bill Clinton and many others have said that the Crusades were the beginning of hostility between the West and the Islamic world. This is a naïve historical view that is based on apparent ignorance, whether willful or not, of the fact that there were jihad wars fought for more than 500 years against the Christian world before there was ever a Crusade. Over half of Christendom was conquered and Islamized in those jihads before there was ever a Crusade.

To say that the Crusades began the hostility between the West and the Islamic world is to buy into the Muslim narrative of victimization that portrays the West as being responsible for all the hostilities between the Islamic world and the West, and never acknowledges any responsibility whatsoever on the part of Muslims.

Although the Crusaders did some things that cannot be excused, the reality is that they were fighting a tardy, small-scale defensive warfare designed not to win back the huge expanse of land lost to Muslims in earlier jihads, but simply to try to secure the safety of the Holy Land for Christian pilgrims.

This goal was ultimately unsuccessful. However, during the 200 years that the Crusaders did have a presence in the Holy Land, there were no jihads into Europe. So, we probably have the Crusaders to thank for the fact that Europe was not ultimately conquered and Islamized.

JEFF KING: Speaking of Europe, tell us what you see in your crystal ball for the future of Europe in light of Muslim immigration and demographic trends.

Bernard Lewis, the great historian, had said flatly that Europe would be Islamic by the end of the century, and I don't see any reason to dispute that assessment.

The Muslim populations are growing very quickly and the non-Muslim populations are not growing. Simply on the basis of demographics, unless there's some drastic change, there will be Muslim majorities in various Western European states within a few decades and then there will be calls for Islamic law. I think those will create great conflict in Europe before we're through, but there's no way that Europe can escape a confrontation on that basis.

JEFF KING: Help us understand what that means. You mentioned earlier that this third wave of jihad has taken some unconventional forms. ICC's take is that jihad is fought on three fronts: military, political, and religious, with the foundation for all these being the funding for these efforts. Can you touch on that and talk about how these arms and strategies are being used?

Military, political, and religious jihad are really all related. It's all the same jihad. The goal is all the same. The goal is bringing Islamic law to the West. That is being pursued by Muslims in different ways and different places. There are some who are waging war, selling bombs, setting IED's in Iraq and so on, fighting against Israel, and some who are waging war in a different way. Some are trying to assert elements of Islamic law in the West and are trying to assert that where Islamic law and American law conflict, American law has to give way.

And then, of course, there's Sharia finance. The idea that the financial institutions in the West must change the way they do business in order to accommodate Muslims and Islam and Islamic laws regarding interests and so on. Ultimately, the purpose of all three is the same—that Islamic law is extended over the West.

JEFF KING: What is stealth jihad, and is it real?

It's eminently real. Stealth jihad is simply the non-violent effort to further the goals of the jihadis who are working with guns and bombs. The stealth jihad is one that is designed to further the goals of the jihadis without violence, but to bring Islamic law to the West in different ways.

JEFF KING: What about legal strategies? What do you see on the legal front?

On the legal front, there is a variety of things going on. There is the suing for libel of various people who speak the truth about Islam and jihad. There is the intent in court to gain advantages for Muslims in various places and society, especially in the workplace. Muslims are demanding special privileges, special break times in various workplaces, and so on, and suing to get them. It's a comprehensive effort on multiple fronts.

JEFF KING: Give us your views on hate speech laws. What's the danger of these?

The danger of hate speech laws is that they are exploited by the powerful to silence their opponents. Any tyrant can use the charge of hate speech to claim that the people who are dissenting from the tyrant's law are haters. The Organization of Islamic Conference, which is the largest building block of the United Nations right now, is the chief sponsor of hate speech laws trying to get Western governments to adopt hate speech laws on a global basis and to criminalize criticism of Islam.

The problem is that they would want to criminalize even honest discussion of the elements of Islam that Islamic jihadis have used in order to justify violence and terrorism. Hate speech laws are really a weapon of the jihad to further the goals of the jihadis.

JEFF KING: Let's talk about some present-day Muslim organizations involved in stealth jihad. Robert, what does the average person wanting to understand Islam need to know about the Muslim Brotherhood?

The Muslim Brotherhood is an international Islamic organization founded in Egypt in 1928 and it's now found all over the world. It's also active in the United States under various names: the Muslim

American Society, the Islamic Society of North America,[10] The Muslim Students Association and so on. These are all Brotherhood entities. Pretty much every major Muslim group in the United States today is linked to the Brotherhood. The Brotherhood is dedicated (in its own words) to "eliminating and destroying Western civilizations from within and sabotaging its miserable house so that it falls" and is replaced by Islamic law.

JEFF KING: Can you tell us about the funding of Islamic radicalism as well as their strategies and approaches towards the West?

The most common source of funding is the Saudi government, Saudi Arabia and Saudi private citizens. The Saudis have so much money, courtesy of our oil pumps, and they use it to finance jihad all around the world.

JEFF KING: You touched on CAIR earlier just briefly. Tell us about CAIR. Who are they? What's their background? What are their aims?

The Council on American-Islamic Relations (CAIR) is an unindicted co-conspirator in a Hamas terror-funding case involving the funneling of money by the Holy Land Foundation, which was once the nation's largest Islamic charity to Hamas, the jihad terrorist group in Israel. The Council of American Islamic Relations is actually a Hamas front that was started by Nihad Awad and Omar Ahmad, who came from the Islamic Association for Palestine, which has since been shut down for being a Hamas front. Nihad Awad has said publicly that he's a supporter of Hamas, and CAIR has had several of its officials convicted of various terrorism-related charges. It is a group who has had several of its officials make Islamic

---

[10] See pg. 347.

supremacist statements about how they want to see the United States have a Muslim government sometime in the future.

This is a group that is trying to further the aims of Islamic law in the United States, and yet, it enjoys a widespread reputation, even in government, as a moderate and peaceful group. That's the result of a sophisticated and ongoing PR effort.

The fight against Islamic radicalism is not a racial issue, and it's not bigotry. It's a matter of defending human rights against the encroachments of an ideology that would deny the freedom of speech, the freedom of conscience, and the equality of various people before the law. But as far as the Council of Islamic Relations is concerned, it's something much different. That is, you're a bigot if you speak honestly about what jihad is all about. They are a very effective group in terms of silencing the honest discussion of Islam and jihad and obscuring the issue about what's really at stake.

JEFF KING: Is radical Islam infiltrating our armed forces and intelligence agencies?

You can look at various military personnel like Nidal Hasan who murdered thirteen people at Fort Hood. He was a major in the US Army and he was an Islamic jihadist. He is clearly a sign that Islamic Jihad infiltrated the military and that they have presence there. He's not an isolated case, either.

There was Hasan Akbar, who murdered several of his commanding officers in Kuwait. A convert to Islam, he threw a grenade at them and said, "You guys are coming into our countries and you're going to kill our children and rape our women." He was an American citizen. It's interesting that he would consider a Muslim country to be his country. When he converted to Islam, he suddenly was no longer an American, at least in his own eyes. The problem is that there are a lot of Muslims in the military. No effort whatsoever, none, zero, zilch is being made to determine their views on jihad, on

Islamic supremacism, on political Islam. Nobody is even checking. Nobody is trying to see where their loyalties lie. So we shouldn't be really surprised if there are more incidents like that of Nidal Hasan and Hasan Akbar.

JEFF KING: What is the role of lying and deception in Islam and jihad? What are the implications for the casual observer of Islam in the West?

The Qur'an says that if you are a believer, you should not take unbelievers as your friend and protectors unless you're doing it to guard yourself against them (3:28). It's saying that you can protect yourself from the unbelievers by pretending to take them as friends and protectors. The idea is that a Muslim can deceive a non-Muslim in order to protect himself and protect Islam. That is something that is based on the Qur'an and that has a great deal of validity within Islam. Muhammad said, "War is deceit," and that lying was permitted in several circumstances during war times.

When we understand that the Islamic jihadists believe that the United States is at war with Islam, and that Islam is at war with the United States, it becomes a matter of concern because this is effectively saying that deception is all right. We should take what Muslims say with a grain of salt because it is a recognized aspect of warfare to deceive the unbelievers.

JEFF KING: Why all the political correctness regarding Islam in the West?

I wish I knew. I think what I'm saying in my work is fairly commonplace and is easily established. All somebody has to do is look at the Qur'an and see if what I'm saying is true. The drive toward political correctness is probably a concerted effort by Islamic groups, Muslim Brotherhood and other groups to obfuscate the truth about Islam and to spread everywhere the idea that Islam is a religion of peace that's been hijacked by a tiny minority of extremists. They say that the extremists are twisting the real Islam, which is actually peaceful.

These [kinds of statements] are comforting thoughts and they're making people feel better about Islamic immigration into the West. This is why I think Islamic advocacy groups in the United States have made a concerted effort to portray anybody who notes the dishonesty of these things and points out that Islamic teaching is otherwise in a bad light. They are portrayed as the bigots, racists, Muslim hatemongers and so on--that's the kiss of death in the United States. People go to great lengths to avoid being labeled as racists or hate-mongers, even if that means that they have to avoid speaking the truth.

FORMER MUSLIMS

SPEAK OUT

Chapter Three:

The Feminist Daughter of a Somali Warlord

*The more of Islam you practice, the more inhuman your practices will be. "Radical Muslim" is a euphemism for practicing Islam pure and simple. For me, this is the definition of a moderate Muslim: [one] who will say: I will **not** follow every example set down by Muhammad. I will __reject__ some of his examples and I will take some of them. Now, there are very, very few individuals in the planet who will say this. Because Muhammad is infallible, refusing . . . his example will take you straight to hell, or get you killed by fellow Muslims for being an apostate.*

Ayaan Hirsi Ali

If you are not already familiar with **Ayaan Hirsi Ali**, you need to be. She is one of the most courageous women on the planet today. Her life story sounds like fiction. Born as a Muslim to the daughter of a Somalia warlord, she emigrated to Holland where she eventually became a Dutch MP. She left Islam and became a feminist. Her honest and outspoken criticism of Islam and the murder of a close friend at the hands of an Islamist led the Dutch government to urge her to leave the country.

She has settled in the US, where she works as a fellow at the American Enterprise Institute. She travels with bodyguards due to the incredible number of death threats she receives.

She is a former Muslim, an atheist, a feminist, an author, and a sought-out expert on Islam.

Books by Ayaan Hirsi Ali:
- *The Caged Virgin: An Emancipation Proclamation for Women and Islam*
- *Infidel*
- *Nomad: From Islam to America: A Personal Journey Through the Clash of Civilizations*
- *Shortcut to Enlightenment*

JEFF KING: Tell us about your background.

Well, I am born in Somalia and I grew up in Saudi Arabia, in Ethiopia, and in Kenya. I lived in the Netherlands for fourteen years, and I now live in the United States, in Washington D.C. I was brought up a Muslim and I am no longer a believer. That's the short bio. In fact, everything about my life is in the book called *Infidel*.

JEFF KING: What prompted you to leave Islam?

Well, I think it was a very gradual process. But the most sudden moment of it all was on the 11th of September 2001, after the terrorist attacks in the United States. That is when there was this international debate: is it Islam or not? And if it is Islam, where do I, as a Muslim, stand? And it was Islam because I heard bin Laden's work and al- Zawahiri. I used to be a former sympathizer of the Islamic Brotherhood. And so, I downloaded the works of bin Laden, took his quotes from the Qur'an and from the Hadith and looked for them in the Qur'an and the Hadith and I found them there. So, for me, it was very clear that it was motivated in the name of my religion.

Then, the next step for me was: If I condemned the attacks, then where did I stand with my own faith? And that set the ball rolling and I just came to a personal, very personal, very private conclusion that I didn't want to be a part of a killing theology or a theology that justifies so much murder and oppression.

And I had been, for a long time before that, fighting and agitating for the rights of Muslim women because they are just given this position in life, which is slightly better than that of animals and, definitely, subhuman.

JEFF KING: Why do you think that Muslims persecute Christians? Would Muhammad approve such persecution?

Well, Muhammad is the one who made it official and righteous to oppress people who rejected Islam. And, as long as there are human beings and as long as there were human beings from the Stone Age until now, human beings have been oppressing one another. What Islam does is: It provides those who want to take away the rights and freedoms of others with the justification for doing that.

It divides the world into infidels and believers [Muslims]. If you are an infidel, you must be killed. If you are a Christian or Jewish, you are given *dhimmi* status, which is a lower status given to [non-Muslim] citizens. If you are a woman, you need to be confined, and covered and subjected to maltreatment.

It makes all of these, I would say, universal traits for humans to oppress one another; it justifies them as long as you invoke Islam, Muhammad, Allah and the Qur'an. And that is just something all human beings, not only Muslims or Christians, but all human beings should fight against.

JEFF KING: In countries such as Egypt, Christians and other Muslims are given *dhimmi* status (status of a second-class citizen). Where does this come from?

If they were all to turn around and accept Islam and reject Christianity, then their *dhimmi* status would be lifted and then they would become fellow Muslims. But they are excluded in the name of Islam. So they're given the choice: You want to have a lower status? Fine, remain a Christian. You want to be one of us and expand the power base of Islam? Then you leave your religion and you come to us.

These are violations of the freedom of religion and conscience as we've come to understand them. Even as many of those countries, including Egypt, have signed the United Nations human rights charter.

JEFF KING: People who decide to convert from Islam to Christianity or any other religion often are killed. Where does this come from? What is your reaction to this?

Again, I tell you, the tendency, the urge to oppress others, deny them their conscience, limit their freedom, is a universal trait. But what makes Islam specific is to say: The Qur'an says only Muslims or those who come to Allah and who recognize the Prophet as the last messenger of God, so who basically adopt a set of beliefs that Muhammad taught, only those ones deserve full human status, but everyone else should be killed.

Now, someone like me saying, "I have known this religion, I accepted and adhered to this set of beliefs, but I now refuse to do that. I changed my mind about it." People like me are threatened with death. Because, you know, like all cults and like all groups that are kept together by means of fear, when you allow the first person to wander away, the second one will go, the third one will go and the people who use Islam as a source of power will end up with nothing.

JEFF KING: In Saudi Arabia, Christians and others can't build their places of worship. Saudis sponsor the construction of mosques throughout the world. Why the double standard?

It is not only churches and synagogues, but in Saudi Arabia even Shiites,[11] who are Muslims, are persecuted.

JEFF KING: Why do Saudi Arabian officials prohibit freedom of religion for people who don't subscribe to their religious view?

The Saudi officials are basing their doctrines on the Qur'an and the Hadith. The Saudi state and the state of the Islamic Republic of Iran – both of them have their law: their social laws, their political laws,

---

[11] See pg. 356.

and every form of legal justice they have, I would say injustice, is from the Qur'an and the Hadith.

JEFF KING: Some people argue that Islam is not the source of the problem, but that it is radical Muslims who are the problem. Would you agree with this assessment?

I don't. Let me put it in my own words: the more of Islam you practice, the more inhuman your practices will be. So, people we call radical Muslims—that is a euphemism for practicing Islam pure and simple.

This is the definition for me of a moderate Muslim. A moderate Muslim is an individual who will say: *I will not follow, consciously, every example set by Muhammad. I will reject some of his examples and I will take some of them, but I still consider myself a Muslim.* Now, there are very, very few individuals on the planet who will say this. Because Muhammad is infallible, refusing or selectively following his example will take you straight to hell or get you killed by fellow Muslims for being an apostate.

JEFF KING: In your opinion, would it be possible to reform Islam? If so, what aspects of Islam need to be reformed?

Well, if you divide Islam into three categories: you would say number one is the spiritual dimension of Islam, which is praying and fasting, and visiting Mecca once in a while and doing charity.

The second dimension is the social dimension. That is the relationship between men and women, parents and children, and how you arrange and socialize society. And the third dimension is the political-legal [dimension]. That is the state versus the citizen.

Only the first dimension [the spiritual dimension] is compatible with liberal democracy or within any functioning democracy on the condition that Muslims accept their religion to be subject to state law.

The social dimension, the second dimension is not compatible with democracy. It denies women their rights and seeks to exclude and kill gay people and apostates.

The third dimension [the political dimension] is also not compatible. It seeks to replace state laws with repressive Islamic laws [which] are not compatible with democracy. They are just not compatible with the modern nation state as we know it.

JEFF KING: Let's unpack the incompatibility of Islam and women's rights.

Once again, there is a spiritual dimension to Islam which is all about praying and fasting, giving charity and visiting Mecca once in a while. That dimension is compatible because it doesn't really threaten the civil liberties. But again, the social and political dimensions of Islam do.

There is a whole list: women will not be able to choose their own husbands; they will be forced into marriage. There will be child brides because Prophet Muhammad married a nine-year-old girl, and all Muslim men who want to marry an underage girl will invoke Muhammad and ignore the constitution of the country they live in. We have a whole institution of marriage and divorce in the West that protects women's and children's rights that will be turned upside down for women. It will discriminate against women; they will not get alimony, they can be divorced on a whim. You know, [in Islam, a husband can say to his wife], "I divorce thee" three times and then they are divorced. It is so easy for them to divorce their wives.

Under Islam, the testimony of a woman is worth half of that of a man. If you are raped, you have to prove with four witnesses that you have been raped. All these civil rights that women have in the West do not exist [within most Islamic States]. Islam really institutionalizes a form of discrimination on women.

What about gay people, apostates? I have left Islam and I have phalanx of police protecting me, and I live in the West. I am not talking about living in Somalia. I am talking about living in America and needing protection because I left Islam. That is scandalous.

JEFF KING: The Muslim population in Europe is growing at an alarming rate. What is your take on that?

In Europe, there is a fast-growing demography of Muslims. The proximity of the continent of Europe to Muslim countries, you know, it makes it easier for people [to emigrate to Europe]. And almost all Muslim states are in some trauma or the other, so people will be leaving them. So, the number of people in Europe will grow [because of] the immigrants and their children. Currently, Europeans in general are not having as many children as they used to or as many children as the Muslim immigrants are having.

If European governments still continue to ignore this demographic problem—but also cultural-religious conflicts between Europeans and Muslim immigrants—then, I think, as all historians and demographers predict (the major one being Bernard Lewis), that within twenty to thirty, or maybe fifty years, the European demography will completely change. Some of the cities, and even countries, will have Muslim majorities.

JEFF KING: Do you think the growth in the Muslim population in Europe will be a threat to liberal democracy in the continent?

If Muslim immigrants assimilate and adopt the values that have made Europe a peaceful continent for a very short while in history, then human rights and the European constitution will not be threatened.

It will be a problem if that demography clings to Islamic Sharia as their way of life. Then, they do have a problem. Right now, as things look, there are a disturbing number of European Muslims who do cling to the old Islamic norms and who reject consciously and openly the European values.

JEFF KING: Do Muslims ask for implementation of Sharia law?

Not all Muslims, but there are those Muslims who are seeking political influence, like the Muslim Brotherhood, as a movement. They have organized themselves in political terms around Sharia law.

Ayatollah Khomeini in Iran did the same thing. For a long time, in exile in France, he propagated the overthrow of Shah and [replaced] the monarchy with Sharia law. And he achieved that. We almost saw it happen in Algeria in the late 1980s. We have seen it in the province of Zamfara in Nigeria. We've seen the Taliban do it and achieve their goals in Afghanistan. We can also see it now in my home country [of] Somalia.

Any political movement that takes as its manifest and its ideas in establishing a utopian Islamic state will introduce, sooner or later, Sharia. Always starting by taking away women's rights, by the way.

JEFF KING: But Muslim groups in Europe are lobbying for the introduction of Sharia law, particularly the family law aspect, in order to litigate cases among Muslims. What is your take on that?

Well, it's true you can see [in] places, like the UK, France, the Netherlands, Belgium and Sweden, there are a growing number of very vocal Muslim organizations that are lobbying the government and employing PR and legal firms to push for the passage of Sharia laws, especially family law. That is a reality.

Can it be countered? I think it can be countered. I think that European governments can oppose or simply refuse to appease or accommodate these demands. But, also, there should be competition, for instance, from Christians and from secular humanists to go out and say that we don't want this. We think it's wrong, just like we think the extreme right wing parties in Europe are wrong to create parallel societies in which some citizens are delegated [relegated] to lower citizenship status. Because when the Sharia family law is employed, the rights of women and girls will go back to the Middle Ages.

JEFF KING: What is your observation of the Islamic movement in the United States, and how does it compare with the Islamic movement in Europe?

Islamic organizations are mostly grassroots, and they are helped in the USA, by wealthy donors from Saudi Arabia and other Gulf states to lobby Washington D.C. using PR companies and law firms.

So, it's not just grassroots movement. The grassroots movement is for Dawa or to proselytize. But elite Muslims push with media and PR the message among the masses that Islam is peaceful and harmless. These developments can be seen especially on campuses and certain cities and neighborhoods. This movement is present in the United States. It's not as developed and as strong as some places in Europe. But it's definitely present. So, that means the danger is there. It is small, presently, but it can always grow.

JEFF KING: Tell us about your upcoming book, *Shortcut to Enlightenment*. What does the book deal with? When is it coming up?

I think it will be on the market in 2011 because I have another book coming up called *Nomad*. *Shortcut to Enlightenment* is about the prophet Muhammad waking up in the New York Public Library and having a dialogue with three of my favorite Western thinkers. One is John Stewart Mill. The Prophet and he will talk about women. The second scholar is Fredrick Hayek. Hayek and Muhammad will talk about the community versus the individual. And the third one is Karl Popper. And Muhammad and Popper will talk about the open state versus the tribal state or the closed state.

Chapter Four:

The Convert to Christianity

I started going to a mosque in America because I wanted to belong to a community, and the first thing I was told was that we shouldn't assimilate because we were here to Islamize America. I was told that we had to stand out as Muslims, to assert ourselves and send a message that we were here, and that we were going to increase in number and eventually rule America. That was our objective. I felt scared. I felt scared for America, and I was shocked because this was a radical agenda. This was not religion; this was an invasion. Muslims who move to America are not allowed to assimilate. They are pawns. We had come to freedom – freedom as women and freedom from Sharia law. But they wouldn't leave us alone. I could not relate to my religion anymore. I felt I was at a crossroads. I could become either a part of America or part of a jihadist agenda against America. I chose to be part of America.

In a few decades we're going to have an area in America that's predominantly Muslim, and we are going to have terror attacks inside the United States by Muslims demanding Sharia law. If it isn't given to them, we are going to be living in fear of bomb attacks whenever we go into a restaurant or a shopping mall.

Nonie Darwish

Nonie Darwish was born a Muslim to a high-ranking army officer in Egypt in 1948. She is a human rights activist and the director of Former Muslims United. She is a Muslim apostate (she left Islam) who converted to Christianity and is now an outspoken critic of Islam, specifically, in relation to Islam's treatment of women and the culture of hatred that Muslims grow up in.

She is on the executive committee of FormerMuslimsUnited.org, an organization that is challenging Western Islamic leaders to sign "The Freedom Pledge." It is a public pledge to reject Muhammad's decree (and part of Sharia law) that Muslims that leave Islam should be killed. Although this has been sent to most of the Muslim leadership in the States, to date, only a few have signed the pledge.

She is the constant target of death threats and is one of the world's most courageous women. Her work causes her life to be in constant jeopardy.

Books by Nonie Darwish:
- *Now They Call Me Infidel*
- *Cruel and Usual Punishment: The Terrifying Global Implications of Islamic Law*

Website: formermuslimsunited.org

JEFF KING: Nonie, tell us about your background.

I was born in 1948 to an Egyptian family right after Egypt's war with Israel, when Israel was created. My father was a high-ranking army officer and participated in that war. After the Egyptian revolution in 1952, he was appointed by the president of Egypt to go to Gaza and start the fedayeen[12] operation against Israel. The fedayeen was a paramilitary group that penetrated Israel and caused as much damage, destruction and death as they could.

These were practically the first terror operations against Israel, but they were not conducted by an underground terrorist group. They were state-sponsored and not in any way denied. Israel suffered a lot because the fedayeen did not only kill Israeli military personnel, but civilians, as well.

Israel wanted to kill my father to end the fedayeen, and they made several assassination attempts on him. I remember one night, in the early 1950s, when Israeli commanders came into our heavily-guarded home. Fortunately, my father was not there and they left the rest of my family unharmed.

I really lived in the heart of the Arab-Israeli conflict as a child. I attended Gaza Elementary School and I learned from early on in life, just like all Arab kids, to hate Jews. Not just to hate them, but to be *proud* of hatred and to feel it was our duty as Muslims to hate them. They must be hated; they were subhuman and God commanded us to hate them.

So I hated them. I didn't know any Jews at that time, and I really didn't know that they were human beings just like the rest of us. This is how Arab kids are brought up, "*Jews are subhuman, they are a*

---

[12] See pg. 340.

mistake by God, and God entrusted us to rid the world of them. " In order to program us to always feel this way, they instilled in us a fear of Jews. For example, I was told not to take any candy from a stranger because it could be a Jew trying to poison me. When you instill such fear in the heart of a child, hatred becomes easy; it's a natural reaction. Terrorism against Jews then becomes acceptable and even good.

This teaching is the core of Islam, and I became a victim of that kind of indoctrination. It wasn't easy to change. It took me a long, long time.

In July of 1956, when I was eight years old, the Israelis finally managed to kill my father. Afterwards, when we moved back to Cairo, my mother wanted to give us the best education possible and I was enrolled in a British Catholic school. When it was time for the Christian girls to go to Bible studies, we Muslims—about half the class – went to another part of the school to learn about Islam. Even though I never really studied the Bible in that school, I became aware of a lot of differences between Christianity and Islam.

We were taught by English nuns, and I was really struck by the difference between the religious figures in Christianity and those in Islam. I heard the nuns tell my mother one day, "We're going to pray for you," and I saw tears in my mother's eyes. She said, "I never heard this before; that people of another religion would want to pray for me. Even Muslims never told me 'we're going to pray for you." It's not a concept in Islam to pray for someone else. People in Islam pray for themselves, not for other people.

At that time, I lived in two worlds. One was of the British nuns where I saw peace, holiness, love and religious tolerance demonstrated. Then there was the outside world, where I heard Muslim teachers cursing Jews and non-Muslims. At the end of almost every Friday prayer, my religious leader would yell and scream and encourage jihad against non-Muslims. It was as if they wanted to provoke a war of vengeance by anger and incitement.

I never felt comfortable in Islam. I felt as if I was fighting my inner drive to be at peace with the rest of the world. I had to constantly think whether the person in front of me was a Muslim or not because I'd have to adapt my behavior in a certain way. It's not a comfortable situation when you constantly feel you have to fight the good side of your human nature to be a Muslim.

I lived my life never really believing in Islam, but I never tried to turn to another religion because that is the absolute worst thing you can do in Islam. It's not just a sin; it's treason. It's treason against the state, it's treason against the religion, and it's punishable by death.

Because of that, I really never tried to think about examining other religions to choose between them. That is not allowed in Islam. You're living in a mental trap in which you cannot believe in anything other than Islam, even though you doubt it. You live in limbo. Most Muslims are in that situation. Most Muslims are living under the chains of this ideology, and they know it in their hearts. They know it subconsciously, but they abide by it and they live with it. Most of them live a life with no true religion, and I was one of these people.

Eventually, I came to America. That brought about true change in my life, but I still could not leave Islam. We were brought up believing that Islam was almost like part of your being; you couldn't change it. I used to laugh at Americans who said, "I became a Protestant; I was this and I became that." I said, "Oh, these people can't convert from something to something; this is unheard of." My Muslim friends and I would say, "Oh, they quit their own religion. How funny! Is that allowed? Wow!"

I started going to a mosque in America because I wanted to belong to a community, and the first thing I was told there was that we shouldn't assimilate because we were here to Islamize America. I felt as if I was in a political institution more than a religious one; as if I was a member of an army waiting to invade America.

Then I was asked, "Why aren't you wearing your Islamic clothes?" I told them I had never worn Islamic clothes in Egypt, and neither had my mother nor my grandmother, so there seemed no reason to do that in America. I was told that we had to stand out as Muslims, to assert ourselves and send a message that we were here, and that we were going to increase in number and eventually rule America. That was our objective. I felt scared. I felt scared for America, and I was shocked because this was a radical agenda. This was not religion; this was an invasion.

I stopped going to the mosque, but most of the other immigrants who had come with us kept going. A few years later, I was walking in a mall here in southern California and I saw two or three women wearing Islamic clothes. One of them greeted me and I realized it was one of the women who had immigrated with me to America and who had previously worn Western clothes. We had all been so excited to arrive in America, so grateful to be here, and we dressed like Americans. Now, she was completely covered from head to toe, except for her face. I was shocked.

Muslims who move to America are not allowed to assimilate. They are pawns. We had come to freedom—freedom as women and freedom from Sharia law. But they wouldn't leave us alone. I could not relate to my religion anymore. I felt I was at a crossroads. I could become either a part of America or part of a jihadist agenda against America. I chose to be part of America.

I lived my life without a religion for many years in the United States, but I sent my kids to a Christian school to learn about good morals and values, just as I had learned in Egypt when I went to my Catholic school. One day, my son came to me and said, "Mom, I want you to go to church. I want you to be saved." Well, I was shocked. I said, "Oh sweetheart, I just send you to that school because it's giving you a good education, but I don't know if I want to go to a church." I laughed it off.

Then, in 1997, years after I had arrived in America, I was having a cup of coffee and watching Sunday morning shows on TV. I was flipping through channels and saw pastors and preachers and church services, one after the other. I was very impressed by one particular pastor, and while I was watching this program I began praying for my people to watch it too. I just kept thinking, "They are so deprived of this kind of holy message. All they hear about are jihadist aspirations, torture in the grave, and God's wrath on the Jews. Why don't they hear this? It's so different."

The preacher was saying that we're all sinners. I was shocked! What a concept! I had thought only non-Muslims were sinners. We were Muslims. Therefore, we were superior, and *they* were all sinners. It made me feel so good to think that I was a sinner too, and that we were all equally sinful before God. Islam teaches you too much anger and hate towards others, and so much pride in yourself that you forget you're a sinner.

Then, my daughter came in the room and asked, "Mom, what's wrong with you? Are you okay? Why are you crying?" I explained I was very touched by what this preacher was saying, and when she looked at the TV and saw the pastor she said, "Mom, this is Dudley. He preaches from the Bible every Sunday at school."

The next Sunday, I woke the whole house up early in the morning and said, "Everybody, get dressed, we're going to go to church." I thought that everybody would think I was crazy, but my husband and my kids got up and got dressed, and we all went to church. All the way in the car I was so excited, and when I entered the church there was a song playing and I heard the words, "And I won't be afraid." Even the song was telling me not to be afraid.

I started crying, and I couldn't stop myself from crying for the whole service. It was almost a relief that I couldn't stop. Then, I looked at the empty seats in the church and said, "Oh, I wish my mum was here in this church, in this chair. I wish my sister was here, I wish my brother was here. They don't know what they're missing. They don't know what true holiness is, what true religion is!"

A few weeks later, I got baptized. It wasn't difficult for my kids to follow me in the Christian faith. They immediately accepted Jesus as their Lord and Savior because they had learned about Him in a Christian school. My life has never been the same again. I don't feel fear in what I'm doing, even though a lot of people tell me they're too scared to speak against Islam in such a way. I feel it's the natural thing for me to do because I've been so hurt by this ideology, and it's hurting so many other people.

JEFF KING: What was the response of the Muslim community when you became a Christian?

The response was total condemnation and threats. I got threatening e-mails. The Muslim community totally rejected me. In Egypt, there were articles written about me, threatening my life. My family had to disown me in public, and here the Council on American Islamic Relations (CAIR) accused me of Islamophobia. They were denouncing me, calling me names. They said I was doing it for the money, or because I hated myself and had suffered in my childhood.

JEFF KING: Were there threats on your life?

Yes, there were threats on my life in Egypt and in America. They called me an apostate, an infidel, and even a Zionist. It's scary because I never know if somebody is going to stab me in the back as I'm out walking. However, ever since I became a Christian I have a peace inside me and an urge to speak the truth about Islam and its goals, especially to unsuspecting Americans. Religion—any religion—should be about peace, tolerance and getting along with the rest of humanity, but the goals of Islam are to conquer the world to Islam. The means to achieve these goals can be done through murder and total control of society. Under Islamic law, anyone who leaves Islam must be killed! What kind of holy religion is that?

JEFF KING: Why do you risk your life in speaking out about the danger of Islam?

Because I care so much about the Judeo-Christian culture in the United States. Expansion of Islam in America is a threat to our democracy and to our culture. Islam does not want to co-exist. Islam wants to rule and it wants to change the state of Christian culture. It wants to change the state of America forever. We only need to look at history to know how Islam has changed nations.

JEFF KING: Nonie, give me a summary of your book, *Now They Call Me Infidel.* What's in there? Why should they read it?

Now They Call Me Infidel is about my life story, reflecting on the true culture of Islam that I grew up in. I reflect on how I felt and how it affected me—as well as on the jihad, the anger, and the indoctrination within the Islamic society. I explain: what jihad is; the roots of jihad against the Jews, against Israel; how I changed; and how I became a Christian. My major in college was sociology and anthropology, so you will find a lot of sociological analysis of Islamic society and the Islamic mind. My second book is *Cruel and Usual Punishment.*

JEFF KING: That's a great title.

The Terrifying Global Implications of Islamic Law is the subtitle. I noticed that a lot of people in the United States were being fooled by Islamic defenders who said Sharia law is compatible with democracy. This is a lie. I studied Sharia law for a year and a half to write my book. Even though I had lived under Sharia for many years, my jaw dropped. It was much worse than I'd thought.

My third book, which I'm writing now, is going to be called *Islam: Ideology or Religion?* In it, I refute the idea that Islam is a co-existing religion and I explain why this unrestrained growth of Islam in America is an ideological threat to American values.

A religion must never infringe on basic human rights. People must be allowed to choose their own religion. If a religion does not comply with the basic human right of choice, then it shouldn't pretend to be a religion at all. What's more, Islam discriminates between men and women, between Muslim and non-Muslim. Discrimination is also an infringement of basic human rights. If you condemn other people to death because they don't belong to your religion or because they have renounced it, then you have crossed one of the basic tenets of a religion.

Islam is not a religion; Islam is anti-religion. It's like communism, cloaking itself with an image of faith. It gives Muslims some ritualistic things to do to feel they have a religion but, in reality, it's a totalitarian ideology that is hell-bent on controlling the world and ending true religion, ending the belief in Jesus Christ, and ending Judaism. Just as they conquered North Africa, Turkey and Southern Spain centuries ago, the desire to conquer the world has never diminished.

Islam is very jealous of any other ideology or religion. It's so jealous that it wants to wipe them from existence. Islam's credibility in its faith in itself is tied to the destruction of other faiths. It perceives religion as a competition, and that's why Muslims are not told about any other ideology, nothing other than Islam. Every other ideology is constantly impressed on Muslims as something to despise, and that's the only way Islam feels secure enough to operate. It must destroy the credibility of other religions.

According to some estimates, sixty-two percent of the Qur'an addresses non-Muslims. It's consumed with curses and ridicule for non-Muslims, while Muslims are not addressed enough. The Qur'an is less concerned with advising Muslims in morality than with encouraging them to compare themselves with non-Muslims and to hate them. Islam is a negative response to Christianity and Judaism, and that's why I really believe Islam is not a religion; Islam is anti-religion. Most Muslims really don't know that this is not a very coherent kind of thinking.

JEFF KING: The inconsistencies are not recognized?

That's right. It doesn't add up, but we were trained to believe in two opposing views at the same time, and it seems perfectly logical. I remember we had an imam at our house one time, reciting the Qur'an, and I told him that my heart was breaking for the many poor people in Egypt. I contrasted the depth of poverty in Egypt to the poor in America, who would be considered middle class in Egypt. What this holy man told me was really heartbreaking. He said, "There is a reason why God made them poor: because they deserve it." They deserve it! His position was: don't break your heart for them; they did it to themselves. I felt this was so cruel.

The word love is never mentioned in the Qur'an; it's never promoted. The concept that God is love, or that God loves me is not part of Islam. There is no concept of redemption. In order for us to be guaranteed to go to heaven we must die in the jihad against the unfaithful. The word jihad means only one thing: war with non-Muslims to extend Islam by a process of converting sinners. The concept of sin in Islam is being a non-Muslim; non-sin is being a Muslim.

JEFF KING: Most non-Muslims are familiar with the idea of what heaven provides in Islam, including the seventy-two virgins, but that has an appeal for men. What did they say to little girls in Islam; what does heaven provide for women?

As women, we were socialized to know that only if we pleased our husbands, listened, and never objected to Sharia law, we would go to heaven. Religious leaders never defined what we were going to do in heaven. It's a place where you have rivers of wine; everything that's prohibited on earth is in heaven. You're told also that most of the inhabitants of hell are women. There are many Hadith [quotations by Muhammad in the Qur'an] in which Muhammad says, "I visited hell and heaven and I saw that most of the inhabitants of hell are women."

They make you feel you're in hell already, and the only way to escape to heaven is by total obedience to men and to Islamic law, which oppresses women. The more women accept oppression, the greater the chances that they will get out of hell and closer to heaven. That's why Muslim women accept their inferior status. They accept their oppression and have very few laws to protect them. All the laws are for the empowerment of men and enslavement of women, and they trick the women's minds to make them guardians of their own oppression, of their own prison.

JEFF KING: You have said the rule of Islamic terror is the rage that exists within the Muslim family. Could we talk about that?

The Muslim family is not like the traditional Christian family. The family dynamic in Islam does not honor the relationship between one man and one woman. Islam gives the right to a man to have more than one wife. And the Muslim marriage contract is very discriminatory. In it, the wife is asked if she is a virgin. If she isn't, the man will take her back to her family, take back his dowry, and she will be honor-killed. The man is not asked if he is a virgin.

There are other unsettling portions of the marriage contract. The husband is asked to write down the names of his other wives, if any. Even if these spaces are left empty, the woman knows they can be filled at any time in the future. She knows that she should not expect loyalty from her husband, so she does not feel she is part of a unit: one man, one woman, one set of children.

In the Muslim marriage, no property is shared. A Muslim man keeps his money; a Muslim woman keeps her money. They are separate in order to protect the woman. She doesn't want to pay for someone else's family. Also, if her husband dies, she will receive very little because the male members of his family will inherit more than she will.

A woman goes into a marriage with a mindset of self-preservation, with all the legal rights of the man against her. For example, a man can beat her and he doesn't have to give any explanation, even to the police. Divorce is in his hands; she has no right to divorce him unless he agrees. He can beat her; he can even imprison her in the house if he thinks she has misbehaved.

Because of all that, a woman goes into a marriage in a very weak position. She has to be very innovative in how she protects herself. She has to protect herself from the man. There is distrust, and when you don't have trust then the marriage is full of conspiracies to protect themselves against each other.

One time, when I was a teenager visiting my aunt's house in Egypt, we watched an American movie. In the 1960s, Egyptian television showed an American movie once a week and we would all gather to watch it. I saw for the first time a Christian wedding in a church in the movie. It was very different from the Muslim wedding. We saw the father of the bride walk her to the husband who was waiting by the priest and he handed the wife to the husband. Then, they both stood as equals in front of the preacher or the priest and they made their vows. They were reciting vows of loyalty. I heard the man say, "I will love and cherish my one and only wife in sickness and in health; till death I will honor you and cherish you."

And the wife said the same thing. I was so shocked. It was very different from the Muslim marriage. They became one unit and then they became one flesh. The idea in Christianity of becoming one flesh, one body under holy matrimony, was a totally different idea of marriage.

JEFF KING: Touching on Muslim families in another way, how prevalent is honor-killing in the Islamic world?

It's very prevalent. Perceived sexual violations by women are harshly punished. Just a simple rumor that a girl likes a man can ruin her. She doesn't even have to be sexually active. She is immediately called a whore, and her father and brothers cannot show their faces to society. Islam harshly punishes women for sexual misconduct of any sort. I personally knew somebody who was honor-killed for actually being raped.

This is another major difference between Christianity and Islam. In Christianity, Jesus stood and prevented the stoning of a woman in the middle of a public square, yet Islam, which came centuries after Christianity, codified the stoning of women for sexual misconduct into law forever. Today, you find women being stoned to death by the government of Iran. Honor killing is also sanctioned by Sharia. A lot of Muslims in America will say this is a cultural thing and nothing to do with Islam, but this is a big lie, because there is a law of Sharia that clearly says a Muslim will be forgiven for murdering an adulterer.

JEFF KING: Even culturally, it's an incredibly harsh custom. Even just being unable to have a boyfriend ...

Sexual segregation is against US law, but it's entrenched in Islamic law. Mixing between the sexes is not supposed to be allowed. I lived in Egypt, which was much more moderate than Saudi Arabia or the Gulf states, and I could never have a boyfriend openly. I could never have smiled at a man or even have looked a man in the eyes without being called a whore. A woman has to be untouched. Yet, walking in the streets of Cairo, in the crowded downtown areas, we would get pinched by men; we would be physically touched and we had to practically run. Because you are a woman who is walking alone without a man, you somehow deserve to be touched.

You are totally segregated, and you are better off keeping yourself segregated to avoid being accused of something.

JEFF KING: Let's talk about the abductions of Christian girls in Muslim countries. Help your average Westerner understand what is going on. How big a problem is it? What recourse does a family have if their daughter has been abducted?

The American public will not want to believe this, but I heard the testimony of a former Muslim who said that when he was a Muslim he was part of a group in Egypt who was paid by funds from Saudi Arabia to marry Christian girls by hook or crook.

Saudi Arabia wants to get rid of the ten or twelve percent of remaining Christians in Egypt. The way they are doing it now is by telling the Muslim men that if they marry a Christian and convert her to Islam, they will be rewarded in heaven. In Islam, the children always follow the father's religion, so Christianity is wiped out at marriage. But how does a Muslim man get a Christian girl to marry him? A Muslim girl who's a friend of a Christian girl entices her into a house where she is given something to sedate her and she's raped, so she's good for nothing. She's ruined. Even among Christians in Egypt, if a girl is not a virgin, she can't get married. It's the same as with Muslims; it's a cultural thing.

The Muslim man who rapes her tells her he will help her by marrying her, but she has to become a Muslim. It's better to be a Muslim than to live in shame for the rest of her life. She actually runs away with him or they take her by force in an unconscious condition. She goes to a *ma'zun*, the man who marries people in Islam, and she signs the marriage contract and is never seen by her family again.

JEFF KING: Let's say the family finds out where she is. What happens?

I've heard it firsthand from fathers who say they reported their daughters as having been abducted and forcibly married, but the policemen just slap the father on the face because she's married and he has no rights to her anymore.

JEFF KING: She could be thirteen. He could say, "Wait a minute; she's underage."

It doesn't help. Even if the [abducted girl's] "husband" is brought in, he's responsible for her now. The father gets nowhere. I heard that even sometimes they bring in the daughter and she's in a half-conscious state [drugged], but that's it; [she's gone] forever.

JEFF KING: What do you see for the future of the United States in regards to Islam?

In a few decades, we're going to have an area in America that's predominantly Muslim, and we are going to have terror attacks inside the United States by Muslims demanding Sharia law. If it isn't given to them, we are going to be living in fear of bomb attacks whenever we go into a restaurant or a shopping mall.

JEFF KING: Where are the main areas you see that happening?

I see that happening in Michigan, but I see it also happening inside the Bible belt. There are many mosques being built specifically in the Bible belt because they want to preach to the vulnerable there. They are not building mosques only in areas that are spiritually empty places. No, they're going to the heart, and there are always vulnerable souls in these areas, those who don't feel they belong; vulnerable young males, especially in the jail population.

JEFF KING: The usual line that you're very familiar with in the West is that every religion has its crackpots, its fundamentalists who distort the essential message, and that Islam is really a religion of peace. What's your take on that?

That is untrue because what I and others are criticizing is not people. We are criticizing the words in the Qur'an, the Muslim scriptures. Muslim scriptures encourage Muslims to kill non-Muslims. Commands to kill are all over the Qur'an. It's not just one or two; it's actually the main idea of the Qur'an: to either subjugate non-Muslims or kill them.

I'm sure there are many good and peace-loving Muslims, but that's not the point. It's the ideology inherent in their scriptures that we criticize.

The doctrine itself is flawed; the doctrine itself is anti-peace. The ideology itself promotes war, hatred, discrimination and lying. It commands Muslims to lie. If a religion commands its followers to lie, then there must be something wrong that it's trying to hide.

JEFF KING: Why are the majority of Muslims silent in terms of condemning Islamic terrorism?

Muslims know that speaking against Islam is punishable by death. Even if they move to America, they all move with their baggage of fear. There are many reasons why Muslims are silent, but the most important reason is that we know in our hearts that what the jihadists are doing is following the Qur'an. Condemning the concept of jihad [which is a mainstream ideology in Islam] is equal to condemning Islam itself.

We're all brainwashed. Some of us have succeeded in removing this brainwashing and we see the ugly reality, but the majority of us are still confused, and those are the people who are Islamists. Things don't add up for them, but they settle that confusion by ignoring it.

JEFF KING: You've said radical Islam has declared war in America and in the West, and that the majority of Muslims either support or make excuses for terrorism. Now, do you stand by that?

No, I didn't say they support terrorism. Sometimes I'm misquoted. A lot of Muslims are really misinformed about their own religion and they don't really know it or defend it, but they are not my concern. My concern is the people who are really committed to the Islamic ideology of jihad as it appears in the Qur'an. They are the majority of really committed Muslims who understand exactly what's in the Qur'an and who want to misinform us about the intentions of terrorists. Some people try to tell us such people are in the minority. But, in fact, their ideology is what's at the very heart of Islam. Islam and the Qur'an encourage terrorism against non-Muslims; it's called jihad.

We just have to read the Qur'an and the Hadith and look at the example of Muhammad himself to know that Islam at its core is an expansionist-by-the-sword religion. It has imperialist aspirations and it has its eyes always on government. It's a political ideology that wants no other party but the party of Islam to rule. That's what's called *Hezbollah*.[13] *Hezbollah* means the party of Allah, and only the party of Allah must rule under Islamic law.

Islam, at its heart, promotes violence. The Islamist definition of jihad is "war with non-Muslims to establish the religion." This is really a misinterpretation, because in ancient Arabic it simply meant "effort to promote the religion."

Wherever you see the borders of Islam with non-Muslim countries, there is war on that border. Wherever Islam goes, conflict, helplessness and war prevail, and there's no peaceful coexistence of religions.

JEFF KING: Let's turn to Egypt. How do you describe the growth of Wahhabism in your own home country?

Egypt is becoming radical; it's close to becoming like Saudi Arabia, unfortunately. Egypt used to be a Christian nation, but gradually the Christians became discriminated against. They had to pay extra taxes and I'm amazed, really, at how they survived because there are very few minority religions in Iran, Turkey and North Africa. Only Lebanon and Egypt defied the odds and survived for many years with Christian populations.

However, Islam itself weakened and became discredited, in my opinion, in the nineteenth century. The British, when they were in Egypt, brought a lot of equality and tolerance towards the Christians. They no longer had to pay the jizya, which is extra taxes because they were Christians, and they started gaining more respect in society. Jews also prospered and gained more equal rights.

In 1920, the first feminist movement happened, defying Islamism. In my opinion, it was all due to Western protection. Huda Shaarawi was an upper class elitist feminist in Egypt. She went to Europe and Turkey, and was inspired by the feminist movement that was

[13] See pg. 343.

developing in America and Europe around that time. When she and a bunch of rich Egyptian women came back from Europe to Alexandria, they took the train to Cairo where Huda Shaarawi took off her Islamic head cover and her hijab and threw it down for the media and the world to see. All the women with her did the same thing. It was a big feminist movement. Nothing happened to them; they were successful, and that is why my grandmother never wore the headgear, and why my mother never wore the hijab.

However, the British officially left Egypt in 1954 and left the Muslim Brotherhood to regain its influence. The Arab world, particularly Saudi Arabia, was growing in economic power because of oil, and that helped bring Wahhabism out of the grave.

JEFF KING: Could you compare more of the Islamic world to the world of the West? What other differences are there?

The cultural differences are huge. The value system is opposite. For example, pride is a virtue in Islam. Envy is very common. I feel that the Muslim world is controlled with envy, pride, and shame. This is a very predominant part of the culture that's very different from that of the West.

In the West, they promote your behavior through encouragement. In Islamic countries, you're shamed into doing something: "Do this or you're not a man; do that or you're not a real Muslim; you should do this or you're going to hell." It's shaming and threatening.

Another difference has to do with envy. One thing I learned in my Christian church is that envy is one of the seven deadly sins. It's something that hurts the person who envies. In the Muslim world, and according to the Qur'an, envy (directed at you from others) is a curse that you must guard yourself against all the time. You always have to watch out for other peoples' evil eyes. Consequently, there is no trust between Muslim people. There is total *distrust*. You have to be on guard against your neighbors, your friends, even against your family. This concept of envy is engraved in Islamic culture.

JEFF KING: What do you think about how Americans deal with Islam? Are we diplomatic enough? What's wrong with our attitudes and what do we need to do?

I have many suggestions in my second book, *Cruel and Usual Punishment*. The main point in that book is that Americans feel something is wrong with Islam but cannot pinpoint it. They believe it's a religion and religions must be respected. We are left in a quandary, and it's all because Islam defines itself as religion.

As Americans, we have to define for ourselves what a religion is before we give protective rights to any ideology which might be seeking to subvert the values we hold dear. There are religions from ancient times that used to practice human sacrifice. Are we going to bring religions from foreign lands that believe in human sacrifice? Islam does believe in human sacrifice. It believes that Jews should be killed wherever you find them. Are we going to give it total freedom to expand in America? Under Islam, a government *must* be ruled by Sharia, but Sharia is totally in opposition to our constitution.

I'm not saying we want to restrict everybody from practicing their religion. I don't care if you want to call your witchcraft a religion as long as you don't hurt anybody. But the minute you want to practice human sacrifice and impose seventh century Arabian law on the government, then you have crossed the line. Islam has violated the most sensible standard of what a religion should be.

JEFF KING: You've spoken about the radicalization of Muslim students at university campuses in the States. What's going on there?

Under the freedom of religion, Muslim Student Associations are in every university. I haven't seen one university that doesn't have them in every college and, again, this is not by coincidence.

I am in communication with students in Yemen and Egypt where there are offers of free scholarships to Arab kids who are tested to see if they are worthy of coming to America. A Yemeni student—an A-student—once wrote to me to say he had been denied the scholarship because he was in favor of peace with Israel and wasn't a radical Muslim.

He said that they gave the scholarships to four radical Muslim students who were for jihad and promoting Islam. It's almost a quid pro quo. If you want to get a scholarship to America, you must become a member of the Muslim Student Association to promote Islam in America and to promote jihad and anti-Semitism. It's not difficult to find people in the Muslim world like that. They are in the majority.

JEFF KING: So, radicalism is growing?

Radicalism is growing. The same people who [were] financing Osama bin Laden are also financing the mosques across the world, including America. It's the same source of money. These are the people who are sitting in Saudi Arabia on bank accounts from petro dollars who want to promote Islam around the world, whether by sending money to terrorist organizations or by the radicalizing of imams who work for them in the mosques.

JEFF KING: It's helpful to get people to understand that there is no real division between the Islamist Brotherhood, Wahhabism, and Al Qaeda.

They all have the same goal. The problem with Islam is that it's attractive to the violent side of human nature. Most human beings, and I believe a majority of Muslims, really don't want to be involved in terrorism. They don't want to do bad things to others; they want to live in peace just as everybody else wants to, but that's not what their religion is telling them.

JEFF KING: Nonie, your name has become associated with something called "the pledge." Can you tell us what the pledge is?

Last November, my organization, www.FormerMuslimsUnited.org wrote a Muslim Pledge for Religious Freedom and Safety from Harm for Former Muslims. This is what's now known as The Freedom Pledge. It was sent to over 165 Muslim leaders and organizations in the USA. In the pledge, we asked them to repudiate the Sharia legal doctrine that requires the punishment and, in most cases, the execution of former Muslims who choose to exercise their rights to religious freedom and freedom of speech. Unfortunately, we only received two signed pledges back, and they were from reformer Muslims, Zuhdi Jasser and Ali Alyami. To date, no Muslim leader, including the so-called 'moderate' Imam Rauf, has agreed to sign or even acknowledge receipt of the pledge. Please read the pledge and cover letter by visiting the site below:

http://formermuslimsunited.americancommunityexchange.org/the-pledge/

Chapter Five:

The Son of a Hamas Founder

My problem is not with Muslims;
our problem is with the idea of Islam, the god of Islam.
I love Muslims, and because I love them I tell them the truth.
My problem is with their god and their religion,
and so I am challenging them.

I say that Muslims are wonderful people; Muslims have more
moralities, responsibilities, and logic than their god. I believe that
their god doesn't have these qualities. The most criminal, terrorist
Muslim has a minimum of morality more than the god of Islam. I say
that this hatred is in their Qur'an, so either they admit that this is in
their Qur'an and this is who they are and they are proud of it, or
they say they are not Muslims anymore.

Author photograph taken by Stephen Vosloo.
Copyright © by Tyndale House Publishers, Inc. All rights reserved.

Mosab Hassan Yousef

Mosab Hassan Yousef has lived as the son of one of the founding members of Hamas, as an imprisoned enemy of Israel, as a spy for Israel, and finally as an apostate from Islam and as a convert to Christianity. He has known the core of Islam and the price you must pay to abandon it.

I wanted to include his perspective because he is one of the clearest voices on the source of Islam. He will tell you that, while Muslims are some of the greatest people he knows, many are unaware or have been deceived by Islam, Muhammad, and Islam's holy books.

Mosab Hassan Yousef has risked his life by publishing his own book that exposes Islam and the organization that his father helped to found: Hamas.

Books by Mosab Hassan Yousef:
- *Son of Hamas: A Gripping Account of Terror, Betrayal, Political Intrigue, and Unthinkable Choices*

JEFF KING: Tell us about your life in Hamas.

I grew up in one of the most religious families in the Middle East. My father was one of the leaders of the Islamic revolution and was one of the founders of Hamas. He's still at the top of Hamas today in the West Bank. He's in an Israeli prison. I grew up in the Palestinian territories where I saw lots of killing, lots of violence. Later on, I was arrested by the Israeli Shin Bet, and with my experience in prison, everything changed.

JEFF KING: Tell us about how Hamas was founded and your father's role in starting the organization.

It was born to destroy Israel and establish an Islamic state in the Palestinian territories in order to establish a global Islamic state that would rule the entire world. Hamas' other purpose is resistance – to defend themselves against Israel's occupation. The international community gives them the right to defend themselves. But they believe that they have the right to defend themselves by blowing people up. Because of that, Hamas has been responsible for the deaths of many Jewish people, and many Israelis.

I also believe they're responsible for Israel's aggression and its reaction to their attacks. Hamas is an organization that wants to defend its people, but I don't believe they know how. They have made the situation worse, and they are responsible for the deaths of many people. They need to stop for a second and think where they're going with their so-called resistance.

JEFF KING: Was Hamas founded as an outgrowth of the Brotherhood?

Hamas and the Brotherhood are the same. The Muslim Brotherhood is the mother of Hamas. They have the same ideology, but they call it Hamas in order to take the Muslim Brotherhood out of the picture so Israel does not attack the entire Muslim Brotherhood. This is how they survive. It was a strategic and smart thing to do, but the two groups are absolutely the same.

JEFF KING: How about funding? Are the Saudis the main funders?

This is a tricky thing. Hamas initially funded the movement from their own pockets, with members' donations. Funding is not what keeps Hamas going. What keeps Hamas going is their motivation — their Qur'an and their Islam. In fact, funding can sometimes be destructive for Hamas because when they have more money, they become more corrupt. They get busy with money. There have been times when they didn't have money, and they were more dangerous.

JEFF KING: And the PLO is getting funding from the EU, correct? The Palestinian territories are receiving funding from the EU and from the US, as well as from the Saudi world. Who actually receives the money? Where does it go?

The official organization that receives funds from Western countries and Arab governments is the Palestinian Authority. The Palestinian Authority is not ruled by Hamas. The Palestinian Authority is ruled by the PLO, which is secular.

They're supposed to report how they use the money. They use it for infrastructure, for education, health, and things like this. But from experience we have learned that in the Second Intifada,[14] Yasser Arafat used money that came from American taxpayers to fund terrorist acts and pay his guards to kill people.

They also built villas and bought fancy cars; they spent the money on personal things most of the time. This is why there was a huge case

---

[14] See pg. 345.

of corruption in the Palestinian authority. Now, I think there's less corruption than there was, but corruption exists in every government.

But I am sure that there is no direct funding from the EU or the United States to Hamas. Indirectly, the Palestinian Authority pays Hamas parliament members from the funds that they receive from the United States. So, directly or indirectly, some of this money will go to Hamas.

But this doesn't mean that the EU or the United States should stop those funds; there are orphans, there are people who are victims of this conflict. They need education, they need health care. At the end of the day, money is not the issue, and cutting the flow of money to terrorists will not stop their motivation.

JEFF KING: You say that Hamas is a ghost, an idea. What do you mean by that?

Say, for example, you're dealing with a mafia. Usually, their motive is a personal motive. You can scare them, put them in prison and punish them, and they will stop on some level and they will be very limited. But, when you're fighting a group like Hamas—that's highly motivated by their beliefs, by the Qur'an, by the promise of their god—the more you put pressure on them, the more they believe in their idea. Hamas is an idea; Hamas is an ideology, and you simply can't kill an idea with a tank or Apache. You stimulate ideas or you change ideas; you challenge ideas. So it's ideological warfare.

This is why everyone has failed to stop Hamas so far. There's no way to stop them if you don't stop their ideology, not even if you cut off all their funding. Hamas has been under sanctions for the last four years now in Gaza. They are responsible for feeding 1.5 million Palestinians and themselves, and they're still surviving. No gas, no electricity, no food, lack of everything, and they can still survive. You know why? Because their motivation still survives.

JEFF KING: If Hamas and Fatah[15] were to get land for peace, what would they do?

The best-case scenario is that they will fight for that. It's finally their decision to have self-determination and do whatever they want in their land. But what I can say is, I cannot guarantee that they will ever get peace.

JEFF KING: That's the point. One of their stated goals is self-determination, but if they gain self-determination, that won't end the war. Why not?

They must understand and gain freedom and liberty in their hearts first. If you give them land now, and they don't understand what liberty means, what freedom means, they will abuse it and they will be victims.

I'm not saying that they don't deserve to have a Palestinian state, but this is their challenge. It's their right to have a state, but will a Palestinian state give the Palestinians peace? I doubt it. Will a Palestinian state build a future for Palestinians? Good education, good health care? A solid government that will make them a better nation? I doubt that also. This is the real challenge.

JEFF KING: You described in the book a time when you were watching an explosion that was being blamed on Israel. Your father was being interview by Al Jazeera. You are looking at the video, and you realize that the explosion came from the ground up. Despite proving this, Al Jazeera ran it as a false story. I just remember in the Lebanon war, there were a lot of staged things from Hezbollah and they largely got pass. How reliable is the news coming out of the region? How easily is it manipulated?

---

[15] See pg. 340.

It's not only manipulated, but everybody there creates his own version of this conflict. There are victims on both sides. Many people are taking advantage of the conflict: religious leaders, politicians, everybody's trying to take advantage of the situation to climb on the shoulders of these victims.

We're dealing with corrupt human beings. Everybody has a percentage of corruption. Because of that I have to keep my focus on individuals, not just on nations. We have to start to change people's hearts.

You can use anything for any agenda. Take one picture; Palestinians will use the picture for their goals and the Israelis will also use the same picture. Whoever has more connections and more power will have more influence.

JEFF KING: What's been the cost of your conversion to Christianity?

Of course, the cost was really high. This is one of the most difficult things for any Muslim who wants to turn their back on the god of the Qur'an. First of all, you turn your back on your entire culture. You turn your back on your god, your family, everything you have learned.

You become absolutely alone. You become hated, and you get death threats. It is a death sentence, or death penalty, for turning your back on the god of Islam. This is Islamic teaching. Muhammad said, "Whoever changes his religion, kill him."

With all that, of course, the consequences are very high, and the cost is very high. It's amazing how you are rejected just for saying the truth. In my case, it wasn't only about leaving Islam; I was also collaborating with Israel. This made me also a traitor—a traitor to Allah, a traitor to the nation. Even Christians in the Middle East call me Judas because they can't think of Israel as anything but the enemy.

Christians in the West were afraid I was a terrorist. I'm sorry, not everybody felt like this, but several Christians thought like this. I couldn't convince anybody of my motive, my heart, and the reality of what happened in my life. There is a huge price for proclaiming truth. Look at Jesus Christ, the perfect one. He was innocent and they shed his innocent blood for what? For what cause? He was telling the truth.

Because he brought the truth, they killed him. Everybody participated in nailing him to the cross. I'm telling you, this is a living example. Say the truth and everybody will hate you for it.

But this doesn't mean that we hide the truth. It doesn't mean that all of us should be cowards.

JEFF KING: What has been the cost specifically with your family?

My family finally disowned me. I kept in touch with them; they were expecting that I would come back to Islam. After my book came out, and with its dangerous facts, they had no choice but to disown me.

Simply, my family is like any other family. I understand their position. If they didn't disown me, it means they were giving me a cover. The consequences for partnering with a traitor like me who turned his back, he betrayed god, betrayed his nation, betrayed his people, his family, everybody. To participate or partner with a person like me, this means that they deserve the same that I deserve. And they are there—they could be persecuted.

So, they have no other option to protect themselves but to disown me. But I know their hearts. This is another cost that I'm not the only one who's paying. My family also is paying a very high price for this. I believe through this project I defeated demons of fear and shame and guilt.

The god of Islam controls the entire Middle East, not just my family, but every Muslim in the world with three main weapons: fear, shame, and guilt. Those are the most dangerous weapons against Muslim society. Because of them, that society doesn't have liberty. They don't have freedom to express themselves, and they don't have freedom to choose.

Even my God told me how he defeated those enemies of man – enemies of humanity – on the cross. He defeated the demon of fear, the demon of shame, the demon of guilt on the cross. I simply took a similar lead in publishing *Son of Hamas* and defeating those dangerous enemies. Those are the enemies you need to defeat to be able to be a productive nation.

JEFF KING: Tell us about the role of shame and fear in Islam.

The entire culture in the Middle East is based on shame and guilt. This is how they define what is good and bad; if a child does something bad, his mother will tell him, "Shame on you." They don't say, "This is bad and this is good."

To people in the Middle East, to my family, to Muslims in general, because their culture is based on shame and guilt, even if I did what was right, even if I saved a human life—the right thing to do—this was shameful. In their eyes, it was wrong. Suicide bombers kill innocent people, but they are honored in that society. People praise them in that society. Why? Because that culture is based on shame and honor.

This is honor; this is shame. They don't care if it is right or wrong. Guilt, shame, and honor, those are the real values of that culture. And of course, the god of the Qur'an uses those weapons against the Muslims.

JEFF KING: Let's dig a little deeper, then. What's at the core of Islam? Who is behind Islam?

Muhammad is behind Islam.

JEFF KING: Who was Muhammad in your opinion?

I believe that Muhammad is a liar. I believe that Muhammad created a lie. He wrapped it in layers of truth, facts, and moralities, and because of those layers it became a perfect lie. It deceived many, many people. He hid his ugly, selfish face behind this religion. He created this religion to serve his personal desires of becoming the king of the Arabs and the prophet of the Arabs.

He wrapped this lie of selfishness, of self-desire, in noble goals with facts and morals that he stole from other religions, and forced everybody to believe in it. At the beginning, he didn't have the power to force it on people, so he convinced some of the poor people, and used them later to create an army and force it on everyone else. He sacrificed humans for this lie, and at some point he believed in it and forced everybody to believe in it. Islam and Muhammad are the biggest lies in human history.

JEFF KING: Who's behind Muhammad?

I can't say in a simple word. You as a Christian will understand what I say, but secularists will not understand because they don't believe in Satan and they don't believe in God. But what I can say is that darkness, ignorance, selfishness, and greed all work together in the personality of Muhammad to create this idea of Islam that serves all those selfish things in his heart. The powers of darkness have fed the desires of his followers until today.

Of course, there are also religious and political leaders who take advantage of poor people trying to find God and something to believe in. They became rich and corrupt, and they caused the deaths of their followers and others. They destroyed civilizations and they built their kingdoms on the rubble of wonderful civilizations. The common point among Muhammad and his disciples is the power of darkness. Simply, it is Satan.

JEFF KING: The material we deal with can make a lot of people hate Muslims. That's not our goal at all. What do you say to people when they hate Muslims?

Our problem is not with Muslims; our problem is with the idea of Islam, the god of Islam. We love Muslims, and because we love them we tell them the truth. Our problem is with their god and their religion, and so we are challenging them.

I say that Muslims are wonderful people; Muslims have more moralities, responsibilities, and logic than their god. I believe that their god doesn't have these qualities. The most criminal, terrorist Muslim has a minimum of morality more than the god of Islam. I say that this hatred is in their Qur'an, so either they admit that this is in their Qur'an and this is who they are and they are proud of it, or they say they are not Muslims anymore.

Chapter Six:

The Outspoken Apostate

Americans are brought up by the Western code of ethics which prevents them from judging people based on their religious background. I appreciate that, but the problem is that people in the West need to understand Islam is more than a religion. We have to define the concept of religion Islam is [also] a dangerous political ideology. Once people in the West understand this point, they will treat Islam differently, in a different way than other religions.

*[When] I came to the United States, I started publishing articles in Arabic newspapers criticizing Islam. A few months prior to September 11, a member of CAIR (**Council on American Islamic Relations**) called me at home and he said in Arabic, "Wafa, you are crossing the red line." In Arabic, when you use this statement, you know exactly what he means, exactly! When you tell a Muslim you're crossing the red line, then after the next offense, you will be beheaded.*

It is not easy to live expecting that someone may shoot you anytime you leave your home. It's not easy to relocate every six months – here in the United States! To live in America and to live under fear twenty-four seven, is beyond many people's ability to comprehend.

Wafa Sultan

During an Al Jazeera interview with a bullying Islamic cleric, **Wafa Sultan** shouted her five famous words ["shut up, it's my turn"] and then went on a rant about problems of Islam. Clips of the interview literally swept around the world. For an Arab woman to speak up, to demand equal space and time from a man—and a Muslim cleric, to boot—was unheard of. For an Arab woman to openly criticize Islam as inherently destructive was equally unheard of.

Wafa was formerly a Muslim. As an atheist apostate and outspoken female critic of Islam, she lives constantly with a price on her head. She is constantly watching over her shoulder and has to move every six months, but she will tell you that she is at peace and feels an energy coursing through her that empowers her to speak out and denounce evil.

Books by Wafa Sultan:
- *A God Who Hates: The Courageous Woman Who Inflamed the Muslim World Speaks Out Against the Evils of Islam*
- *Cruel and Usual Punishment: The Terrifying Global Implications of Islamic Law*

JEFF KING: Wafa, tell us about your background. Where were you born and how did you come to the United States?

I was born as a Muslim in a very traditional and devout Muslim family in Syria. In college, I met and fell in love with my husband, who was raised as a Muslim but was introduced to the Christian culture at an early age. He played a major role in making me who I am today. On our very first date he told me that Islam is not a real religion. I was very shocked. I was a medical student in 1978, and there was a very bloody conflict brewing between the Syrian government and the Muslim Brotherhood movement. One day, my professor was killed before my eyes and, at that time, I didn't really realize who the killers were. But they were shouting, "Allahu Akbar, Allahu Akbar (Allah is great)." At that moment, I started to question what kind of God we [Muslims] worshiped.

For years, I argued and debated with my husband, telling him the problem was not with Islam, but with how Muslims understood Islam. By the late eighties, the US had put Syria on a terrorism blacklist and enforced economic sanctions. We had a terrible life for half of the eighties. Everyone was thinking about leaving the country, and somehow we managed to emigrate to the United States in 1989.

When we first arrived, I was working very hard to find the truth, especially in regards to the Jews. As Muslims, we were taught that it was our mission to fight the Jews to the last day of our life. I remember a few incidents in the United States where I was shocked, completely shocked. I remember the first time we visited a shoe store in Hollywood. I was trying on some shoes and my husband asked the salesman, "Where are you from?" He said, "I'm a Jew from Israel." You wouldn't believe what happened. I screamed. I absolutely screamed. I jumped out of my shoes and ran from the store, screaming. My husband tried to calm me down, but I said, "But he's a Jew!!" You know, I was a medical doctor! I practiced medicine in

Syria for nine years and I never believed the Jews had human features. Can you believe the power of brainwashing?

I was shaking, just shaking. For the first time in my life, I met a Jew and I could see he was a human being. But I wasn't able to comprehend that he was a normal human being. About a year later, my son had a hearing problem and he had a special teacher helping with his speech. Around Christmas, this teacher sent me a note saying, "Wafa, I am a Jew by choice and I know you're Muslim, and I like to give my students a little gift for Christmas. Do you mind if I give him one?" She was so nice to us—she didn't want to offend me.

At first, when I read, "a Jew by choice," I didn't understand what she meant "by choice" because I didn't know that people could choose their religion. She said, "You're a Muslim." How did she know I was a Muslim? I went crazy. I called my husband and he said, "We may need to watch her. We're going to report any discrimination against our son." Within a few months, we realized she was a gift from God. Over time, she became a member of our family.

I had been brainwashed to not see the true nature of our Islamic teachings. You know what forced me to open my mind and my eyes? I started to study Islam, the Qur'an, and the life of Muhammad. I remembered a story my teacher proudly told us when I was eight about a moment in Muhammad's life, when he beheaded eight hundred Jewish men in one night (see author's note #1, pg. 125). He then slept with a Jewish woman whose father, husband, and brother he had killed that night. I was eight when I was brainwashed to believe that was a beautiful story and how brave Muhammad was to kill eight hundred Jewish men, to behead them. Could you imagine telling a child, an eight-year-old child, this story and making him or her believe her prophet is a brave man? So, after four or five years of being in a free country and practicing my life as a free woman, I opened my mind. I said, "Oh, my God, how can I teach my daughter this story and brainwash her to believe her prophet was a brave man?"

I believe education without values has no value and I mention that in my book *A God Who Hates*. The problem, the crisis, in the Islamic world is a moral crisis.

Do you know that Islam lacks a code of ethics? Do you know it was only after I came to the United States that I learned how to say "I'm sorry," and "I apologize." I had never said that in my native country because ... the Qur'an says that you don't apologize to anyone but Allah and Muhammad. So, in our faith, Islam, the only responsibility is to worship Allah and Muhammad. Once you pray, nothing else matters. So, our crisis is a moral crisis. When I came to this country, I was free to judge. I was free to look and evaluate. I learned that the problem is deeply rooted in Islamic teachings, and we are victims of Islam.

The President of the United States once said that Islam is hijacked by a bunch of criminals, but he is deceived. We [Muslims] are hijacked by the life and teachings of Muhammad. There is proof we can re-read the Qur'an in a more peaceful way, but the problem is not with the Qur'an. The problem is with the life of Muhammad. If Muhammad killed eight hundred, beheaded eight hundred men in one night – how do you read this story to your children in a peaceful way?

JEFF KING: Yes, and what about his consummating his marriage to a nine-year-old or that he had his way with the women he captured in battles, etc.

Yes! The lesson is that Muhammad is the problem since the Qur'an says that Muhammad is the role model for every Muslim and Muslims believe that the Qur'an is the absolute word of Allah, of God. I don't know how you're going to rewrite the life of Muhammad. That's why I don't have any hope when it comes to the reformation of Islam. You can reform Muslims, but not the religion by itself.

JEFF KING: Yes, that's the problem. The holy books are there and all the violence is encoded, it's all written down. You have a hard time explaining so much of it away.

Exactly. I don't know if you're familiar with the principle of abrogation. In Islam, "abrogation" is a principle that evolved within Islam to deal with contradictory verses in the holy books. Under abrogation, where there is a conflict between two passages in the Qur'an, later verses overrule earlier verses.

For instance, early in Muhammad's life, when he had little power, he tended to be peaceful and say peaceful things. Later, as he gained political and military power, he said and commanded many violent things which contradicted those earlier sayings.

The Qur'an was written in two different times of Muhammad's life. The first time, he was in Mecca and then when he moved to Medina; they're totally different times. The first time, he adopted some peaceful teachings that were taken from Christianity and Judaism, and then, when he established a strong army in Medina, he canceled it. He said abrogate all the previous teachings, and he established the new rules. So, I don't know. I believe the only way to change Islam is to grant Muslims the freedom to choose and you wouldn't believe the power of that. I am a well-known writer in the Arab world. Come read my e-mails that I receive from my readers in the Arab world.

And, by the way, I believe the only way to see meaningful change in Islam is through the Arabic language because Islam is purely an Arabic religion. And ninety-five percent of the Islamic texts—the original ones, at least—were written in Arabic. I believe ninety-five percent of them have never been translated to any other language.

JEFF KING: Recently, I was speaking with a high-profile Christian from the Middle East who used to be a Muslim and he said the same thing. The people are in a prison of fear.

Yes, absolutely! Read my book. There are three or four chapters about how destructive fear is. The first few chapters mention that Islam kept itself intact by forcing the Islamic teachings upon people. Let me tell you a story. My sister came to visit me maybe five, six, seven years ago, and we were sitting in my living room when I asked her a few questions about Islam and she started shaking and said, "Please, please, the walls have ears."

JEFF KING: Incredible! She was alone with you?

Yes, she was alone with me, in America. Can you imagine? She said, *"Don't forget, I'm going back to Syria."* She was afraid to express herself, alone in my living room in the United States, thousands of miles away from her country. I'm giving you an example of how manipulated, how controlled by fear Muslims can be; Islam micromanages our life. We're even taught how to use the bathroom, can you believe that? You have to use your left leg first because the bathroom is dirty. It's a very complicated story, but even when you enter the bathroom, you are focused on how to use your feet. Can you imagine?

I still remember they taught us how to eat. You have to use your right hand and we always say in the West that they use the fork with their left hand because [the right is] evil. Even with this, you're not free to behave spontaneously.

JEFF KING: Islam's influence is all encompassing. Just as an example, wherever they are they hear the call to prayer five times a day; there is no god but Allah and Muhammad is his prophet. It's more than a religion (in Western terms) it's hard for Westerners to understand because there is no equivalent. It's

just so all-encompassing. It's morning to night; throughout all of the culture, it is cradle to grave.

Even the concept of prayer in Islam is totally different. If I become sick, as a Christian, you would pray for me: "God, please help her to get well." This is not the way Muslims pray. We have to recite a prayer. We're not free to say whatever we want in our prayer. We have to recite certain verses of the Qur'an. We're not allowed to say, "Please God, help my friend." No, that's not prayer. So, we are micromanaged, even when we pray. We have to follow exactly what to say.

JEFF KING: Talk more about what happened with your worldview and how your views changed. What was the last part of the story?

The very first week I came to the United States, I started publishing articles in Arabic newspapers published here in California. Day by day, I was criticizing Islam more and more. I was afraid, believe me I was afraid! My writing was sugar-coated because I didn't want to be in danger. I was so afraid. I believe a few months prior to September 11, a member of CAIR [Council on American Islamic Relations] called me (See author's note #2, pg. 125). Yes, he called me at home and he said in Arabic, "Wafa, you are crossing the red line." In Arabic, when you use this statement, you know exactly what he means, exactly! When you tell a Muslim you're crossing the red line, then after the next offense, you will be beheaded.

If you tell an American this, it's like, "So what?" But in Arabic, I knew exactly what he meant. I tried to defend myself and defend my writings but he was not trying to be nice. He was calmly trying to convince me to stop writing, but then he went wild. "We can take you to court here in America because you're insulting our religion." I didn't know much about the American justice system [at] that time. I thought they could take you to court just to drain you financially, and I was afraid. Many friends, even Christian Arabs, advised me at that time to slow down. They said, "Please, please, it's for your life, and they can take you to court."

I was afraid. I had just bought my house. So, to be honest, I slowed down – until September 11. Thank God he called me only two months prior to September 11. September 11 was the major, major turning point of my life. The second I heard what happened [on 9/11], I said to myself, "Let them take me to court." I left Islam prior to September 11, but on September 11, I was released from my fear. I became free, totally free, at that moment. So from that moment on, it was easy.

JEFF KING: That had to be a good feeling!

Yes, my mind was unleashed! People always ask me why we don't hear more Muslim women do what I'm doing. I always say, "It's not easy." I understand Muslim women. I receive many e-mails from them telling me: "You are the only hope in our lives. Please keep going." It is very draining, very draining to go against your culture, against your religion, against your family.

It's not easy to live in a different kind of fear. A fear, I call it, of my choice. It is not easy to live expecting that someone may shoot you anytime you leave your home. It's not easy to relocate every six months—even here in the United States! If I do that in Syria, my old country, it makes sense. But...to live in America and to live under fear twenty-four seven, is beyond many people's ability to comprehend.

JEFF KING: Is that your life right now? You are moving every six months?

Absolutely. Prior to my book release, I had to move from my home and now it has been even more often than every six months. Today, we were thinking about moving again.

JEFF KING: What events led up to a video of you being broadcast around the world? How did that happen?

That was my first television interview. Prior to that Al Jazeera interview, I had become a well-known writer in the Arab world. People ask me why they invited me on Al Jazeera, and I think their plan was to destroy me.

They wanted to kill me emotionally. In Arabic, the language is totally different than any other language. Actually, we have two languages: the classical one and the spoken one. In order for you to defend yourself well and be perceived as respectable on national TV, you need to know how to speak classical Arabic. Even my husband doesn't know how to do it. They knew I had been in the States for sixteen years at that time, so they didn't expect me to be able to speak it.

They called me two days before the show and the host told me, "Now, we're familiar with your writings. We're going to ask you very simple questions. Do you think there is a link between terrorism and Islamic teachings?" I said, "Yes, yes! Absolutely, yes!" When I went to the studio in Hollywood, I found myself facing a human beast [the imam with the opposing viewpoint on the show]. He called me every bad word in the book. The next thing I know, my interview is all over the world. I didn't know at that time that my interview would be translated to so many languages. The very next day, a friend of mine called and said, "Wafa, do you know what happened?" I said, "What?" He said, "An organization called MEMRI translated your interview. It's all over the news."

And I couldn't believe it. You know, when I left the studio, I was crying [because I felt like such a failure]. My husband tried to calm me down. He said, "No, you did a great job." I said, "No, I didn't have enough time to defend myself. Nobody will believe in me anymore. I actually lost it—I was screaming!" The very next day, I was introduced to the West.

JEFF KING: What does that mean?

You know, it means prior to the interview, I thought I only needed to educate my people in the Arab world. After the interview, I found out that the West needed to be educated on Islam, too. I think the problem is that the West lacks an understanding of the Muslim mindset.

JEFF KING: Certainly.

You will never be able to win over your enemy until you understand their mindset and absolutely, absolutely, the West doesn't understand it, so far. So, hopefully, little by little, we're getting there.

JEFF KING: Yes. What did you say in the interview that caused it to go around the world? Al Jazeera taped it but then MEMRI put it out, it went on the web and it just went everywhere. It was a fire throughout the world!

Believe it or not, MEMRI didn't translate the whole interview and people in the Arab world take from the interview something different than what the West focused on. In the interview, this imam, because he didn't believe I had the right to speak, would constantly interrupt me. At the end of the interview, the host told me, "Wafa, you have only two minutes to sum up your position." I started, and the imam still kept interrupting me—wouldn't let me speak. I looked at him and shouted, "Shut up! It is my turn!" I believe this statement opened a new history in the Arab world!

JEFF KING: Yes, it's radical in the Islamic context.

Never in Islamic history did a woman tell a man to shut up, and not only that, but I said, "It's my turn." You know, women have no turn in the Islamic culture!

Afterwards, I received unlimited e-mails saying, "Shut Up, It's My Turn!" I gave a speech here in California and the man who introduced me told the story to my audience. He said, "Wafa turned to the imam and told him, 'Be quiet, it's my turn.'" I said, "Please don't be politically correct. I didn't say 'be quiet,' I said 'shut up.'" So, that's what I said. Even the word "shut up" in Arabic cannot translate into English. It's a really bad word. You know, sometimes the real meaning is lost in translation.

JEFF KING: So, then what? In those last two minutes, what did you say?

I told him that, "The problem with terrorism is that it is deeply rooted in your [Islamic] teaching. Go read your prophet's life and then you will know where the problem is." This was my major statement.

JEFF KING: Unbelievable! [Defaming Muhammad is a death sentence and she said this on Al Jazeera.]

If you open your mind and read your prophet's life, you will understand where the problem lies.

JEFF KING: What has happened as a result of that interview in terms of security and threats?

Oh, I was threatened even prior to the interview, but it increased my risk, I can tell you. You know, I receive many death threats on a daily basis. I can forward a million of them in Arabic telling me, "*We know what school your children go to.*" As a parent, how can you take that? It is...

JEFF KING: It's terrible.

But believe me, at the same time, somewhere deep inside me, I feel peace, and that's what keeps me going. Sometimes—even though I don't believe in any religion—I ask myself why I did it.

Two seconds later, I feel like I am empowered to keep doing it. I don't know what it is. I believe in some kind of supreme power, but I cannot say God, but I feel this empowering. I feel like I'm connected to a source of energy, where every time I feel drained, somehow I get recharged again.

JEFF KING: Many people in the West are uneducated in regards to Islam and just hear and absorb that "Islam is a religion of peace," and they assume that Muhammad is kind of a Jesus equivalent. What do you say? What's been written in the Islamic holy books? What's revealed in the Qur'an and Hadith about Muhammad?

Americans are brought up by the American or Western code of ethics, which prevents them from judging people based on their religious background, and I appreciate that. I don't want anybody to be discriminated against based on his religious background, but the problem is that people in the West need to understand Islam is more than a religion. We have to define the concept of religion because you [can't fit Islam under any definition of religion]. Islam is a dangerous political ideology. Once people in the West understand this point, they will treat Islam differently, in a different way than other religions.

JEFF KING: Flesh that out for me.

There is no spirituality in Islam at all. I believe the most spiritual moment of your life is when you pray. When you pray, you feel somehow spiritually connected to a super power. Even at that moment, Islam deprives us from feeling spiritual because we have to follow and to recite certain verses. We're not allowed to add one more word. If we want to ask God, "Please help me pass this test," we're not allowed to do it while we are praying. So, there is no spirituality in Islam. How can you feel spiritual when you are convinced you should kill anybody who doesn't believe in your religion? What kind of ethics do you follow?

People say, "But the Christians were able to reform Christianity." I believe that's not true, because they reformed themselves, not Christianity. In the Middle Ages, Christians went back to the life of Jesus. They were able to reform the Church.

JEFF KING: The Church drifted away from living out the principles of Jesus. The Reformation was getting them back to the original teachings.

Exactly, but can you imagine if we went back to the life of Muhammad?

JEFF KING: Yes!

Actually, Osama bin Laden's followers are trying to take us there.

JEFF KING: Exactly, that's what they want.

Back to their version of Islam. And that's why I say the original Islam is radical, but the Islam that most Muslims practice now probably is less radical than Muhammad's Islam.

JEFF KING: Wafa, one of the politically correct things people say and believe is that the violence coming out of the Islamic world is a response to Western aggression. What do you say to that?

It's not true. Islamic aggression goes back to Muhammad's life and, at that time, there was no Israel. There was no United States. It is written in our book that a Muslim's mission on earth is to take over. Your mission on earth is to fight for the sake of Allah and to kill or be killed in this fight. This was written fourteen hundred years ago. It wasn't a reaction to Western foreign policy. No, it is written in the

Qur'an. Read [about] the life of Muhammad and you will find out the aggression started there.

JEFF KING: What percentage of Muslims do you think really understand Muhammad and who he was? Most of them haven't studied Muhammad or Islam. They don't know his life and actions. Would you say that's true?

Listen, statistics speak. Eighty percent of Muslims are not Arab.

JEFF KING: What is the significance of that?

At least sixty-five percent of the world Muslim population is illiterate. So there is this statistic, plus, as I told you, the Islamic text was written in Arabic. I believe many of the Islamic texts in Arabic have never been translated to any other language. Extremely few people know the truth about Muhammad and Islam. You understand my point?

JEFF KING: So, for instance, in Indonesia, the largest Islamic country, the services in the mosque are in Arabic. Therefore, the average Indonesian has no idea, really, what's going on. It's kind of like the old Catholic system, when the church services were conducted in Latin so the average churchgoer had no idea what was being said. Is that correct?

Absolutely. I even mentioned that in my book *A God Who Hates*. I gave prayer as an example. When we pray, we have to pray in Arabic, regardless of our background or our native language. We pray five times each day. In each prayer, we have to recite the first Qur'anic verse and in this verse we curse the Jews and the Christians. So five times five—twenty-five times—a day, the Muslim recites this verse where he curses the Jews and the Christians. Most of them have no idea what they are saying. Do you understand my point? So, I always say the damage that has been done by Islam to Arab Muslims goes much, much deeper.

JEFF KING: Wafa, why does Islam persecute other religions?

You have to go back to the life of Muhammad in order to understand this. He wasn't a prophet. He was a warrior and he killed everyone who stood in his way. So, in order for him to convince his followers to do what he was doing, he told them, "It's us versus them." He divided the world in two: "us" and "them." Always in the Qur'an, in the Islamic teachings, when you read, you see "us and them." So he divided the world into Dar al-Harb, the House of War and Dar es Salaam, the House of Peace. So, we [Muslims] have to finish with the House of War. We have to destroy everybody who doesn't believe in Islam because we are convinced at a very early age that one day the whole world will be Muslim. So, you've got to understand the fight of Muhammad in order to understand why Islam is against any other religion.

JEFF KING: That's excellent. This is such a key point. In your speech at UCLA you said, "I don't personally [use, or believe in the terms] 'radical' Islam or 'militant' Islam."

No, I don't. Islam, by its very nature, is radical, and growing up in Syria, I believe I was taught the real Islam. You know, during my childhood, and even up to the moment I left Syria, I had never heard of terms like radical, militant, political, or Wahhabi Islam. I truly, from the bottom of my heart, believe that the West invented those terms for the sake of being politically correct. I truly believe this. What else could be more radical than teaching a child that her prophet beheaded eight hundred men in one night? What could be more radical? Tell me.

JEFF KING: And framing it as a beautiful thing. Wafa, talk to me about your niece, Mayyada.

I am deeply, deeply wounded about her, and I don't know if I can ever heal this wound. I lost my father in a car accident when I was almost ten years old and I lost my brother the very day I gave birth to my first child. I don't know why the death of my niece [affects me so much]. I don't know why.

JEFF KING: How did she pass? Was it connected with Islam?

Of course, because she was eleven when she was forced to marry her cousin.

JEFF KING: Oh my goodness.

He was over forty. She was eleven. I was thirteen when she was forced to marry her cousin, who was an alcoholic and a very abusive man. Extremely abusive. Every week, she would run to her father's house, begging him, "Please [take me back]." We were very young. I still remember. I can see her face now, crying, "Dad, please let me stay here, I will be your maid for the rest of my life." And he would say, "I called him and he promised he wouldn't do it again. It's changed. You want our neighbors to hear that you run away from your husband's house?" A year after I moved to the United States, she committed suicide.

JEFF KING: I'm so sorry.

I feel powerless. Sometimes, subconsciously, I avoid mentioning her story because I don't want to be hurt over and over and over. She was a beautiful girl, full of life, full of energy and, before my eyes, she was reduced to something even smaller than a fly. I have witnessed many crimes committed under Sharia law. I tried to smother them all for nine years in my country. People tell me there are abused women even here in the United States. I say only because they choose to be abused, because here the law respects you as a woman. Why you don't go and fight your abusers [men]? But in our country, under Islamic Sharia, abusing women is valid.

To deceive the West, even if you go to the Qur'an—this is another point I would love to mention—that even if you go to an English copy of the Qur'an, you will see the [Islam's deception of the West]. In Arabic, the verse says, "*beat them.*" But, when they translate it to English, they say, "beat them lightly." I don't know where they got the word "lightly" from.

JEFF KING: Unfortunately, there's a lot of that!

They know it is forbidden in the West, under Western law, to beat women. So, to be politically correct, they say, "Beat them lightly." So, all the crimes [against women] I've witnessed are valid under Islamic Sharia. So, when a woman is sentenced to death in Iran under Sharia law, and she is a virgin, they will rape her before they kill her because you're not allowed to kill a virgin woman. So, they rape her then they kill her. Can you believe it?

JEFF KING: Sadly, I do.

I've asked many [fundamentalist Muslims] and they say, yes, that is written in the Islamic Sharia [law]. It is a very, very barbaric culture, extremely barbaric culture, and I believe the West for many, many, many years has been turning a blind eye to it all. I cannot believe that America can be friends with Saudi Arabia.

In the Arab world, in the Islamic world, people are powerless, hopeless because they are defeated. I received a letter from a twenty-year-old girl. She told me, once she went to court for some reason and her mom approached the judge…She was little; she was eight years old. It was something very terrible. She heard her mom asking the judge, "When my husband sleeps with me, he wants to do this and that." The judge said, "Yes, yes, you do whatever he asks you to do." This girl was eight years old when she heard the judge tell her mom that.

So now she lives in England and suffers from severe depression and she believes this statement—the judge's statement—destroyed her fight and destroyed her for the rest of her life, because he didn't give her mother any shred of freedom to protest against her husband's abuse. It's a very bad statement. He said, "Yes, you let him do whatever he wants." And now she's asking me, "How can I repair myself? How can I heal my wounds?"

She's living in England now, and she said she sees Islam taking over. She's very young; she's twenty-something. So she can't comprehend what's going on now, because she lived under Islamic Sharia and now she's free and living in England. But, right before her eyes, Islam is taking over England. So, out of frustration, she's asking me, "What can I do?" Do you believe it?

JEFF KING: Both Democratic and Republican administrations have followed what is, in our estimation, an intelligence agency strategy where they want to build up moderate Islam and marginalize fundamentalist Islam. Part of this strategy is to say these statements that they know are not true, like *"Islam is a religion of peace,"* over and over.

Have you heard Obama's speech in Cairo? Unbelievable! He almost killed me when he said America and Islam share the same set of principles. I could not believe it. It is a disgrace to every woman in the Islamic world. Do you mean women under Islamic Sharia are treated the same way women are treated under the American Constitution? This is a disgraceful statement to my niece Mayyada. This is not acceptable to be said by the president of the greatest country on Earth. I was in shock and humiliated. I felt like my niece, in her grave, was humiliated by this statement. Unfair, absolutely unfair. Since he said that, I cannot reconcile with him. I respect him as the President of the United States of America, and I wish him the best, but I cannot even relate to him anymore because I believe he poured more fuel on the fire. You know, my niece committed suicide by setting herself on fire, and I believe he set more fire on her by saying America and Islam share the same set of principles. What a lie, what a lie.

JEFF KING: Yes, it's a shame more people don't stand up and condemn these kinds of political statements.

For many years, all over the world, the Saudis have tried hard to Arabize and radicalize Muslims. Even in Afghanistan, even in Pakistan, I believe it's different than it was there years ago.

JEFF KING: Yes, since the '70s, I think the Saudis have spent $100 billion spreading radical Islam, building radical mosques, radical madrassas, et cetera, et cetera.

Exactly, I have heard of that, yes. I don't know if we can undo the damage that has been done so far. It is a huge task. Even here, in the United States, they're infiltrating everywhere.

JEFF KING: Let's talk about that. How are they infiltrating? What are they doing?

Any school you go to, you see Islam is infiltrating their curriculum. I have a friend, who is originally from Egypt—he's a Coptic Christian from Egypt—a Christian. He lives in San Diego, California. His son goes to middle school. The history teacher is pure American. He's not from a Muslim background. He gave his students a project for extra credit to fast a day in Ramadan.[16] I believe for most Americans, if you tell them to do this, they would say, "So what?" But, for Muslims, it's a totally different story. That's why I said you need to understand their mindset. For Muslims, it is a sign that they are taking over.

It is a very encouraging point [in Islamic terms] that an American history teacher is encouraging his students to fast one day of

---

[16] See pg. 345.

Ramadan. It is a divine sign. This is how they perceive it, as a divine sign that they are taking over.

JEFF KING: Yes, it's seen as God's favor.

To some point, I believe it. I heard that a history teacher in an elementary school asked her students to each choose an Islamic name. She told them—she gave them a list of Islamic names: Muhammad, Ahmad, Mahmoud, Abdullah, whatever—and she asked everyone to choose an Islamic name, which, for me, is the end of it. You know, once I was reading a website in Arabic—just to give you an example of how they think—and there was some news about the American actress Halle Berry.

And the story said she had a baby, a girl, and she named her Nahla. Nahla is an Arabic name, that means the honeybee, and it was mentioned in the Qur'an. So, many readers left comments about the news and they said, "You see? We're taking over." So, that's why I wrote in my book *A God Who Hates*, about when I was asked about Mr. Obama. I said I mostly care about his middle name, Hussein. Believe it or not, if he is a Muslim or not, I don't care [because], for Muslims, his middle name is a big sign from God that they are marching inside the White House and this has, by itself, encouraged them to go even further. This is the way they think.

JEFF KING: You talk to American society about the danger that their democratic and constitutional systems face from Islam. Well, what is the danger? What does Islam want to do? What means are they willing to use to achieve their goals?

You mean fundamentalist Islam? Their only goal is to take over. In the very first years of my life as an immigrant here, I was very much involved with my Muslim community in California. You know, you get homesick in the first few years, and I was very much involved with them and I heard it said a million times that eventually we will replace the American Constitution with Islamic Sharia.

I always mention this story and I will never forget it. In 1992, I was very new to this country. We were having lunch with a friend of ours, a Syrian Muslim friend. We were arguing over the Western values and Islamic values. He got mad at me and said something I will never forget. He said, "Write down that we are in 1992. I give this country only ten years to survive." And believe it or not, in 2001, after almost nine years, September 11, happened.

I used to read the Arabic newspaper published here in the United States and I used to ask my husband, "Do you think the American government, the FBI are aware of what is written in these newspapers?" because they would clearly state in Arabic that they were here to take over.

JEFF KING: The American-Arabic newspapers in the United States would say that?

Absolutely. Previously, they would say that but now they've changed because they brought in the concept of al-Taqiyya. Now, they're changing their language a little bit. They sugarcoat it.

JEFF KING: Explain al-Taqiyya.

Al-Taqiyya is a concept in Islam that means you can lie, cheat, and deceive [sanctioned by Muhammad for strategic purposes in conflict with unbelievers]. Muslims are allowed to do it and, at that time [the Arabic newspapers in earlier years], they were strong enough not to practice al-Taqiyya. They were loaded with Saudi money. They were strong enough to express themselves clearly and openly in the newspapers.

You know, when September 11, happened, I was absolutely shocked, but I wasn't surprised. I knew something big was going to happen because I read it a million times; I heard it a million times, that this country wouldn't survive for long.

JEFF KING: Wow.

And I believe—it's bad to say it, but I always say I believe, (God forgive me if there is God)—September 11 was—I don't want to say it was a blessing, but...

JEFF KING: It woke the country up?

Yes, something turned for the better to some degree; it helped to wake some Americans up. I believe now I can see some people trying to wake the rest of us up. It is a very tough war and it is tougher when I fight at the American front, believe it or not. I have more hope when I deal with my readers in the Arab world. It is tougher for me to deal with Americans because, as I said, Americans are brought up to respect all religions and I agree with that principle but, at the same time, you have to define what you mean by "religion." If my religion allows me to kill you if you don't believe in my teachings, do you accept that as a "religion?"

JEFF KING: We also have to respect the truth. We have to deal with truth. So let's not put our head in the sand. Let's deal with reality. Let's talk openly about what the reality of what fundamentalist Islam is.

Absolutely. I don't want this beautiful country to be lost. I hope one day Syria will be another America. I don't want to see America become another Syria. I don't want to see any woman in America living the same way I lived for thirty years in my life. I'm sure there are too many women abused everywhere on earth, but I don't want to see their abuse validated by their laws and by their constitution, this is the point.

AUTHOR'S NOTES:

#1: Qur'an: Sura 33.26 **YUSUF ALI:** And those of the People of the Book who aided them—Allah did take them down from their strongholds and cast terror into their hearts. (So that) some ye slew, and some ye made prisoners.

Volume 5, Book 58, Number 148: Narrated Abu Said al-Khudri: Some people (i.e. the Jews of Bani bin Quraiza) agreed to accept the verdict of Sad bin Muadh so the Prophet sent for him (i.e. Sad bin Muadh). He came riding a donkey, and when he approached the Mosque, the Prophet said, "Get up for the best amongst you." or said, "Get up for your chief." Then the Prophet said, "O Sad! These people have agreed to accept your verdict." Sad said, "I judge that their warriors should be killed and their children and women should be taken as captives." **The Prophet said, "You have given a judgment similar to Allah's Judgment (or the King's judgment)."**

#2: CAIR (Council on American Islamic Relations) is ostensibly a Muslim rights group in the US. Many allege that CAIR was created as a Hamas front group and is a terrorist front group whose primary goal is the establishment of Sharia Law in the US.

THE ROLE OF

SAUDI ARABIA

Chapter Seven:

The Islamic Reformer

The first book [of the Hadith] was written centuries after the Prophet Muhammad's death. They claim that someone who heard this Hadith heard it from someone who died, and another and another who listened to the prophet Muhammad. This is a falsehood, but they attribute it to the Prophet Muhammad. No one can imagine or give the number of all these Hadith. Millions! There are different books and different interpretations, full of contradictions and differences and falsehoods

Dr. Ahmed Mansour

Dr. Ahmed Subhy Mansour is a Muslim who was born in Egypt in March of 1949. He is a graduate and former professor of Al-Azhar University, the pre-eminent Islamic university in the world.

As a scholar studying the Hadith (one of Islam's two holy books that comprises the events and sayings of Muhammad), he became increasingly skeptical of the historicity and reliability of the Hadith. This led him to found a sect known as the Qur'anists. Qur'anists are Muslims that no longer believe the Hadith can be relied on and say the Qur'an is the only reliable holy book of Islam.

As you would imagine, this made him many enemies in the Islamic world and he spent time in Egyptian jails for this "thought crime." He was exiled from Egypt and now lives in the United States. He has served as a visiting fellow at the National Endowment for Democracy and at the Human Rights Program at Harvard Law School. He was also a one-year visiting fellow at the US Commission on International Religious Freedom and a one year visiting fellow at the Woodrow Wilson International Center for Scholars.

The reason that he is so significant is that much of the violence of Islam can be traced to the Hadith and related Islamic jurisprudence.

His rejection of the reliability/historicity of the Hadiths is based on solid scholarship, not on a philosophical or theological rejection of the Hadith's content.

The Qur'an is not without violence. But, if his position was more widely adopted it would allow Muslims a way to move forward and modernize and become less violent without the internal conflicts that would be caused by a lack of adherence to Islamic core teachings.

Note: This interview was conducted prior to the revolution.

Books by Dr. Ahmed Mansour:
- *Al Sayed Al Badway: Fact versus Superstition*
- *Using Religious Texts to Inform Muslim History*
- *The Personality of Egypt after the Muslim Invasion*
- *The History of the Historic Sources of Arabic and Muslim Fields*
- *The Fundamental Rules of Historical Research*
- *The Invasions of the Moguls and the Crusaders in Muslim History*
- *A History of the Cultural Development of Muslims*
- *The Muslim World between the Early Stage and the Abbasy Caliphate*
- *The Prophets in the Holy Quran*
- *The Sinner Muslim: Common Mythology Regarding the Sinner Muslim*
- *Egypt in the Holy Quran, Al Akhbar* newspaper
- *The Quran: the Only Source of Islam and Islamic Jurisprudence* (published under the title *The Quran: Why?* using the pseudonym Abdullah al-Khalifah)
- *Death in the Qur'an*
- *The Penalty of Apostasy*
- *Freedom of Speech: Islam and Muslims*
- *The Al Hisbah between the Quran and Muslims*
- *The Torture of the Grave*
- *Naskh in the Qur'an Means Writing Not Abrogating, Al Tanweer* magazine
- *The Introduction (mokademat) of Ibn Khaldoun: A Fundamental Historical and Analytical Study*

- *Suggestions to Revise Muslim Religion Courses in Egyptian Education to Make Egyptians More Tolerant*
- *Religious Thought in Egypt in the Mamluke Era: Islam versus Muslim Sufism*
- *Al-Aqaid Al-Diniyah Fi Misr Al-Mamlukiyah Bayna Al-Islam Wa-Al-Tasawwuf*
- *Al-Tasawwuf Wa-Al-hayah Al-Diniyah Fi Misr Al-Mamlukiyah*
- *Misr Fi Al-Quran Al-Karim*

JEFF KING: Dr. Mansour, it's an honor to meet you. Tell me about your background.

I am a Muslim scholar, a Muslim thinker. I used to work at Al-Azhar University. Al-Azhar is like the Vatican for the Catholics. It is the leading seminary for more than one billion Muslims. It was built in the same year that Cairo itself was built (AD 972). I graduated from Al-Azhar in 1973 and worked at the university until I was fired in 1987 because of my struggle to get Muslims to accept religious freedom, human rights, tolerance and democracy.

I am the founder of the Qur'anist Muslims. Qur'anists believe in Islam as a religion of tolerance, peace, justice, human rights, freedom of speech and freedom of belief. We consider all peaceful humans as Muslims. We consider the ones who kill people, like Osama bin Laden, as *kafir,* or infidels. Not according to his belief, but according to his crime.

So in the field of belief, it is [a matter between them and] God. We have nothing to do with this; no one has the authority to judge others in the field of faith. Behavior is the primary thing. Are you transgressing against people? Are you killing people, persecuting people, terrorizing people? We do not believe that any of these people are Muslims, due to their criminal behavior. So, anyone like you, like me, whatever—regardless of their faith—we regard as brothers and sisters. This is what the Qur'anists believe.

The Qur'anists suffered four waves of arrests because we are very active in advocating for what we believe. During the second wave, I escaped to the United States for political asylum in 2001.

JEFF KING: When was the first wave?

I was in prison during the first wave in 1987 with about sixty-two of my colleagues. Six months after I was fired from Al-Azhar, they put us in jail for two months because of our ideas. The third and fourth waves were 2007-2008.

JEFF KING: Are any other Qur'anists still in prison?

No, no. But imprisonment is persecution that comes from the government. There's another daily persecution that comes from the Muslim Brothers and other fanatic organizations that control the Egyptian states and villages. They control the mosques, the neighborhoods, and the streets. So [Qur'anists] are suffering at their hands because they are criminals.

JEFF KING: So according to the belief of the Qur'anists, the Qur'an is the only text that's acceptable to Muslims? What about the Hadiths?

All Muslims believe that the Qur'an is the primary source of Islam, but they add to the Qur'an what they call the Sunnah,[17] other Hadith, other man-made scriptures. As Qur'anists, we make a solid distinction between what belongs to Islam and what belongs to Muslims. The Qur'an belongs to Islam—it is the only source of Islam. What Muslims wrote after the Qur'an belongs to Muslims. The traditions, the literature, the history, the civilization, all of these are man-made things; they do not represent Islam.

JEFF KING: But the vast majority of Muslims accepts and believes in the Hadith and Sunnah. What is the difference between the Hadith and the Qur'an?

A big difference! It's the same difference between truth and falsehood. The Qur'an, from a scientific point of view, is limited to 114 chapters and a specific number of verses. No one can add anything, no one can delete anything. It is intact from the time of

---

[17] See pg. 345.

Prophet Muhammad until now. You can find the same text of the Qur'an over the centuries.

But when you go to the Hadith, you find the first book was written centuries after the prophet Muhammad's death. They claim that someone who heard this Hadith heard it from someone who died, and another and another who listened to the prophet Muhammad. This is a falsehood, but they attribute it to the prophet Muhammad. No one can imagine or give the number of all these Hadith. Millions! There are different books and different interpretations, full of contradictions, differences, and falsehoods.

Just like lies, you find them everywhere. In my scholarship as a Muslim scholar, I began, as most Sunni Muslims, to try to refine the Hadith, to reform the Sunnah [the biographies of Muhammad] from within. I worked on this from my early scholarship. I went to the Qur'an and found that the Qur'an contradicts many Hadiths. So I re-read the Qur'an with a new method: to understand the Qur'an, not according to the Muslim tradition, but according to the Qur'anic terms themselves.

The Qur'an was written in a very unique Arabic language, fourteen centuries ago. The Arab language from that time until now has really changed. As a language, it has survived until now, but it has changed in its meaning and in its vocabulary. When you read the Qur'an according to the meanings of today, you find differences. And that's why Arab people misunderstand it. To understand the Qur'an or to understand any book, you have to read it according to its language, its terminology. That's what we are doing. When you read the Qur'an, you find a very big gap between what [today's] Muslims write and think and what is in the Qur'an. The Qur'an, according to its unique language, grants all the humans, [the] rights that we now recognize as [part of] modern civilization.

JEFF KING: Fascinating. Are you saying the Qur'an is compatible with democratic ideals?

Yes, yes (and I'm not the only one saying that). This is what all my research has been about for more than thirty years. When I came to the United States I got my first fellowship at the National Endowment for Democracy and my research was "The Roots of Democracy in Islam." I completed a couple of books: *Democratic Islam* and *Muslim Tyranny*.

JEFF KING: You say that the Qur'an is perfectly in line with democratic ideas, but what about Surah 51:5, which says, "*All ye who believe take not the Jews and Christians for your friends. They are friends to each other...*"

I have written about this on my website, and you can find it there. This is speaking [in terms of] allies, not friends. This is [an example] of what I [mentioned earlier] about the language of the Qur'an. It's speaking of a specific event in the time of Prophet Muhammad. Some people around the prophet Muhammad allied themselves with the Christian and Jewish tribes at the time when they were fighting and transgressing against Muhammad and [the Muslims]. Those people allied themselves with the enemy who were attacking them. That is what the verse says.

JEFF KING: And what about Surah 4:54, which says, "*If a man sees disloyalty from his wife, first he has to admonish her; second, refuse to share a bed with her; thirdly, beat her.*" According to your opinion, what does this mean?

The Arabic word "beat," it is like "beat [hit] the road"—it has many meanings. But, going to the Qur'an, to verse 19 of the same Surah, it gives you the rules of how to deal with your wife. Qur'anic law has three categories: order, rule and target. Order [regards]: do or do not. Rule is that which governs or rules the order. I'll give you an example:

God says in the Qur'an: "*Fight in the cause of God those who fight you and do not transgress the limit.*" This is the law of fighting in the

Qur'an, or the law of jihad. The order is "fight." The rule, "in the cause of God those who are fighting you," is governing the order. If you took the order itself, [cut it away] from the rule, you will become a terrorist and fight the innocent people, civilians in the street who are not fighting you.

So the word "fight" is under the rule of "those who are fighting you." This is the rule. The objective comes after that in another place. You have to understand the rules of the Qur'an according to its system. What Muslims usually do is take the order, and split it from its rule. They say that "fight" means fight anyone. That is what Osama bin Laden is doing.

It is the same in Surah 4:54. The order is: *"Advise them, abandon them in bed, and beat them."* "Beat them" has many meanings. "Beat them" means give them advice or simply beat them. But this is the order. Going to the rule, in the same Surah, in number 19, it says: *"And deal with your wives in the most honorable way even if you dislike them. If you dislike them and deal with them honorably, God will reward you."*

Going to the Qur'an, you have to understand the system of its law. It is not only in this, but in many things. In dealing with others, in dealing with your wife, in dealing with your neighbor—everything has orders, rules.

JEFF KING: In Egypt, there are millions of Christians and other religious minorities that complain about discrimination and persecution at the hand of government officials and the society/culture. Why do Muslims discriminate against the Christians in Egypt, in Saudi Arabia, and in many Islamic states?

One of my research topics is about the persecution of the Copts after the Muslims invaded Egypt in the seventh century. According to

Muslim and Egyptian history, some persecution happened, but the main aspect was tolerance. This is what Egypt is all about.

Egyptians—Muslims or Christians—are very tolerant people because they are farmers. And farmers are different from Bedouins, people of the desert. Everything changed in Egypt after the Saudi State was established in 1932. The Saudis believe in the fanatic Sunnah (Hadiths and biographies) which are compatible with their own fanatic desert culture. Their culture is reflected in their understanding of Islam.

The Saudi State established the Muslim Brothers [Muslim Brotherhood] in 1928. For many political and social reasons, the Brotherhood stretched to Egypt and, in only twenty years [1928 to 1948], the Brotherhood had [established] more than 50,000 branches in Egypt. They had their own international organization and their own secret army.

Then they helped the Free Officers start a coup or, as it was called after that, the Egyptian revolution in 1952. The Muslim Brothers and the officers of the army went against each other and Nasser persecuted them. Their leader escaped to the Saudi state, and then in the time of Sadat they came back. Sadat allied his regime with the Muslim Brothers and gave them all the authority over Al-Azhar, which is the seminary that controls Muslims' daily religious life. They control the mosques, they control education, they control the media, [and] they control the culture.

From the time of Sadat, about 1971 to now (over forty years), the Egyptian education and Al-Azhar University became poisoned by the Wahhabi's. I'll give you an example. In 1905, Sheikh Muhammad Abdou died. Sheikh Muhammad Abdou was a big scholar, a big thinker, and a big reformer. He struggled to reform and modernize Al-Azhar. His first assistant was a Syrian. This man's name was Rashid Reda. Since he was a Syrian and not an Egyptian, he was not as strong as Imam Muhammad Abdou. He became an agent for Abdel Aziz Al Saud, the founder of the Saudi state. Reda was the engineer that established the Muslim Brothers. The leader of the Muslim Brothers, Sheikh Hassan al-Banna, was a student of Reda. All that Muhammad Abdou had done was destroyed.

When I came to Al-Azhar in 1977, more than seventy years after the death of Abdou, it was very hard to repeat [the views and positions] of Muhammad Abdou from seventy years before. Because we tried to do what he used to do, to say what he used to say, we are persecuted. Look what happened!

JEFF KING: So you are saying the Muslim Brotherhood is the cause of the radicalization?

Yes, but the Muslim Brotherhood is just a weapon of the Wahhabis. The Wahhabis, the Saudis, are the axis of evil for Muslims and for Islam and for the Middle East.

JEFF KING: The influence of Wahhabi Islam is, of course, growing in many countries because of the petrodollar?

Yes it is.

JEFF KING: If the Muslim Brothers come to power in Egypt, what will happen to non-Muslims?

They are far from coming to power now. But look what they are doing while they are not in power. They're killing Christians. They attack anyone who tries to build a church. When Christians so much as try to repair the bathroom of any church, they attack them. They kill, usually to tease the government. Muslim Brothers kill not only the Christians, but also the secular leaders who are against them. They do this while they are not in power. So imagine when they come to power what they will do.

JEFF KING: But even now, the actual core of the Egyptian constitution says that the principle of Islamic Sharia is the principal source of Egyptian legislation. That's what the constitution of Egypt says.

In a meeting with the BBC, I called for changing the second article of the Egyptian constitution to use the universal declaration of human rights as the principle source of legislation, instead of Islamic Sharia. I declared it and it was a very big surprise for many people.

I said, I testify before my Lord, Allah, that the universal declaration of human rights is the nearest human writing to the spirit of the Qur'an. It is very accurate and systematic, and you can depend on it.

Going to the principle of the Sharia, it is good, but how can you find [defend]? How can you find the principle of the Sharia? If you want to go to the Sharia of the Qur'an, it disagrees with Muslim Sharia. And going to the Sunni Sharia? They are killing people in the streets!

So, let's not go to the Sharia of the Qur'an or the Sharia of Sunnah. Let's go to the universal declaration and it will be protected by the international society itself. The international society will be the monitor of applying these laws that come directly from the universal declaration of human rights.

JEFF KING: According to interpretation of Sharia by the Muslim Brotherhood and Egyptian officials, Sharia does not tolerate other faiths and doesn't allow for building churches. Sharia doesn't allow for the conversion of Muslims to other religions.

I just want to explain to you the mentality of the Brotherhood. They have slogans and refuse to allow anyone to discuss these slogans. They say, "Islam is the Solution." But if you ask them how [it is the solution], you will be their enemy. They say, "Apply the Sharia." If you ask them, "How? Which Sharia?" they will assassinate you.

The second constitutional article itself is good because it does not say "Sharia." It says "the principles of Sharia." The principles of Sharia, according to the old scholars, are: justice, freedom, tolerance and all the values. It is about the values, not about the rules. It is about the principles and the values. In terms of values, no one can deny that Islam is a religion of peace, of justice, of freedom – this is mentioned in the Qur'an. There's no argument about it.

But Muslim Brothers, according to the understanding of the masses (the masses do not know), they want this because it has the name "Sharia." So, let's get rid of all of this and go directly to the universal declaration of human rights because no one can ignore it or play with it.

JEFF KING: In Egypt, for Christians to build a place of worship, they need permission from the governor. It used to be the president. I think it came through Ottoman rule?

Late in the Ottoman era, there was a law called the "Faraman" to systemize or organize the building of churches. And it was good, at that time, but you are talking about more than one hundred years. Everything's changed, so it does not fit our day.

JEFF KING: What does the law say?

I don't remember all its articles, but it makes it impossible to build a church. One of them says [the church] should be far from any Muslim buildings. This is obviously very difficult to have. Egyptian towns and villages are very crowded and attached to each other, so how can you build a church—in the desert?

There is still a law that no one can repair a church unless they have permission from the president. We struggled for three decades until Mubarak, last year, gave this authorization to the governor to give permission. But the law stands.

At the same time, anyone who wants to build a mosque will be given help from the bureaucracy inside Egypt. They will be given help and cement and all the things that can help them. That's why you find a mosque between every three buildings. More [mosques] than people need. Most of these mosques are built by the help of the government, and the money comes from the Saudis and they are controlled by the Wahhabis.

JEFF KING: What do they teach inside the mosques?

Hatred against non-Saudis, non-Wahhabis, and non-Muslims. Their principle is: any Muslim—any Muslim from Bangladesh, from Pakistan, from India, from China—is my brother, but any Egyptian who is not Muslim is not my brother.

JEFF KING: What would you say is the distinct nature of Wahhabism? Can you say these are the points where Wahhabi's are wrong?

Only one word: blood. They believe that anyone who is not Muslim should be killed, should be fought. As mentioned by Muhammad ibn Abd al-Wahhab, the founder of this faith, their goal is to hate and to fight the non-Muslims. They call the Christians, Jews and non-Muslims infidels. The Muslims who are not Wahhabis are called idol worshippers and should be killed also.

As a historic fact, from the time of Muhammad ibn Abd al-Wahhab and the first Saudi state, which was established in 1745, until 1818, more than four million people were killed because of the Wahhabis. Most of them were Muslims.

You know, India was divided and Pakistan created because of the Wahhabis. It was a big mistake in the twentieth century. And until now, Pakistan is a trouble-maker in Asia. They created the Taliban, al-Qaeda, and the Muslim Brotherhood.

JEFF KING: But in Saudi Arabia, Wahhabism is the State religion. Correct?

Yes. That's why I usually say, to reform the Middle East you have to reform American foreign policy. In the field of the war of ideas, the number one enemy of the Americans is the Saudis. They now have more than 1,000 mosques and Islamic schools under the control of the Wahhabis in the United States, and more in Europe, because America and the West opened their doors for the Saudis to come at the time when they were together against the Soviet Union. Osama bin Laden at that time was a fighter for America against the Soviet Union. So this is the big problem, the big mistake.

JEFF KING: How do you think the US has helped in promoting rights such as religious freedom in Egypt? The US gives a lot of money to Egypt.

American policy is doing it the wrong way. I'll give you one example. From 1979 until now, more than thirty years, America has given Egypt more than $100 billion! Yet, when you look at Egypt over these thirty years, you find the American image has become very tarnished. Why? Because Hosni Mubarak uses this money to tarnish the American image. Why? Because he needs to. He needs to twist the anger and the frustration of the people towards an outside enemy instead of him. Everything that goes wrong is blamed on America and Israel plotting and conspiring against Islam and against Muslims and Arabs.

So, to stay in power, he has to create an enemy inside and outside Egypt. Inside Egypt, he is the one who protects the Muslim Brothers' culture because he needs them to say to America: I am against them, I am fighting them. But he needs them to stay in power to justify why he is there. At the same time, he needs to create the image of America as the enemy of Islam and the enemy of Muslims, to [inflame] the anger and the frustration of the people towards America and Israel instead of towards him. That's why he gets all these funds from America. All the aid money from America, he uses it against America. The funny thing is that we say this all the time and no one listens.

JEFF KING: So what should be done? What should the United States do? Should the US stop giving them money?

No, I'm not saying this. The solution is to deal not only with Mubarak but every dictator over there. Many, even my friend Adel Ibrahim, talks about how to diminish the millions in aid to Egypt. I said no. Even this money, most of it is corrupted and stolen by Mubarak and his regime. But that is not the issue. The issue is to punish Mubarak himself, not to punish Egypt. And this is very easy because the people who are guarding Mubarak's life are Americans. So they can threaten him if they want, about his life, about his money. They can pressure him if they want.

But I don't know. I think there's something wrong in the mentality of the American policy makers. They deal with Mubarak as a president like the president of France or the president of Spain or Italy. He is not a president. He's a criminal. The president of France is elected by the people and he's serving his people. But President Mubarak is not elected by the people. He's using his army to scare the people, to torture people. So there's a difference. Do not look at him as a president, don't respect him as a president, or look at King Abdullah of Saudi Arabia and respect him as a real king. Those people are surrounded by hatred from their own people.

The mistake here is that the American policy makers deal with them as real leaders or real presidents or real kings. They must deal with them as criminals and pressure them to make a democracy and to make real reform. Otherwise, everyone here will come to hate America.

JEFF KING: According to your research and according to your understanding, how is Saudi Arabia using its money and

influence to expand Wahhabism? How are they doing it? Do you have any research?

I have. In fact, a book [of mine], which isn't published yet, is about the Saudi State, the Wahhabis, and the opposition inside Wahhabism itself. This opposition produced Osama bin Laden.

The first revolution against the prophet Muhammad was in Najd [Central Saudi Arabia]. From the same place came Muhammad Abd al-Wahhabi [clan leader form the 1700s that Wahhabism is named after]. Many leaders, blood-shedding leaders, came from that same place. Always from the same place. They [produced] bloody revolutions, movements, and Muslim States in Iraq, Syria and Egypt, even in the times of Andalusia. Tribes came from there to Egypt and destroyed many things in Egypt. Then they went to North Africa, to Andalusia, Spain and destroyed many things in Spain.

Another factor is the stance of Egypt. Because Egypt was a big country, before and after Islam, it used to stand against the Wahhabis. Egypt was the state that destroyed the first Saudi state in 1818, and destroyed its capital, Diriyah. They also arrested the Saudi emir and brought him to the Ottoman Empire to be killed.

So the Saudis have in their mind to hate Egypt and hope to control Egypt in order to survive. As fanatic Sunnis, they have many Muslim enemies. They have Shi'ites in Iran and the Gulf, inside the Arabian Peninsula, and in Yemen. So, they are surrounded by Shi'ites and by Sufis. The Shi'ites and Sufis are against Wahhabism. For most of its history as a Muslim state, Egypt was Sunni—but, moderate Sunni—not fanatic Sunni like the Wahhabis.

Abdul Aziz reestablished the third Saudi state in 1902, and he gave it his family name and called it the Saudi Kingdom. This man was like Hitler. He understood that for his newborn state to survive, he must have Egypt on his side.

Egypt, during most of its time as a Muslim state, directly or indirectly controlled Al-Higaz [the eastern part of the Arabian Peninsula, which contains Mecca and Medina, where all Muslims come for pilgrimage]. The one who controls Al-Higaz will be the leader of Muslims. So Adel Aziz conquered the ruler of Al-Higaz, the grandfather of King Abdallah of Jordan. When Abdel Aziz invaded Al-Higaz and added it to his kingdom he controlled the pilgrimage. This was in 1924–1925. From that time, all the people came from Egypt for the Hajj, and he chose some Egyptians to become Wahhabis. And, in 1928, the Muslim Brotherhood appeared.

The best part of the story is oil. Saudi Arabia was a poor state, but after Abdel Aziz allied himself with America after the Second World War, he gave them the opportunity to search for oil. His sons had all this money from oil, so by oil and by America they spread Wahhabism in the name of Islam.

JEFF KING: In many countries, Muslims try to apply Sharia law to non-Muslims. For instance, in Saudi Arabia, they say: don't build any church; this is a holy land. They use it as an instrument to discriminate.

Yes. It's very important to classify or to identify the term. Call it the Wahhabi or Sunni Sharia, but not the Islamic Sharia. Wahhabi Sharia says that anyone who is a non-Muslim has no rights at all—he should be killed or enslaved. You know, even up to now, they (the Saudis) have slavery inside their palaces and homes—even now! They are dealing with the Arabs or Muslims who come to work in the Kingdom under the *Kafeel system*.

Kafeel is a new kind of slavery. When you go there to work, there's supposed to be a sponsor, but not a sponsor that cares about you. He takes your passport and he owns you. For any reason, he can destroy your passport, call the police to put you in jail, or even kill you with any accusation. So the sponsor is the one who owns everyone who goes to Saudi Arabia.

This is a very satanic country and a satanic law by all means. No one goes to Saudi Arabia and loves it or respects it. Poor Egyptians go there because they are starving.

JEFF KING: Are the Wahhabis infiltrating the US and Europe?

Yes, because we are talking about money. You can find the Saudi influence through money everywhere. I'll give you an example from my personal experience. Three decades ago it was said that Jewish scholars were controlling Islamic studies in the American universities. It was true, but no longer. Now, Saudi money is the first player in this field. Saudi money is given to American universities, to the Islamic and Arabic departments, to prevent them from discussing Wahhabism.

The Islamic field is very vast and has much diversity: about history, about the Qur'an, about Sunnah, about tradition, about civilization, about art, many, many things. But, when you talk about the war of ideas and the enemy that threatens this country, you must understand your enemy from within its culture. Your first weapon is your think tank, your universities. And, the first of those are the departments that deal with Islam and Muslims. So, these departments in American universities must, as a necessity, deal with Wahhabism to understand how to combat it. But it is prohibited.

JEFF KING: What do you mean prohibited?

[These departments] need people who are experts in this. [Based on my scholarly background] I should be able to find a job in any American university, but my reputation as one who is against [Wahhabi Islam] is well known in all circles of the Islamic field. I tried [to get a job in American academia] but only got one fellowship—at Harvard. In Harvard, there is a big center, the Center of King Fahad for Islamic Sharia. It's owned by the Saudis who give money to Harvard. I couldn't find a job there. I was given my fellowship with the help of Scholar at Risk, which is an organization that helps persecuted scholars find jobs and survive. At the same time, the Saudi influence is still after me here as it used to be in Egypt.

So, we find they sneak with their money inside everything. I'll give you an example. There was a big mosque in Boston. Youssef Quaradawy, a big sheikh of the Muslim Brothers, was behind the building of this mosque. Abdul Rahman Al-Amoudi, a sheik who is in prison for life, was also behind the building of this mosque.

I discovered that this mosque was fanatic, [so I and others] became the founders of a center for citizens for peace and tolerance, and we stood up against this mosque and the ideas of hate it harbored against Christians and Jews and so on. I was the only Muslim founder. Another was Jewish and another was Christian. Do you know what they did? They sued us in court. Imagine! I have nothing. I have no job. How do I survive in court? Fortunately, some people helped me [and the others] in court. There were big lawyers [since] it wasn't only me. Fox News and others talked about this case.

Our lawyer responded by giving all the documents they asked for. He also asked them to give some of their documents and they found a lot of money coming from the Saudis—a lot of money. So, they asked for more documents. So, the [radicals suing us] said, "OK, we quit. We want to stop." And it was stopped. You know what happened? They built this mosque and the mosque invited the governor. There is a tape of their imam saying the Jews and Christians are filthy!

We held press conferences at that time and asked the media to come. The media refused because they are scared of getting sued. Because the Islamic radicals have money, they can sue you. You have to pay for a lawyer. Rather than going through with the [suit], the [fundamentalists] say, "OK, that's enough. We can stop." But you've already given money to the lawyer and you can lose millions. It's nothing to them because they have a lot of money.

JEFF KING: In Ethiopia and other places, they use their money to build huge numbers of mosques. After they build the mosque, they teach Wahhabism. Poor local people have been given money to go and kill Christians, and they have.

Yes. It is a real problem in Nigeria because in Nigeria you find 50% Muslims and 50% Christians. If a civil war arises it will be a disaster.

JEFF KING: And that's what they want?

Yes. So this is a real axis of evil. The question is how to diminish or terminate the Wahhabi danger. I said it is a war of ideas. A war of ideas has two links. One link is to reform Muslims from within Islam peacefully and intellectually.

Reform, not only religious life, but political life, social life, economics, everything! Educate them in the culture of democracy before establishing a democratic regime. This is the reform [needed]; reform [in] legislation, reform in politics, reform in everything, including religious life and thinking.

The second link is to combat terrorism and the fanatics from within their own Sunni culture by having Islam on your side, because they get their power from claiming Islam is on their side. So when you make a distinction between their understanding, when you prove the contradiction or the gap between their understanding, you dismantle them, you dismantle their power. They become the enemies of Islam because they are misusing Islam for their own political agenda. And it is horrible in Islam to use the name of God for something bad. It's horrible. This is what they are doing.

To prove this—and this is very easy—the example is our website. It is a very poor website, but it is very powerful because it has the truth. For example, our website was hijacked by the Saudis for one month! Until now, it is blocked in the Saudi kingdom and the Gulf states. It can't be viewed [in Saudi Arabia]. Look at the Saudis! They have thousands of centers and mosques and websites and TV stations, thousands of ulama, or sheikhs, and imams and millions of followers and they are unable to face us. We who are very limited in power, we are facing them with [only] our bare arms. But, we are so successful that the only way they have is to persecute us and imprison us and torture us—not to have arguments against us. The biggest Muslim website is owned by the Wahhabis: Islam Online. The biggest Arabic channel, Al Jazeera, is owned by the Muslim Brotherhood. Everything biggest in the Muslim world, it is owned by them. Yet, they are defeated in the field of ideas against us.

Suppose we have a TV channel. Suppose we have a company for producing movies and dramatized history. Give me two years. Give me two years and one company for producing Arabic movies and one Arabic TV channel and one website, and I will terminate the Wahhabis. I'm very serious. Because, you know, I'm struggling to survive. I came to this country in 2001. Only three months I was employed at The National Movement for Democracy, one year at Harvard law school, and now this is the beginning of the third fellowship here. This is from 2001 until now. Eight years. In all of this time I haven't worked, but I give all my time for struggling against them. Suppose I have all the ability to face them online and on TV and by drama. It is a matter of money.

JEFF KING: Have you ever been threatened with death?

Yes, yes. There's more than 150 fatwas against my life. I couldn't go back to Egypt because there are many cases against me in the courts just because I am writing here. And guess what? They accuse me of despising Islam. Me, Ahmed Mansour, is despising Islam? They have the power and they can do whatever they want.

JEFF KING: So if they find you they will kill you? That's what the fatwa says?

Yes. A fatwa that [declares] someone is against Islam [grants] permission for anyone to kill him. Anyone! Anybody want to go to paradise? Okay, go kill Ahmed Mansour and his family. All the members of my family are mentioned in many fatwas. And many fatwas are even translated into English on websites.

JEFF KING: So are you taking any special precautionary security measures?

No, no. When I was in Egypt, I lived for more than twenty-six years in a very notorious neighborhood, full of fanatics. I was not scared of them. Because, as a Muslim, I believe that when my time comes, no one can delay it and no one can speed it. So many people around me were killed. One of them was very famous, Dr. Farag Fouda. He was assassinated in 1992, and we were together in the same fatwa. We were about to establish a new party in Egypt for defending the Christians. Its name was The Future Party. Once we announced the party, a fatwa from Al-Azhar and others [was announced] calling for our death and giving our names.

One week later, Farag Fouda was killed. He was assassinated in front of his office. Because of this, I wrote my book *The Penalty of Apostasy*. I wrote this book in 1993, proving from more than 1,000 verses from the Qur'an that there's no such penalty in Islam and this is a fabricated punishment written two centuries after the prophet Muhammad by the Abbasid Empire at the time. As I said, more than 1,000 verses of the Qur'an uphold unlimited freedom of speech, freedom of belief, and freedom of religion in Islam.

Chapter Eight:

The Convert to Islam

In Muslim countries the [Saudis/Wahabbis] essentially come in and begin distributing their literature and preaching that they are the only true and real Muslims... Basically they go in and divide the Islamic community to set up a separate Wahhabi jamaat community to agitate against the established Muslims, to provoke family quarrels, to agitate against other religions if they're present and then to train people in the military arts and arm them, and to provoke armed conflicts. They do this over and over again, even in Muslim countries.

In countries where there are Muslims and non-Muslims living side by side, like India and Ethiopia, they attempt to provoke conflict between the Muslims and the non-Muslims [mainly the Hindus in India] in order to support their image of themselves as the great jihadists, the great warriors for Islam, the only real/true Muslims.

Stephen Suleyman Schwartz

Stephen Suleyman Schwartz is an American journalist, columnist, and author who converted to Islam (Sufi) in 1997. He is a vociferous critic of Islamic fundamentalism and especially targets Wahhabi Islam. Schwartz is the executive director of the Center for Islamic Pluralism and has written many books.

We wanted to interview Mr. Schwartz because he is a rare bird. That is, he is a moderate Muslim (Sufi) who is willing to stick his neck out publicly to denounce radical Islam. He has developed, among Westerners, a unique position as a confidante of Shiite Muslim religious leaders and intellectuals, notably with Iraqis as well as Shias living in the US.

Sufism is a spiritual tradition within Islam that focuses on the mystical. It is a movement within Islam that seeks to find Allah's love and knowledge through the direct personal experience of God and focuses on unity and harmony. They are known, and violently attacked by radical Muslims, for their appreciation of other religions, mainly Christianity and Hinduism.

Stephen's investigative reporting on Islamist extremism has led to repeat appearances on Fox News and other TV and radio networks.

His articles have been published in the *Wall Street Journal, The Spectator*, and the *Weekly Standard*, to name just a few. He also was a staff writer for the *San Francisco Chronicle* for ten years.

His articles have been printed in the world's major newspapers, including *The New York Times, The Wall Street Journal, The Los Angeles Times, The Toronto Globe and Mail*, and many more. He is a regular contributor to *The Weekly Standard* and *The Spectator* as well as to the *New York Post, Reforma* in Mexico City, and leading periodicals in the Balkans (from Center for Islamic Pluralism http://www.islamicpluralism.org/about/).

Books by Stephen Suleyman Schwartz:
- *A Sleepwalker's Guide to San Francisco: Poems from Three Lustra, 1966–1981*
- *Brotherhood of the Sea: A History of the Sailors' Union of the Pacific*
- *Spanish Marxism vs. Soviet Communism: A History of the P.O.U.M* (with Victor Alba)
- *A Strange Silence: The Emergence of Democracy in Nicaragua*
- *From West to East: California and the Making of the American Mind*
- *Kosovo: Background to a War*
- *Intellectuals and Assassins: Writings at the End of Soviet Communism*
- *The Two Faces of Islam: The House of Sa'ud from Tradition to Terror*
- *Sarajevo Rose: A Balkan Jewish Notebook*
- *Is It Good for the Jews? The Crisis of America's Israel Lobby*
- *The Other Islam: Sufism and the Road to Global Harmony*

JEFF KING: I want to start with a personal question. Tell us about your personal journey towards Islam, and just give us some general background about your life.

I will be brief about my life. I grew up in a household that was anti-religious. My mother was a communist, and so, being a good typical American, I rebelled against my parents, but I realized when I was eight years old, I believed in God. From the time I was a teenager, I started to look at and study different religions, but I didn't choose a particular religion until 1997 when I went to Yugoslavia. I was writing a lot of articles regarding the war and recovery in Bosnia for several publications. When I went there, I was very struck by the moderate form of Islam followed by the people of Bosnia and how they had not engaged in terrorism during the war. That was very important to me. I saw that they had organized a regular army and defended themselves, but they did not engage in terrorism, even though terrorism would have been easy for them because they looked like Serbs, they spoke the same dialect, and many of them had married Serbs.

I had also always been interested in Sufism since I was a teenager and actually became interested in Sufism because of its influence on Catholic mysticism. But, when I went to Bosnia, there wasn't really much Sufism in Bosnia. There was moderate Islam (that appealed to me), but then I went to Kosovo. [I found that] Sufism is a very, very vibrant, living movement. In fact, 40% of the Albanians living in the west of Kosovo are Sufis and that is where I actually became a Sufi as well.

I didn't intend to become someone famous for converting to Islam. I believe the situation was forced on me after 9/11 when it was necessary for moderate Muslims to organize and speak out against the terrorists. One week after 9/11, I published my first major article about Wahhabism and I became known as the critic of Wahhabism. In the course of that, I became known as a Muslim critic of Wahhabism. Everything became public.

JEFF KING: All right. A lot of people here in the West don't understand the difference between Sufism and Wahhabism and different types of Islam. Please tell us the difference.

Very briefly. Sufism is not a type of Islam. It's not a sect like Sunni or Shia Islam and it's not a subset like Wahhabism. It's a set of spiritual practices that are well known to both Sunnis and Shias. Sufism is essentially self-discipline aimed at purifying itself and getting closer to God.

Everybody thinks Saudi Wahhabism is ancient, traditional and conservative. It's not ancient; it only started 250 years ago. It's not traditional; it destroys tradition. It's not conservative; it's radical. And part of the jihad of the Dawa[18] of the Wahhabi is that they hate the Sufis. They hate the Sufis because the Sufis developed positive relationships with Christians and Jews, and the Sufis were interested in the views and traditions of the other religions—mostly Christianity, Buddhism, and Hinduism—and the Wahhabis hated this. The Wahhabis hated the fact that the Sufis became the dominant Islamic religious interpretation under the Ottoman Empire. The Wahhabis were a purification movement coming out of Arabia. They hated the Ottoman Empire and they hated the Sufis. They still hate the Sufis.

In fact, in classical Islamic theology [al-Ghazali], Christians were praised for their love of Jesus, even though Muslims don't believe Jesus was God's son. But the Wahhabis hate anything in Islam that seems to resemble anything in Christianity. But, mainly, they hated this Sufism because of its association with the Ottoman Empire, and so they have killed Sufis and still do it today. It's very strange for Christians and Jews to hear this.

---

[18] See pg. 340.

JEFF KING: You mentioned that Wahhabism is something that came from Muhammad ibn Abd al-Wahab and ibn Saud from the Arabia Peninsula. Can you give us some background on that? It's very important for people to understand how Wahhabism developed in [what is now] Saudi Arabia and the symbiotic relationship that the kingdom of Saudi Arabia has with Wahhabism.

Well, there wasn't a Saudi Arabia when Wahhabism emerged. It was: Arabia, the Kabaah, Mecca, and Medina—all controlled by the Ottomans—as well as the area around Kuwait and further south. The interior of Arabia was a wild desert called Najd, where there has been no economic development, no agricultural development. The only income was robbing the caravans that went from Kuwait to Mecca. There was a powerful clan in Najd, headed by Muhammad ibn Saud (the House of Saud), and they formed a partnership with the House of Muhammad ibn Abd al-Wahhab, the founder of Wahhabism.

The agreement was that the House of Saud would control political, financial, governance practices while the house of the descendants of ibn Abd al-Wahhab would control religious life and the two families married and they continue to marry among themselves. This created the situation of a joint Wahhabi/House of Saud plan for control of Arabia. They took over for the second and last time in Mecca and Medina in 1924 and the Saudi kingdom was established in 1932.

I was once on Canadian television and the interviewer said to me, "Well, of course, Muhammad was born in Saudi Arabia." I said, "Well, no he wasn't, because there was no Saudi Arabia then." It was Arabia; he was born in Hijaz, but Hijaz was not then in Saudi Arabia. Saudi Arabia emerged only in the last century.

JEFF KING: How is Saudi Arabia spreading Wahhabi ideology and violence in the world? What mechanisms and structures are they using?

Basically, they go in and divide the Islamic community to set up a separate Wahhabi jamaat community to agitate against the established Muslims, to provoke family quarrels, to agitate against the other religions if they're present and then to train people in the military arts and arm them, and to provoke armed conflicts. They do this over and over again, even in Muslim countries.

King Abdullah came to power in 2005 and he doesn't like the Wahhabis and has wanted to limit and restrict them and abolish their religious monopoly in the kingdom. Abdullah has made efforts to reform the kingdom socially, but he hasn't been very successful because he's up against the Wahhabi clerics who are very powerful. He's up against thousands of Saudi princes and princesses who support Wahhabism, as well as other wealthy Saudi individuals and families. They support Wahhabism as an ideology for internal control within the country, but they also contribute to the spread of the *dawa* of Wahhabism to Sunni Muslims around the world. They essentially call Sunni Muslims around the world to accept Wahhabism, and they've been successful in some countries. They've been less successful in other countries, and even unsuccessful in some countries. But, they have tremendous [financial] resources and, with those resources, they accomplish a lot in terms of establishing their control over Sunni Muslims.

JEFF KING: What is their strategy for expanding radical Islam?

There are three strategies. There's the strategy for Muslim countries, there is [a] strategy for countries where there is a large Muslim population, and there is a strategy for countries with a small Muslim population.

In Muslim countries, they essentially come in and they begin distributing their literature and preaching that they are the only true and real Muslims. This is not an Islamic idea. In [Sufi] Islam we believe that at the end of time God will judge who is sincere and who was insincere according to their intentions. The argument that somebody is a true Muslim, or is a real Muslim, this is rare in [traditional] Islam.

But the whole argument—the argument from ibn Abd al-Wahhab—p was that, in order to be a true Muslim, you have to follow his guidance and that you have to not only reject polytheism and the worship of idols, you have to get rid of all these practices in Islam like Sufism. This is all new; it's not part of classical Islam.

In countries where there are Muslims and non-Muslims living side by side, like India and Ethiopia, they attempt to provoke conflict between the Muslims and the non-Muslims (mainly the Hindus in India) in order to support their image of themselves as the great jihadists, the great warriors for Islam, the only real/true Muslims.

In a country where there is a small Muslim community, they really get away with a lot. The United States is a perfect example. Islam did not really emerge as a significant religion in the United States—that is not to say real Islam or true Islam, but authentic Islam (as opposed to a Black Muslim movement)—did not emerge in the United States until after the 1980s.

When it began to emerge in numbers it had no hierarchy, because you don't have a hierarchy in Sunnism. It had no apparatus, it had no organizations. [As a result], these Saudi-financed Wahhabi organizations like The Council on American-Islamic Relations, the Islamic Society in North America, and some Pakistani jihadist organizations like The Islamic Circle in North America, suddenly emerged. They set up, essentially, a [social/political] and religious apparatus for the Muslims in America. All of a sudden, the Muslims in America had organizations that claimed to speak for them.

A lot of this was in some part inspired by the Muslim Brotherhood, but I think it's a mistake to think it was mainly a brotherhood operation because Arabs are actually a fairly small share of the

Muslim population in America. The largest groups of born Muslims in America are South Asians from Pakistan and India, and they were more under the influence of Pakistani jihadism than of Arab Saudi Wahhabism. But, Pakistani jihadism and Sunni Wahhabism are based on the same concepts with very slight differences, but they have [both] been financed by Saudi Wahhabism.

They ended up creating a structure in the United States with Saudi money, South Asian functionaries, and Brotherhood literature, because most Americans, ordinary American Muslims or new Muslims, can't understand Wahhabi literature or Pakistani jihad literature. They don't understand it. Muslim Brotherhood literature is written much more simply and has much more of an appeal on the basis of being easy to understand.

JEFF KING: That's a great explanation. When you look at global Wahhabism, are there structures/organizations, or one organization that controls the spread of Wahhabism?

I don't think it's a single organization now. There was, under King Fahd, the previous king of Saudi, an organization called the Rabita [The Muslim World League] and they have/had branches. One of them was the International Islamic Relief Organization.

These organizations took the initiative and directed the spread of Wahhabism around the world, but with Abdullah in power—and with a lot of attention focused on these groups after 9/11—it seems to be more splintered now. It doesn't seem like there is a specific organization that is in charge of spreading Wahhabism around the world. It's just done by Wahhabi groups that get Saudi money and appear in different countries and have different names in different countries.

JEFF KING: And that makes it very hard to control?

It's going to be hard to control unless Saudi King Abdullah can be convinced to turn off the money faucet. Like with communism: when the Soviets stopped giving money to communist parties around the world, the communist parties disappeared. In 1988, there were communist parties in almost every country in the world. Now there are almost none. Once the Soviets turned off the money tap, the [organizations died].

JEFF KING: In your book, you mentioned CAIR (Council on American Islamic Relations), ISNA (Islamic Society of North America) and other Islamic organizations in the United States. Tell us about these organizations. What kinds of strategies do they use in order to exert their influence?

Well, CAIR claims to be a civil liberties organization that exists to protect the rights of Muslims. But in fact, CAIR is a front for Hamas and it exists to spread Islamist ideology and spread the image that Muslims are victimized in the United States, that Muslims are in danger in the United States and have to protect themselves. It's a radical group; there is no question about it.

ISNA is a strange phenomenon, in that, a lot of young Muslims are cynical about it. They go to their annual meetings to meet the members of the opposite sex because it's easier than at home. Almost all the Muslim organizations have these wedding services or match up services, but the fact is that ISNA was founded by, and with the support of, the Muslim Brotherhood, the Saudi Wahhabis, and the Pakistani jihadis.

ISNA has always stood in defense of those groups, they have always acted along the same line as Professor Esposito and his group at Georgetown University, which is to defend and promote the ideas of radical Islam as the only Islam there is, as the authoritative voice of Islam.

JEFF KING: There are a number of well-known universities and academic institutions which are being funded by Saudi money. Is this correct, and what are the ramifications?

They receive Saudi money, yes. I will give you the one example which is the most infamous example: the situation of Georgetown University. Georgetown received a lot of Saudi money. They established The Center for Muslim Christian Understanding, they [the Saudis] support the work of Professor John Esposito, and he is an upfront, un-apologizing or unrepentant apologist for radical Islam and for Wahhabism in particular.

He brags about how often he visits Saudi and how proud he is of the Saudi connection between Georgetown and Saudi Arabia. If you look at the work that comes out of Georgetown, inspired by Esposito and people close to him, it is clear that the work is intended to support radical Islam and the position of Saudi Arabia. There is no question about it. It is to whitewash Wahhabism and make Wahhabism sound as if it doesn't exist, it's not a problem, it's reformed, or various other claims they make in order to basically deny the existence of radical Islam.

Now, with the Obama administration, we're in a period where basically the administration is denying the existence of radical Islam. Radical Islam isn't a problem because it doesn't exist!

JEFF KING: So, what do you think is the goal? Is it to indoctrinate the younger generation with the idea that there is no Wahhabism?

Rather, it is that there's just one Islam and the Sunni radicals define Islam.

JEFF KING: How many mosques in the United States are under control of the Saudis/Wahhabism?

Well, there are twelve hundred mosques in the US [getting accurate numbers is very difficult], but in 2010, at least 800 or 900 of them [were] under Saudi influence, Saudi control.

JEFF KING: How do they exert control, and do they plant imams at these mosques?

They control them through the North American Islamic Trust, which is part of the Islamic Society in North America. [In regards to planting imams], yes, when they build mosques, they train the imams and they send imams from abroad, from Saudi. Imams are either trained in Saudi or trained in Yemen, or trained in other countries with radical ideology and then sent as imams. A lot of them are also from Pakistan and even India.

JEFF KING: That's frightening but a few people like you [and other Muslims] are speaking out against this. How effective are you?

Some of us are speaking out and some of us are effective. I mean, the fact that you're even having this interview with me shows that we have some effect, but we're very isolated and it's very difficult. In the United States, the moderate Muslims who are speaking out against Wahhabism are rare, that's the reality.

JEFF KING: What about the government of the United States? In terms of dialogue, are they talking more with moderates or with the Wahhabi?

Under the Obama administration, the position of the government of the United States is that they want to talk to the radicals. They want dialogue with the radicals; they want dialogue with the extremists in Afghanistan. They want to pretend there is no such thing as radical Islam and any problems that exist can be handled through negotiation, through talking, and money.

JEFF KING: Another thing that you mention in your book is your experience in the Balkans, how the Muslims there are being infiltrated by the Wahhabis. How much the Wahhabis are expanding there. Tell us a little bit about what methods they are using to expand.

Money, money!! People in the Balkans are poor. People in the Balkans came out of communism and they came out of a horrible war, series of wars. They're poor. The European Union has not done [anything] to help them rebuild or reconstruct their society. Being that they're poor and the West has done little to help them reconstruct, [this is more in Bosnia than Kosovo] the Islamic elite are susceptible to bribery; they're susceptible to money and the Saudis bring money. But, of course, there is something attached to the money: and that they have to have the right to preach Wahhabism. They've built mosques in Bosnia, and they install Wahhabi imams there, and they use the Saudi-built mosques in Bosnia to spread Wahhabism. But it's always money.

Extremism without money remains obscure and nobody ever hears about it. All forms of radicalism, extremism, revolutionism, communism, socialism, Wahhabism—if it weren't for the money, you'd never hear about it.

JEFF KING: You know we work on behalf of persecuted Christians. We get continual reports of: violence against Christians, imprisonment, even killings of Christians (especially those who convert to Christianity from Islam). There are laws that relegate non-Muslims in general to second class citizens in Pakistan, Saudi Arabia, and Egypt, to mention a few. We get reports of persecution continually. What's your take on that? I mean, as a Muslim, how do you deal with that?

Well, I'm opposed to persecuting anybody over anything having to do with religion. Religion is a matter of private conscience. People follow the religion they follow because God has chosen them to do that, and I'm against any Muslim's interference of anybody's choice of religion. If people go out of Islam, no—very few religions are happy when people become apostates, you have to understand that.

JEFF KING: That's true.

Everybody has that. Christians don't like it when Christians become Muslims. Jews don't like it when Jews become Muslims or Christians. Every religion resents its people leaving the religion, but it's one thing to say you disagree with it, with their action, and it's another thing to promote violence or some sort of legal sanctions against them. If people are going out of Islam to other religions, my answer is, then, let's make Islam better. That's a sensible answer. Otherwise, I respect the individual choices people make since I made an individual choice myself, and I don't support any action to discriminate against anybody on basis of religion. I'm opposed to it, and I think the role of Sufis is to protect non-Muslims who are under attack by Muslims, by radical Muslims. But one has to admit that the issue of apostasy is not a simple issue. What we need in Islam is we need a debate about this. We need a debate about what it really is, what it means. We have to redefine the terms of all of this. We can't let the terms on this debate be set by radicals.

We have to find a way to make real the statements in the Qur'an that Jews and Christians who are sincere in their belief have nothing to fear in the last day and will be rewarded. We have to respect that Muslims are commanded to show [respect] towards Christians and Jews; we have to make that real.

Now, the question of Muslims who leave the religion, as I say, this is not a major problem in most of Islamic history. It's not commented on in most of Islamic history. But, we have to have a different attitude about this and we have to recognize that in the modern world people make choices just as at all times people make choices. It would be interesting to research cases of Muslims who became

Christians in the past because I know that it did happen. In the Ottoman Empire there were families where it was unclear whether they were Christian, Muslim or both, frankly. All of this history and all of this debate has to be carried out within the Muslim community, but the first thing is that nobody should be subjected to violence or legal sanction because of their religious choices.

JEFF KING: Also in your book, you described Wahhabi funding the makers and importing of bombers in Palestine. As we know, the majority of the hijackers during 9/11 were Saudis. So, there is a very clear link between Wahhabism and terrorism?

Absolutely! The Wahhabi apparatus that was emanating from Saudi Arabia at the time of 9/11. I mean, bin Laden [was] a Saudi and bin Laden didn't create al-Qaeda to advance Islam. He created al-Qaeda, in my view, to prevent social change in Saudi Arabia by proving to the world that if anybody tried to limit the Wahhabis they would have to deal with very violent, brutal people. I always say that 9/11 wasn't aimed at America or Israel; it was aimed at the Muslims. It was an illustration to Muslims to show the brutality and the lengths to which the Wahhabis were willing to go.

JEFF KING: So, what is the solution then for Wahhabism? Is there any? Because this looks like it's a danger for the peace and security of the world.

[There is a] very simple solution. King Abdullah should cut off all money going to foreign Wahhabi [preaching/evangelism]. He should break the relationship between the royal family and the house of ibn Abd al-Wahhabi. He should [have said] that Wahhabism is no longer the state religion, that Muslims are free to follow any form of Islam they want, and that all religions are free because about a quarter of the population in Saudi Arabia are foreign workers, millions of whom are Christians. So the fact that there is no right to build Christian churches in Saudi Arabia is absurd. I mean, it's anti-Islamic.

Christians living in Saudi Arabia should have the right to have their own churches. You know, all the other countries around there [what the Saudis call the crescent of normality]—from Kuwait, Jordan, and even Iraq now, all the way down through Yemen—have Christian churches. There are even some Jewish synagogues.

The fact that [building of churches] is not permitted in Saudi, this is not Islamic. This is a new thing that the Wahhabis invented. Because, there were Jews living in what's now Saudi Arabia until the 1950s, and there is a Christian cemetery in Jeddah, an old Christian cemetery, and there is a Christian church in Jeddah, though it's not used as a church now.

It's very simple. King Abdullah should say, "Wahhabism is no longer a state religion in this country. We'll no longer allow any money to go to finance international radicalism by Wahhabis," and that that will be it. It will be just like it was when the Soviet Union stopped being communist. With an end to the flow of money, the phenomenon will end. The phenomenon will decline very quickly.

Now, there is a fact and I've said this elsewhere, radical Islam is more volatile than communism was. When communism collapsed, it was psychologically exhausted. That isn't true with Wahhabism. Wahhabism is still violent, and it still has an appeal to certain types of people. It still has this appeal of planning, and it's the purest form of [perceived Islamic] response. So, cutting off the money won't get rid of the problem completely, but it will certainly diminish the problem.

JEFF KING: One of the challenges in dealing with Saudi Arabia is the relationship between the Saudi royal family/government and the United States. What is your suggestion for the United States government in general and to United States citizens in positively influencing Saudi Arabia?

I think that the only thing that one can say about the present situation of the US government is that the Obama administration has to change its direction, has to stop playing this absurd game of pretending that there's no such thing as radical Islam. [It] has to take a position like that of the Bush administration, that we are opposed to the spread of radical Islam, and the United States has to tell the Saudis, "We want to be your friends, but we want to have a transparent relationship where terrorism is not a side effect of the friendship."

I think King Abdullah would respond to that, but the problem is President Obama won't do it. But that's what Americans can do. Focus attention on Saudi Arabia. Write about it, read about it, pay attention to what's going on there, and demand that the US take a critical position on everything that's wrong with Saudi Arabia.

JEFF KING: Coming back to the book in general, what message do you intend to convey in your book *The Two Faces of Islam*?

My intention is to establish that the majority of Muslims in the world are moderate – they're not radical, they're not violent, they are not jihadists. They do not want to engage in conflict with their neighbors who are not Muslims or with their neighbors who are Muslims. And that people in the West, people who are not Muslims, should do everything they can to help the moderate Muslims and to support the Sufis, the moderate Sunnis, the moderate Shias, and other Muslims who want to defeat radicalism.

But one cannot deny that radicalism, right now, seems to have gotten a new life, because the Obama administration and Western European powers—when they say they want to get out of Afghanistan, when they say that can't win the war in Afghanistan, when they're passive about the threat of the fall of Pakistan—they are encouraging the growth, expansion, and rise of radicalism.

JEFF KING: We want to challenge your thesis of *The Two Faces of Islam*. Overwhelmingly, Muslims take the Qur'an to be the direct word of God and the source of Islam in general. What are you going to do with violent verses which are used by the Wahhabis and others to justify violence, to justify radical thinking—I'm sure you know some of them.

I would rather have a copy of Qur'an here if we're going to discuss it. Maybe we can do that in a separate interview, but the point is we believe that the verses that the Wahhabis and other radicals use to justify their activities are taken out of context. That all the verses have—all of the verses that are used to justify the alleged jihad of the radicals—have other verses that balance them out.

For example, the verse which says *"Let there be no compulsion in religion (Qur'an 2:256),"* has a famous verse that says: *"Fight those who believe not in Allah nor the Last Day, nor hold that forbidden which hath been forbidden by Allah and His Messenger, nor acknowledge the religion of Truth, (even if they are) of the People of the Book, until they pay the Jizya with willing submission, and feel themselves subdued."* (Qur'an 9:29)

Well, no country in the world actually charges the jizya tax today. The jizya tax does not exist today, there is not one country in the world that has [it]. Saudi Arabia doesn't have it. I think the thing is, there are things that applied earlier in Islamic history, and we can say now don't apply in Islamic history. I mean, the Qur'an is a book open to interpretation; we can interpret it. We can interpret how to apply it, and I think we should apply it in a manner that lessens conflict and promotes conciliation (see author's note, p. 173).

I'm not going to use a stupid cliché about Islam being a religion of peace. Islam will be a religion of peace if the Muslims make it a religion of peace. Now, as far as the Qur'an goes, it's God's word, but we can interpret it. We do interpret it; we don't take it literally. Literalism doesn't actually, doesn't exist today. It disappeared in

Islam a long time ago. Even the Wahhabis take themselves on an interpretation. They stress certain verses; we stress other verses.

AUTHOR'S NOTE:

I agree with Mr. Schwartz's need for a new willingness of Islam to interpret various verses of the Qur'an within the context of modernity. But, there is a bedrock principle of Qur'an interpretation known as abrogation. There are many conflicting verses in the Qur'an and more recent (chronologically) verses supersede the earlier verses. The problem is that as Muhammad gained political and military power he became for violence and most of the violent (more recent) verses supersede the less violent (older) verses.

Chapter Nine:

The CIA Director

[Saudi Arabia and al-Qaeda]) both believe in an extreme form of Sharia, they both believe apostates and homosexuals should be killed, in stoning women who are convicted of adultery. The Saudis' [and] al-Qaeda's underlying beliefs are, for all practical purposes, identical. And the Saudis would like to see a steady and major expansion of their brand of Islam, but they don't want it to happen in a way that disrupts their lifestyle.

R. James Woolsey

Woolsey describes himself as a "Scoop Jackson-Joe Lieberman Democrat" and argues that the West is in the middle of fighting a "long war" against radical Islam.

Mr. Woolsey previously served in the US Government on five different occasions, where he held presidential appointments in two Republican and two Democratic administrations, most recently (1993-95) as the sixteenth director of Central Intelligence.

During his twelve years of government service, in addition to heading the CIA and the Intelligence Community, Mr. Woolsey was: Ambassador to the Negotiation on Conventional Armed Forces in Europe (CFE), Vienna, 1989–1991; Under Secretary of the Navy, 1977–1979; and General Counsel to the US Senate Committee on Armed Services, 1970–1973. He was also appointed by the president to serve on a part-time basis in Geneva, Switzerland, 1983–1986, as Delegate-at-Large to the US-Soviet Strategic Arms Reduction Talks (START) and Nuclear and Space Arms Talks (NST). As an officer in the US Army, he was an adviser on the US Delegation to the Strategic Arms Limitation Talks (SALT I), Helsinki and Vienna, 1969–1970.

Mr. Woolsey was born in Tulsa, Oklahoma, and attended Tulsa public schools, graduating from Tulsa Central High School. He received his B.A. degree from Stanford University (1963, With Great Distinction, Phi Beta Kappa), an M.A. from Oxford University (Rhodes Scholar 1963–1965), and an LL.B. from Yale Law School (1968, Managing Editor of the *Yale Law Journal*).

JEFF KING: This is going to be a lot to unpack, but sum up the role of Saudi Arabia in terms of their connection with Islamic terrorism and the spread of radical Islam.

Wahhabi Islam and Sharia, in their extreme form, are the governing religion and essentially the governing constitution of Saudi Arabia. It is quite explicit that Sharia law is its constitution. It is not just a place which has individuals in the country, who from time to time, support radical causes. That could be true of any Muslim country, but Saudi Arabia is a special case for several reasons.

One is the adherence to the most extreme forms of Sharia that were present in the Arabian Desert going back to times even before Muhammad. This really consolidated with the influence of the Wahhabis in the 18th century and the alliance with the House of Saud that eventually produced the country of Saudi Arabia.

It hasn't always been completely smooth between the Wahhabis and the House of Saud, but generally speaking, they need each other and they work very closely together. That has had a major impact on the direction that Saudi Arabia has taken, even before the '70s, but especially beginning in 1979.

In 1979, when the Shiite extremists took over Iran (Saudi Arabia's and the Arabs' great historic rival) there was a simultaneous seizure of the Great Mosque in Mecca by pre-al-Qaeda radicals. Press reports indicated that they had to take the radical step of inviting the French to help clear the Great Mosque of the Islamic terrorists. This would have been a huge blow to their pride.

The Saudis regard Shia Islam as polytheism, as apostasy. The Shia, from their point of view, are as bad as Christians that believe in a Trinity.

I was in Saudi Arabia a year before, in 1978, as Undersecretary of the Navy. A couple of times during my stay there I was invited to the homes of individuals that I was working with. These were individuals, on two occasions, who had spent a lot of time in the West. Their wives were at the dinner in modern Western cocktail dresses, there was jazz on the stereo, aperitifs before dinner, a *New York Herald Tribune* open on the coffee table, and wine with dinner.

That would be unimaginable in Saudi Arabia today. In the early part of the last decade, a girls' school in Mecca, I believe, caught fire. After the first responders arrived, the religious police showed up and either ordered the firemen, or they themselves threw the little girls back into the burning school because some of them didn't have their veils on.

It's almost unimaginable to be that fanatic, but it would not be particularly surprising to see something like that happen again if Prince Nayef, the head of the interior ministry and the head of the religious police, becomes the next king.

Now, with that as the culture, little girls being burned to death for not having their veils on, there is really very little hope for any kind of moderation. I do hear from Saudi dissidents that there are one or two members of the next generation who are, at least to some degree, thinking of reform.

In terms of reform, I think that the issue to watch is women's rights. They won't make fundamental changes first in the religious area, but if the role of women in the society begins to change—if women are no longer stoned for adultery, if honor killings cease—even if the culture is extremely conservative, I think it would be a glimmer of hope for the rest of the world.

Until then, because of its combination of oil, wealth, and the alliance between the House of Saud and the Wahhabis, we have two serious problems in moderate Muslim countries.

One problem is, of course, terrorism. Saudi [princes], and quite possibly some parts of the Saudi government [the border between government and non-government is almost non-existent], are giving money to organizations that in turn fund al-Qaeda.

[In terms of the Saudis and al-Qaeda] it is the [same] issue that the Stalinists in the '20s and '30s had. Although they had the same ideology, for all practical purposes, as the Trotskyites, they loathed and hated the Trotskyites, feared them. The idea of Trotskyites, that you ought to be able to go off and start revolutions whenever and wherever you wanted, was a threat to Stalinist control. And Trotsky died with a Stalinist axe in his skull in Mexico City in 1940. But their underlying beliefs were the same: they wanted a dictatorship of the proletariat and they wanted to liquidate the bourgeoisie in order to get there. But the Stalinists hated and feared the Trotskyites. They would have done anything, including work with us—if we'd been in that business then—to try to track down and kill Trotskyites before Trotskyites could get control of their own system or do some damage to it.

Their argument was not on substance, or on what kind of society one eventually wanted; the argument was on tactics, and who's in charge. Could Trotsky start revolutions wherever he wanted or did he have to obey Stalin? That's roughly—very, very roughly—a comparison between al-Qaeda and similar organizations today and the House of Saud. They hate each other and they kill each other. The Saudis work with us to try to capture al-Qaeda or kill al-Qaeda. As long as it is a terrorist organization that is oriented against them, they will work together with us on it, and they have probably been of some help in thwarting some of these terrorist attacks.

But we shouldn't get starry eyed about that. After all, just after Trotsky's death, the United States and Stalinist Soviet Union became close allies. The war began in September of 1939 when the Stalinists and the Nazis allied with one another. In '41, when we came into the war, for three years and eight months we had a close alliance with the man who, up until that point in history, had killed more people than any other individual in the world. Because we needed him!

We needed him to defeat the Nazis. Sometimes foreign policy and geopolitics are like that. And some Americans got a little bleary eyed, and a little touched, and even the very hardheaded Franklin Roosevelt used to call Stalin "Uncle Joe." But, for three years and eight months we were allied, until the end of WWII.

So today, we have to cooperate and do some things with the Saudis in order to help defeat those terrorists who are [our joint enemies], which is certainly not all terrorists. There is support, probably not from the top level of the Saudi government, but certainly from some members of the royal family, that goes to terrorist organizations. Certainly, very heavily to Hamas, and any group that's working against Israel. That support is a very serious problem: for Israel, for us, for our allies in the West, and the rest of the world.

The other thing which oil money makes it possible for the Saudis to do—and they do this in spades—is to fund Muslim Brotherhood-type organizations around the world. Lawrence Wright, in *The Looming Tower*, says that with essentially a little over one percent of the world's Muslims, the Saudis cover about ninety percent of the cost of Islam around the world. When I was chairman of the board of Freedom House, back in the early part of the last decade, we had a group of American Muslims come to us with material that the visiting Saudi imams kept putting into their mosque.

The American Muslims were just appalled by it. They said, "This isn't the Islam we know, this is not what we want. We've translated it. Translate it yourself. You'll see what it says..." So we had it translated by other people and, sure enough, it was as hate-filled and hideous as one could imagine.

We published it at Freedom House. Nina Shea took the lead in this as the head of the Center for Religious Freedom. And it was certainly not popular in the Saudi embassy. They said some things about how they would review their education materials and make changes, but nothing has changed. Those types of documents and that type of teaching is standard fare in Saudi-funded education institutions, whether they're in Fairfax County or Lahore or in Nablus, and that is a big part of the problem.

I tell people that the next time they pull into a filling station and are, by any chance, thinking about the problems and the war we have with Islamic terrorism, and they're wondering who's paying for all of those madrassas to be teaching this very hate-filled doctrine of Wahhabi Islam—that before they get out of their car and get their billfold to get their credit card, they should sit in the car for just a second and turn the rearview mirror a few inches so they're looking into their own eyes. Now they know who's paying for those little boys to be taught at age eight that their highest desire should be to be a suicide bomber because the Christians and the Jews and everybody except them are so hideous.

Anybody who thinks oil is a free market is delusional. Whether it's the money that the wealthy individuals in Saudi Arabia give to groups that support terrorism, or whether it's the support through Muslim Brotherhood-type organizations of civilization jihad, we have a very, very serious problem, and we need to move very quickly and decisively to get away from our dependence, not just on foreign oil, but on oil – period. I think we can do that with biofuels, with electricity, with greater efficiency in internal combustion engines, and the like. No one of those things is sufficient, but together they could make a substantial dent.

JEFF KING: That's a great overture. Let's unpack a number of themes you touched on. So, with Saudi Arabia, you're saying that there's no great difference, ideologically, between them and the Taliban?

They both believe in an extreme form of Sharia, they both believe apostates and homosexuals should be killed, they both believe in stoning women who are convicted of adultery. And, by the way, a woman who is raped and doesn't have four male witnesses who will testify on her behalf is deemed to have participated in the sex voluntarily. When they stone a man, they bury him only up to his waist and he is able to scrape the dirt away, often extricating himself before he's hurt too badly. And if he can get out and get away from where he's being stoned, he's let go. The woman is buried up to her neck and tied in such a way that she can't escape.

The Saudis' [and] al-Qaeda's underlying beliefs are, for all practical purposes, identical. And the Saudis would like to see a steady and major expansion of their brand of Islam, but they don't want it to happen in a way that disrupts their lifestyle. So, at least in that sense, they're something of a status quo power. But meanwhile, under the table, they're paying for little Muslim children in Fairfax County, Virginia, to be taught to hate.

JEFF KING: While Saudi is the main player, they're not the only Gulf state to fund Islamic radicals. Talk about the role of different states involved.

Well, the Saudis are the heart of the matter, but all of these countries have wealthy individuals who are either essentially Wahhabis or sympathize with Wahhabis. When they give *zakat,* many of the organizations that take that money send that money on to Hamas. They operate some social services as a way to ingratiate themselves to the population, but their main effort is jihad. So a Kuwaiti or a wealthy member of the UAE ruling family, or just a wealthy individual who gives money to Hamas (or to an organization like Hamas), is functionally aiding terrorism, no matter how much he says, "Well, what I really liked about that is that they were running social services in the West Bank or in Gaza."

JEFF KING: Would you say Wahhabism is closer to a strict adherence to the Qur'an and Hadith, or is it an aberration? What I'm asking is this: Are Wahhabis adding extra theological material to Islam or are they purists/fundamentalists who are seeking to obey what's in the Qur'an and Hadith?

That's my understanding [they are fundamentalists], but I think there are some variations. Female genital mutilation is an example. As far as I'm aware, that's in only one early document. It's not in the Qur'an and, consequently, you have a fairly substantial variation in Muslim countries. But the really shocking aspects of Sharia—the killing of apostates and homosexuals, the stoning of women for adultery—it's my understanding they are, at least in some form, in the early documents and many of them in the Qur'an.

JEFF KING: As someone with experience in the Cold War, how do you compare Saudi Arabia's influence with the communists' influence in terms of a threat to the world?

The Soviets were a lot easier for us to deal with. It took us a little bit of time to get sorted out how to deal with domestic non-violent communists or agents of communists. We had some false starts. For example, around 1940 or so Congress passed a bill that made it illegal to be a communist and the Supreme Court struck it down on First Amendment grounds. As things developed in the '50s and '60s, we came up with a panoply of ways we dealt with essentially domestic communists and people who were doing the Soviets' will, essentially trying to bring about a dictatorship of the proletariat, but doing it by spying, lobbying, whatever. We didn't let them serve in the Armed Forces, we didn't let them hold government positions, we made them sign oaths about every time they turned around, and their organization was very heavily penetrated by the FBI.

[Laughing] There was a quiet little accountant who was the treasurer of the American communist party for thirty years or so. They smuggled him over sometime in the '70s or early '80s to Moscow and he was personally given the Order of Lenin by Brezhnev. After a few years, it was disclosed that he had been with the FBI all along and President Reagan awarded him the Presidential Medal of Freedom. So I think he's the only individual ever to win both the Order of Lenin and the Presidential Medal of Freedom.

The problem with Islamism is that it is connected to one of the world's great religions. Almost all of the world's great religions, at one time or another, have spawned some kind of a totalitarian offshoot. And this is a country of religious refugees and their kids, basically. We don't tend to judge people or deal with them. We're not comfortable dealing with them on the basis of their religion. Let's say you and I have just moved into a new a neighborhood and they had a neighborhood barbecue. We're all standing around, and I somehow let slip that I'm a Branch Davidian. You're probably not likely to say, "Why did you end up getting those people killed in Waco?" You're far more likely to say "Oh, I'm a Methodist myself. Have a beer."

We don't treat people, usually, based on their religion. If we do, we do it far less than virtually any society in the world ever has. This really is a First Amendment country. And, as a result, we probably would have had a really hard time dealing with Torquemada, Thomas Munzer, the Sicarii, or the Shintoists (who backed the kamikazes), if they'd been part of the United States.

And if you or I said to an American Muslim, "This business of throwing little girls back into a blazing school because they don't have their veils on is wrong. What's going on?" The response you will get from a Muslim Brotherhood-type is, "You're an Islamaphobe." The Christians, Jews, and Muslims who opposed the Spanish Inquisition were not Christianaphobes. They were people who saw that there was an offshoot from one of the world's great religions that had effectively become a totalitarian movement. And the Islamists are totalitarians. However much they wear a smile, they're totalitarians. And we need to be able to think about them and deal with them the way we dealt with Gus Hall [US Communist leader], which is, "No, we're not going to throw you in jail. Go make a speech on the street corner if you want. If you want to run for president, run for president, but you're not going to be like Major Hassan. You don't get to go into the Army and kill your fellow soldiers. You're not going to be able to work for the federal government. You're not going to have a security clearance." There are a number of things you're not going to be able to do. And it will be very difficult for us to work ourselves into a mindset that is as both rational and effective in dealing with the Islamists as we were able to do in dealing with domestic American communists.

JEFF KING: How much hope do you have of us getting a grip on radical Islam in our borders?

We have a lot of things we've got to do before we can. The first thing we've got to do is stop talking in euphemisms and dancing around the issue. I mean, this business of the government filing a report of Major Hassan's killing of his thirteen fellow soldiers and never mentioning the word Muslim or Islam, or anything. He's just a random violent extremist. That's nuts.

Orwell, as on many things, has the best answer to that: anybody who thinks that's the way to run things ought to read his marvelous *Politics and the English Language*. He has a very marvelous satire in there of political euphemism.

We can't begin to deal with this until we can talk straight about it. That's the first thing. Al Qaeda's [focused] on jihad. The Muslim Brotherhood's [focused] on civilization jihad or grand jihad. Different kinds of jihad, same objective: establish a worldwide caliphate. I think the press and the politicians owe us that, at least, and owe us some direct, solid and totally dismissive comments about people like these Muslim Brotherhood organizations when they call someone an Islamaphobe because he points out that Major Hassan's belief in one form of Islam may have had a little something to do with those thirteen people he killed after shouting "Allahu Ahkbar."

JEFF KING: So, to what do you attribute this politically correct madness? Where we're not allowed to speak the truth, we're not allowed to call things as they are?

I don't know. If you don't admit there's a problem, then maybe you avoid having to deal with it, or having people call you to account for not dealing with it.

I mean, I sometimes you feel like they'll go to the extreme of thinking up euphemisms. For example, instead of calling terrorists "violent extremists," maybe they would call them "Anger Management-Challenged Candidates for Therapy."

This whole issue could use an Orwell—someone who writes with pungency.

JEFF KING: Yes, truth is a great solvent. In fact, a lot of ex-Muslims will say the key to winning this ideological war is to help Muslims come to understand who Muhammad was and what Islam is truly about. They will tell you that most Muslims don't know who Muhammad was and when they discovered what kind of person he was, that created a fork in the road for them. People, for the most part, don't sign up for violence and hatred. What do you think about that?

I don't know. I don't have a very good feel for that issue. I think we're not going to win this thing without getting on our side the real moderate Muslims. The Abdurrahman Wahids and the Zeyno Barans and the Zudhi Jassers, etc. We've got to operate in such a way that we hold on to whoever would like to be allied with us. And my very loose analogy would be: let's not turn George Orwell and Helmut Schmidt away because they call themselves socialists or because they believe in a more progressive tax system than I do. Or because they believe in implementing, to some degree, from each according to his ability to each according to his need. They are, were, marvelous, staunch supporters of human freedom and the fact that they were socialists at the same time is something, sort of, okay with me. So I, I'd like to find some way to...

JEFF KING: ...build the moderates...

Right, to support them, and that will really get the goat of the Islamists.

JEFF KING: And yet, it is a little like a man on the beach with a bucket trying to turn back the ocean, with the Saudis and what they're doing.

Well, that's one reason that I spend so much time and effort working on oil issues. Because I think they have two Achilles' heels: one is oil, and the other is their treatment of women. If we could bring substantial pressure on either issue, I think we could see some very substantial changes. But, we've got to work really hard on both of those issues.

JEFF KING: You brought up Prince Nayef. What happens if he becomes the next king of Saudi Arabia?

I think it would be very bad. He's never given any evidence, as far as I'm aware, of any inclination toward reform. I think he's a very fanatic Wahhabi. And I don't know what we could expect. I don't think we can expect anything positive from him.

JEFF KING: And I would assume that he can exert a lot of influence on trying to line up his successor?

The successor determination in the House of Saud is complicated, and there aren't many people I think who really know anything about it. They have a sequence. I think they have a crown prince, that's Defense Minister Sultan, but he's been quite ill. I think there may be something whereby Nayef has now moved into functionally being one step below moving up to be king. King Abdullah was just here for medical treatment in the United States. I don't know anything about the state of Nayef's health or his exact age or any of that, but there are reportedly one or two members of the next generation who would be at least considerably less fanatic, although their basic views might be pretty much the same.

JEFF KING: You've talked about madrassas; just unpack that a little more. How big a problem is it? How many have been started around the world?

I don't have the exact numbers, but what's taught in these Saudi-funded institutions is Wahhabi Islam. And so, little boys, just after they learn to read, when they're six or seven years old, are taught from the beginning: to hate Christians and Jews, the subordinate position in society of women, that apostates should be killed, and on and on. By the time they're teenagers this is all they've seen or known.

JEFF KING: So, they're known as Islamic boarding schools, but school is a misnomer.

Well, it's a misnomer insofar as we think of school.

JEFF KING: In the past decade, Saudis have poured, what? Tens of millions, hundreds of millions, into US universities? What are they trying to accomplish?

Although there was some sympathy for the Soviets derived from the wartime alliance back, in the US, in say the '50s and the '60s to some extent, nobody let Stalin establish a Lenin chair for political philosophy and pay for it at Harvard or Georgetown. You know? I mean, among the things that we shouldn't be doing is permitting the acceptance of Islamist funds in education.

JEFF KING: What do they get out of it?

They get sympathetic faculty.

JEFF KING: Less critical discourse?

Take jihad. There's this kind of party line from the Muslim Brotherhood that the great jihad really is self-examination, inner struggle. And the lesser jihad is fighting defensively in case anybody should attack you. Well, something like that probably appears in some religious document. But, far and away, the preponderant meaning of jihad is war and, further, war of conquest.

Perhaps, if their chair has been paid for by the House of Saud, perhaps, they'll neglect to talk about abrogation. But abrogation is a doctrine of interpretation for all four of the main schools of Sunni Islam, and it means that the later Medina suras[19] take precedence over the earlier, more peaceful Mecca suras. It's hard for outsiders to sort out because the Qur'an is not organized in such a way that it comes by a chronology at all. I think it's organized by the size of the chapters, but you have to know which ones are later, and some of the harshest ones are the latest ones, such as "fight and kill them [that is, Christians and Jews] wherever you find them."

These supersede the earlier ones. But there are a lot of places where you won't be taught that because it makes it harder for the teacher to explain how *jihad* doesn't really mean *jihad*.

JEFF KING: Anything you want to say about CAIR?

Well, it's a Muslim Brotherhood organization. It's one of the ones that was named as an unindicted co-conspirator in the Holy Land Foundation trial. There was a decision by an appellate judge later that said the federal government should not have released *publically*

---

[19] See pg. 346.

the names of the unindicted co-conspirators, but it *didn't* say that they were not unindicted co-conspirators.

JEFF KING: Recently voters in your home state of Oklahoma voted to oppose any application or use of Sharia laws by the state courts. What prompted the voters to do something like that?

They got in touch with me and asked me if I would make a robo-call and I did. The problem tends to come up in the West with respect to women's rights—particularly the beating of wives and the killing of daughters—as so-called honor killings. It's come up a lot in Britain, the Netherlands, Germany and Italy. What happens is a husband will beat his wife and she'll bring charges against him, but he'll say it is his right under his religion. One of these cases went all the way up to the Italian Supreme Court of Cassation and the beater was upheld. There are several cases that have gone in that direction in Germany as well.

We've only had one case I know of in the US where that kind of a defense was offered, when a man beat and raped his wife and was upheld at the trial level in New Jersey. This was a year or so ago, and then he lost at the appellate level. Because Sharia, in so many ways, has these various discriminatory, and worse, things about women, that's where it tends to come up. When they asked me to make this robo-call, they said, "We haven't had any cases like this in Oklahoma," and I said, "I don't know that you have to have one woman per state beaten, and a beater exonerated, before you pass a Constitutional amendment."

We faced the issue of polygamy in the nineteenth century with the Mormons. A unanimous Supreme Court case in the 1870s held a Mormon guilty on appeal of violating a statute against polygamy. When he said he did it because it was his religious duty, the answer was, "Well, thank you. We're delighted that you believe that is your religious duty, but it's also against the law, and you go to jail."

So, I saw no reason not to help the voters of my home state understand that it's perfectly reasonable to move out this way even before women start getting beaten. The reason it's raised the ire of the Islamist organizations is that it stands athwart their long-term goal to replace the Constitution with Sharia, and if you can't even cite Sharia in a court opinion...

JEFF KING: It'd be nice if they could implement that law in Britain or Germany...

If you look at Europe, you have both the Archbishop of Canterbury and the Lord Chief Justice saying that they believe some aspects of Sharia law are going to or should be incorporated into British law.

JEFF KING: What about August 2010, *The Free Speech Act*, passed by Congress?

The so-called "Rachel's Law." Rachel Ehrenfeld's book was not even sold in the UK, except for a few copies on the Web, but she was sued in Britain by bin Mahfouz, who's a very wealthy man, who really made a habit of this libel tourism. He got some books destroyed by Cambridge University Press by two Americans. It's kind of amazing, one of the oldest universities in the world, beacon of freedom, destroying books. Incredible.

He bit off more than he could chew when he went after Rachel. And, to make a long story short, she's gotten statutes passed in New York and two, three, or four other states, and then finally the federal statute which effectively stops libel tourism.

JEFF KING: And, briefly, what's libel tourism?

It's bin Mahfouz saying, "This sentence in this book libels me, so I'm going to go Britain, where the courts are extremely favorably disposed toward plaintiffs, and get a judgment against Rachel Ehrenfeld." Even though she isn't in Britain and has no ties to

Britain, nonetheless, the British courts interpret that if there was even a handful of books sold in Britain over the Web, that that gave them jurisdiction over her.

So, he received a judgment for several hundred thousand dollars. Normally, he would bring it to the United States to enforce it, but if the American courts are now, as they are, barred by American law from his enforcing it, then that stops this Saudi libel tourism game. Rachel deserves a lot of credit for fighting on this because a lot of American institutions, publishers, newspapers and so forth caved.

ISLAM'S TREATMENT OF PEOPLE OF OTHER FAITHS

Chapter Ten:

The Expert on Islamic Oppression

["After Saturday comes Sunday"] is a general slogan often repeated by Muslims, Jews and Christians, since the three groups know the long history of persecutions in the Dar al-Islam. It is probably rooted in the Qur'an and the biographies of the prophet who first dealt with the Jews in Medina and then with the Christians when they refused to convert. It means that after the persecution of the Jews, the Christians will follow.

Bat Yeor

Islam is more than a religion. It is a religious and political system combined. Understanding this statement will help the average person greatly in the study of Islam. *Dhimmitude* is the system of rules and regulations laid out by Muhammad to be enforced on "People of the Book," and it later extended to some other conquered peoples. *Dhimmi,* an Arabic word meaning "protected," was used to describe those who surrendered by treaty (*dhimma*) to Islamic rule. Essentially, dhimmitude meant that, as long as Jews and Christians agreed to live as third-class citizens, they would be allowed to live at peace in an Islamic state.

Far from some esoteric concept, dhimmitude existed in its purest form for many centuries, and its remnants still exist at one level or another in most Muslim cultures today.

While some of the Islamic laws and regulations that comprise dhimmitude have been enforced since the eighth century, the actual term dhimmitude was coined by Lebanese president Bachir Gemayel and popularized by **Bat Yeor**. Bat Yeor is probably the world's foremost popular authority on dhimmitude. For this reason, I felt it was imperative for her to be included in this book.

Books by Bat Yeor:
- *Les Juifs en Egypte*
- *Le Dhimmi, Profil de l'Opprime en Orient et en Afrique du Nord*
- *Les Chretientes d'Orient Entre Jihad et Dhimmitude*
- *The Decline of Eastern Christianity Under Islam*
- *Islam and Dhimmitude: Where Civilizations Collide*
- *Eurabia: The Euro-Arab Axis*
- *How Europe Became an Accomplice of Muslim Expansionism*
- *Europe, Globalization and the Coming Universal Caliphate*

JEFF KING: Bat, tell us about your background and how you got into what you're doing.

I was born in Egypt into a Jewish Italian family, and was educated in a French school. After the anti-Semitic laws of Mussolini, my father changed his nationality and became an Egyptian. I came from a mixed European background, with a French mother and English grandmother. During and after the Second World War, the atmosphere in Egypt was very anti-Semitic. During the Arab-Israeli war, the situation became very difficult for the Jews. Many were arrested, expelled, and had their goods confiscated. A campaign of hate was launched. There were many former Nazis in Egypt at the time.

I didn't understand all that at the time; I was too young, but in 1956, the situation became worse. The whole Jewish community started fleeing Egypt, abandoning everything, as Jews were not allowed to work and were simply expelled from the country. Finally, under very harsh circumstances, my parents' goods were confiscated, and we left Egypt, stateless. A whole community, 3,000 years old, disappeared before my eyes. I wanted to keep these moments of anguish and death I witnessed in my memory, so I was constantly taking notes. But every paper had to be submitted for censorship on departure, so I burned the notes before leaving. By this time, I was old enough to understand the terrible human tragedy and injustice of which I was just one victim.

During this period, I had Christian and Muslim friends. They were very kind to me. Since Jews were forbidden to go into clubs, restaurants, cinemas and other public places, my friends came to my home. I realized it was a political situation, not a question of people. A Coptic friend told me, "What is done to you is done to us." Christians were feeling like the Jews, a persecuted minority, which I had not known. When I left, we lost contact.

After my marriage, we settled in Switzerland where some of my family had emigrated from Egypt. I collected information and historical documents on the Jews of Egypt and realized that my departure was part of the uprooting of nearly a million Jews from Arab Muslim countries.

During the 1979-89 Lebanese war, I noticed the heinous pro-Palestinian/anti-Christian propaganda in Europe against Lebanese Christians. By then, having published a short booklet on the Jews of Egypt and the end of their community, I understood the dhimmi status reserved for Jews and Christians. Remembering my Christian friends in Egypt, I wrote articles on the situation of the Copts and the Lebanese Christians' fight to keep their freedom and dignity. I explained they were persecuted minorities. At this time, no one knew about dhimmitude and I was ridiculed and attacked for siding with the Christians.

In my research regarding the persecution of the Jews, I had found an equal number of documents regarding Christian persecution, since their condition was similar. Hence, while my French book, *Le Dhimmi* [1980], focused on Jews, it also contains information about Christians.

After its publication, Lebanese Christians contacted me. They were grateful because I had given them back their history, which had been deliberately obfuscated and forbidden. I then added many documents on the Christians for the English translation, *The Dhimmi* [1985]. I was asked for a French publication of the English version, and I embarked on a deeper research, focusing on the Christians. This became my book, *The Decline of Eastern Christianity: From Jihad to Dhimmitude*. It was then, while examining the Christian dhimmi history, that I conceived the concept of dhimmitude.

This study was about the demographic and cultural destruction of the rich and powerful Christian civilizations under Islam. I followed their slow death through the centuries. As I studied this process, it was easy for me to recognize the same symptoms today. My work earned me both sympathy and animosity because I had contradicted a politically imposed version of history aimed at demonstrating Islamic tolerance and proving that the happy Muslim-Christian relationship had been destroyed by Israel. The main proponents of this version were the former European colonial countries, the churches, and the Palestinian Christians.

JEFF KING: For the uninitiated, can you define the term, dhimmi?

Dhimmis are the people who have been conquered by expanding Muslim armies. They were tolerated in their countries and protected from additional jihadist attacks only if they submitted to discriminatory laws mandated by Islamic legislation under a dhimma pact. Pagans in general were killed or converted. Wherever there is Muslim rule, there are dhimmis. Jihad—the Islamic war of conquest against infidels—and dhimmitude are connected and interrelated. Dhimmis are the pre-Islamic people that have survived Islamic occupation and colonization of their own lands conquered by jihad. In the Middle East, it is the Jews and Christians that are the dhimmis. In Asia, it is the Buddhists and Hindus. Today, the Christians and the remnant of Jewish communities living in Muslim countries are dhimmis.

JEFF KING: What is the origin of dhimmitude? Is it mentioned in the Qur'an or the Hadith?

Dhimmitude is the protection against massacre, enslavement, and expropriation given by the Prophet to Jews and Christians on some conditions, including payment of a tribute. It is mentioned in the Hadith and Islamic jurisprudence. It also appears in Qur'an 9:29, which directs Muslims to fight the infidels, and Jews and Christians, until they pay the tribute linked to harsh treatments.

JEFF KING: Talk about the restrictions on dhimmis, especially in regard to religious freedom.

Religious freedom does not really exist in Islam, not even for Muslims, who are forbidden under pain of death to convert to another religion. Religious restrictions were numerous, ranging from prohibitions in [the] building, repair, and enlargement of synagogues and churches, to regulations imposing humility, silence and secrecy in prayer and during burial. The destruction, confiscation and Islamization of synagogues and, more often, churches, were common and are often mentioned in legal treatises and dhimmi chronicles. Dhimmis do not have the right to convert to any religion other than Islam.

Laws forcing dhimmis to billet and provision soldiers and horses were imposed; soldiers and beasts had to be lodged in the best houses, or in churches or synagogues, which were then abandoned because they became refuse dumps or stables. In the nineteenth century, British and French consuls and travellers mentioned this obligation in Bulgaria, Bosnia, Greece, Armenia, Syria and the Holy Land—all provinces that belonged then to the Ottoman Empire.

In the Maghreb [present day Morocco, Algeria, Libya, Mauritania, and Tunisia], during periods of instability and a change in monarch, Jewish quarters were plundered, men slaughtered or ransomed, and women and children abducted by tribes en masse around the towns.

The abduction of women and children for slavery or ransom in times of war and rebellion, or during peace time raids, was recurrent. This is documented in some Jewish dhimmi sources, but mainly in Christian chronicles [Syriac, Coptic, Armenian, Greek, Bulgarian, and Muslim]. Coptic chronicles of the Middle Ages mention the abduction of Christian children as slaves or as a deduction of unpaid taxes. In Yemen, Jewish children under the age of twelve, upon the death of their father, were removed from their families and converted to Islam. The law was retroactive, and was enforced until the departure of the Jews to Israel in 1950.

JEFF KING: There is a slogan: "After Saturday comes Sunday," meaning after persecuting Jews we will persecute Christians. Tell us about this statement.

It is a general slogan often repeated by Muslims, Jews and Christians, since the three groups know the long history of persecution in the Dar al-Islam.[20] It is probably rooted in the Qur'an and the biographies of the Prophet, who first dealt with the Jews in Medina and then with the Christians when they refused to convert. It means that after the persecution of the Jews, the Christians will follow.

JEFF KING: What is the political domain of dhimmitude in terms of protection, disarming, deportation, territorial dispossession, etc.?

The political domain is linked to the military since the dhimmi is vanquished by a war, jihad, which ends only when dhimmis surrender to Islamic power. This submission protects them from jihadist attacks as long as they obey the rules prescribed to them.

They are dispossessed from their country, now belonging to the Dar al-Islam, and cannot hold land. As former enemies, they are forbidden to have arms and must be deported from villages or cities existing on the borders with enemy countries. During the Arab conquests, many populations were deported as booty from Iraq, Palestine, Egypt, Armenia, and other regions. Muslim, as well as Armenian and Coptic, sources mention deportations in the eighth and ninth centuries during rebellions. Muslim chronicles refer to the deportation of dhimmi populations from towns and villages during

---

[20] See pg. 340.

warfare. Seljuk Turk rulers imposed deportations during the eleventh century from Armenia and Anatolia. Prof. Speros Vryonis has extensively documented this phenomenon for Anatolia, using contemporary Greek and Muslim sources, as did Greek, Serb and Bulgarian historians for the Ottoman period. Deportations from the Holy Land were carried out by Arab tribes in the middle of the tenth century, and in Anatolia under the Ottomans during the fifteenth to seventeenth centuries.

Population transfers, motivated by economic factors, affected dhimmi populations and were not restricted to newly subjugated or enslaved populations. Departure of deportees had to take place on the same day or at very short notice (two or three days), making it impossible for the deportees to sell their possessions. In order to discourage flight, they were counted, closely supervised, and forbidden to move from their new place of residence, which was generally very far from their places of origin. After all had been deported, their houses were burned down and the entire village was destroyed. We see the same pattern in the recent war in Sudan against the Christian and animist populations of the South.

JEFF KING: What about its economic domain [jizya, kharaj and other payments]?

They are submitted to several tributes, the main being the jizya, a Qur'anic ransom mentioned as obligatory in the Qur'an 9:29, which should be paid by Jews and Christians while they are humiliated, in exchange for having their lives saved. The jizya was mandatory under threat of jail, conversion, slavery, the abduction of dhimmi children, or death. Dhimmis paid double the taxes of the Muslims and were subjected to the most degrading forced labor. Other payments included kharaj, the land tax. Dhimmis had to pay double the amount of taxes paid by Muslims and were subjected to the most degrading corvées. They were also subjected to continuous ransoms and extortions.

JEFF KING: Tell us about its legal domain.

Specific laws ordained permanent inferiority and humiliation for the dhimmis. Their lives were valued at considerably less than that of a Muslim. The penalty for murder was much lighter if the dhimmi was the victim. Likewise, penalties for offenses were unequal between Muslims and non-Muslims. A dhimmi had no right to defend himself if he was physically assaulted by a Muslim; he could only beg for mercy. He was deprived of two fundamental rights: the right to self-defence against physical aggression and the right to defend himself in an Islamic court, as his testimony was refused.

Many sources document the prohibition on carrying arms for Jews and Christians in Palestine, Syria, Egypt, Armenia, the Maghreb, and Persia. Its debilitating and tragic consequences were analysed by foreign consuls. Dhimmis became prey to marauding, pillaging, and massacre—especially during periods of insecurity, such as rebellions and invasions. With the spread of the Islamic conquest, this prohibition was applied also in Anatolia and in the European Islamized provinces.

JEFF KING: Is the oath made by the dhimmi in the court of law acceptable? If not, what is the implication?

Litigation between dhimmis could be judged under the provisions of their own legislation. However, dhimmi legislation was not recognized in Muslim courts, whose judgments superseded dhimmi legal decisions. Jews and Christians could testify for one another, but their oath was refused if a Muslim was involved. In such cases, only Muslim courts could judge because Sharia law always prevails.

The refusal of a dhimmi testimony against that of a Muslim meant that the dhimmi could never defend himself against an accusation made by a Muslim. We see this situation in Pakistan now, where Christians cannot legally deny the accusation of blasphemy made by

Muslims. This situation of vulnerability ruined the dhimmi communities obligated to buy their security.

JEFF KING: What kind of labor was demanded of dhimmis? Talk about the concept of "corvées" under dhimmitude?

In North Africa and Yemen, repugnant occupations, such as executioner, gravedigger, cleaner of public latrines and the like, were forced on Jews, even on Saturdays and holy days. Likewise, Christians were obliged to be executioners or to execute economic corvées for Muslim landowners or for the State.

JEFF KING: Are dhimmis allowed to hold public office?

No. Dhimmis were forbidden to have authority over Muslims, to possess or buy land, to marry Muslim women, to have Muslim slaves or servants, or to use the Arabic alphabet [confirmed by Colonel Charles Churchill in Syria and Lebanon during 1840-60]. Legally, they could not hold public office because this was honorific, although many dhimmis rose to positions of influence. This breach of the law was often punished by the massacre of the whole dhimmi community.

JEFF KING: Talk about the process of colonization via jihad and dhimmitude and how that helped Islam take over the Middle East.

The process of Islamic colonization was part of the Islamic law referring to jihad and the dhimmis, the former owners of the conquered lands. Often, the dhimmis revolted but were crushed by massacres, deportations and slavery, like the Coptic rebellions in the early ninth century. This retribution, fixed by religious laws, represents a permanent pattern throughout the Islamic world. Hence, after the Greek and Serb revolts in the nineteenth century, thousands of women and children were enslaved. At the fall of Missolonghi (22 Apr. 1825), 3,000 to 4,000 Greek women were sold in slavery.

Countless Armenians were enslaved during the massacres at the end of the nineteenth century and during the genocide of 1915-17. In the following years, Greek and Assyrian Christians also suffered genocide in Turkey and Iraq.

Religious slavery was widespread throughout the Islamic lands. Christian Nubia was obliged to deliver contingents of slaves from the beginning of the Arab conquest. The Mamluks, non-Muslims who ruled Egypt and Syria for centuries, were kidnapped, bought or captured, and integrated into military slave troops. In the Ottoman Empire, for over 300 years, Christian dhimmi children were regularly requisitioned for slavery in Albania, Greece, the Aegean Islands, Bulgaria, Serbia, Bosnia, Croatia, and Hungary. In Persia, the koulars, or military slaves, represented a similar institution. This system of Christian slave soldiers also existed in Andalusia [Spain], where military slaves were particularly numerous. These Christians had been captured in razzias, or as booty, during regular jihad campaigns, and abducted from throughout Europe.

The continuous abduction of Christian children over many centuries in Asia, Africa and Europe, with the deportation and enslavement of whole populations, as well as their fiscal exploitation (with their torture described in dhimmi and other sources) was the main cause of the demographic decline in their homeland and, often, their extinction.

JEFF KING: Can you tell us about the humiliation the dhimmis suffered in their social interactions with Muslims?

Dhimmis had to be recognized by their discriminatory clothes, whose shape, color, and texture were prescribed from head to foot. Likewise, the color and size of their houses and their separate living quarters were prescribed. Dhimmis and foreign Christians were forbidden to ride a horse or a camel, since these animals were considered too noble. A donkey could be ridden in towns but only on a packsaddle, the dhimmi sitting with both legs on one side and dismounting on sight of a Muslim as a sign of respect. A dhimmi had to hurry through the streets, always passing to the left (impure) side of a Muslim, who was expected to force him to the narrow side or into the gutter. He had to walk humbly, with lowered eyes, to accept insults without replying, to remain standing in a meek and respectful attitude in the presence of a Muslim, and to leave him the best place. If he was admitted to a public bath, he had to wear bells to signal his presence. Stoning Jews and Christians, especially in Arab-populated regions, was not unusual. Likewise, disdain, insults and disrespectful attitudes toward them were customary. Some regional rules represent an aggravation of this pattern. In Morocco and Yemen, Jews were forbidden any footwear outside their segregated quarter.

These laws were the basic regulations set down in the classical texts on dhimmis and they had to be enforced throughout the lands of dhimmitude. Muslim jurists strongly condemned the alleviation of these measures when it temporarily occurred. Dhimmitude covers more than a millennium of Christian and Jewish history and is a comprehensive civilization encompassing customs, legislation and social behaviour. Its various constituents were constantly imposed with lesser or greater severity, depending on circumstances, in the Balkans, Anatolia, the Levant, Persia, Yemen and the Maghreb.

JEFF KING: What are the symptoms of dhimmitude in Western countries?

Fear of terrorism, flattery, the denial of modern jihad and modern dhimmitude, the Western mercenary war against Israel to comply with Muslim policy, and the Western policy of Islamizing its culture, demography, media, and universities.

Dhimmitude represents a comprehensive system based on Muslims' fundamental religious scriptures, covering every aspect of their perception, attitude and behavior toward Jews and Christians. It has permeated Islamic civilization and culture from its inception, and is being revived today through the Islamist resurgence and the return of the Sharia in some countries. This pattern is permanent, although most Muslims are unaware of it and some reject it.

On examining dhimmitude, one of its main features appears to be the ongoing Muslim policy of dominating and imposing on the dhimmi a servile behavior accompanied by the constant marking of respect toward Islam. Today, the OIC [Organization of the Islamic Conference], the body representing the Muslim world, formulates this same demand—particularly the Turkish Islamist government—toward Europe and Israel. European and Israeli leaders often start their speeches by paying homage to Islam. The reverse never happens, nor would Western leaders expect it.

Ironically, the success of Islam in Christendom—Iraq, Egypt, Spain, Greece, and in Byzantium—was brought about by Christian leaders, who collaborated for their own political interests with the jihadist forces and with the Islamic forces. I explain that in my book *The Decline of Eastern Christianity: From Jihad to Dhimmitude*. I consecrated a whole chapter to describe this process of Christian collaboration with the forces of their own destruction.

JEFF KING: Talk about the concept of Eurabia—what is that? When did this concept come about?

In my book *Eurabia*, I examine European politics within the historical pattern of jihad and dhimmitude since they are only frameworks used by the Muslim world to relate to Europe. This context shows that the policy of the European Union and Western leaders since 1973 has triggered a dynamic of Europe's disintegration and the demise of its Judeo-Christian values. In other words, the descent of its population into dhimmitude.

The title "Eurabia" was a term invented by European politicians who aimed at uniting Europe with the Arab Muslim world. As a condition to improving its relations with Europe, the Arab world required that Europe recognize the PLO [Palestinian Liberation Organization], which was, and is, a jihadist movement to destroy Israel. Europe submitted to this demand, and has since become the biggest provider of funds and support for the PLO.

Eurabia is also a political strategy that hopes, through immigration, to create a new Mediterranean continent. It promotes multiculturalism to accommodate the millions of Muslim immigrants Europe has welcomed in order to disintegrate European national cultures and the Judeo-Christian legacy. To simplify, Eurabia is a gigantic transnational network aimed at Islamizing Europe, whose cogs and dynamic are European.

JEFF KING: You're saying it's an Islamist strategy. You're not saying that European leaders reject Sharia [law] in Europe or that they've got different motives for inviting the Muslims in, such as cheap labor, etc. That's typically what is said.

No, I don't agree with this because I have the supporting documents. It is a political, strategic, and ideological movement promoted by the Europeans leaders since the 1970-80s. The Arab Muslim countries imposed their demands, threatening with oil boycott, economic retaliation and terrorist reprisals, and the Europeans submitted to their conditions.

I published documents from the European Union in *Eurabia,* asserting the determination of the European leaders to join Europe to the Arab Muslim world. This is the core of the Barcelona Declaration [1994] that has established the whole Mediterranean strategy with political, commercial, cultural, financial, and social institutions to implement it.

You can argue that European politicians didn't expect that millions of Muslim immigrants would bring in polygamy, the discrimination of women, Sharia law, and Islamic banking and schools, totally changing Western societies, but I do not believe that politicians are that naïve.

Multiculturalism, which they impose through the mixture of populations, helped destroy cultural and historical nationalism and reinforced the path toward globalization. Javier Solana urged the EU to encourage globalization by reinforcing United National jurisdiction and to have it supersede the laws of the states.

JEFF KING: Yes. Now, Bat, many people would say, "Oh that's far-fetched, that's just too much to believe." What would you offer to the skeptic as support for this theory?

Well, first, one just has to look at Europe to see that we are living under some Sharia laws—like its blasphemy law, that punishes by death, or legal pursuit for any criticism of Islam. The defamatory trend in the media and the self-censorship in public discourse bring us closer to a dhimmi society, rather than one that applies the International Bill of Human Rights. Although our societies have great economic problems, Muslim immigrants pour into Europe because the OIC wants to maintain, as a right, a constant Muslim immigration to the West. Moreover, for decades the EU has paid billions to the Palestinians and to several economic projects in the Arab countries. I do not object to the idea of international help and solidarity, but I object to the principle of extortion and ransom intrinsic to the jihadist mentality. Furthermore, money shouldn't be wasted behind the backs of the European citizens, but should be linked to outcome and achievement.

I have now published two books giving all the sources of my documentation, which are easy to control since most are from the EU. One source is the French Ministry of Foreign Affairs, the Quai d'Orsay as, in the beginning, it was mainly France's policy to maintain its aura in former Arab colonies.

JEFF KING: List some of the documents.

The documents I just referred to are the minutes of the meetings of the so-called Euro-Arab Dialogue, a body that conducted an unofficial Euro-Arab joint policy under the co-presidency of the Arab League Secretary-General and the European Commission from 1974 until 1994. This collaboration later became official under the name of the Barcelona Process. Israel was accepted in the Barcelona Process but not on conditions equal to those of the Arab states. The Palestinians were already integrated from 1974 in the Dialogue. Those unofficial Euro-Arab agreements were followed through by the European Parliamentary Association for Euro-Arab Cooperation, whose president, secretary and members are known as well as its founders. The Euro-Arab Dialogue policy is mentioned by American and European historians and in OIC and other Muslim sources. Its numerous activities constituted rich material for research. We can say they have molded present-day Europe.

Another important document is the *Dialogue Between People and Cultures in the Euro-Mediterranean Area* (2003), which provides the template for a Euro-Arab fusion and led to the creation of the Anna Lindh Foundation, followed in 2006 by the Alliance of Civilizations. 2003 also saw the creation of the Euro-Mediterranean Parliamentary Assembly (EMPA), and in 2007 another network was created: the Union for the Mediterranean. Besides these, there are many more EU documents....

JEFF KING: A starting point would be *Eurabia*, for those who want to dig into this?

Yes, my book, or other books. You can look in the bibliography.

JEFF KING: Tell us about the demographic increase of Muslims in Europe. Talk about the factors, what's driving it. What are the statistics and, looking forward, where are we going?

Before 1973, all immigration was very strictly controlled. Immigrants could reside in different European countries only if they had a working contract and had to leave when it expired. After 1973, when the European countries made unofficial agreements with the

Arab countries, those measures were abandoned. Then started the waves of big family immigration with the numerous accommodations it required, listed in the minutes of the Euro-Arab Dialogue meetings. This was the beginning of a vast immigration movement, which aims at settling Arabs permanently in Europe.

JEFF KING: Now, tell me this. Was the oil embargo held as blackmail over them? Was that part of this?

Yes, of course. There was Palestinian terrorism and the oil embargo against Europe and America, especially against countries that were friendly with Israel. France, Germany and Italy immediately gave in. The only one who resisted was Holland. But Holland was struck by Palestinian terrorism and eventually gave in.

Finally, the then nine countries of the European community agreed to recognize the PLO. This was a condition for the lifting of the oil embargo. They also had to recognize Arafat as its only chief, and support the Palestinian war against Israel. In tandem with this, another strategy consisted of developing Muslim immigration into Europe and creating Muslim and Arab cultural, political and religious centers. These two movements were correlated.

JEFF KING: Now that's the background. What was Muslim immigration like between World War II and 1973?

It was non-existent, or very little, and only to the former colonial states. Germany's case is special. Ian Johnson published an important book on the origin of the Turkish community in Germany: *A Mosque in Munich: Nazis, the CIA, and the Rise of the Muslim Brotherhood in the West*. The tight German-Turkish alliance in World War I had developed important links in the military sectors, used later by the Nazi organizations of Muslims opposed to the Soviet regime in the Muslim Soviet Republics. This is the origin of the German-Turkish community.

JEFF KING: So, after '73, the floodgates open.

Yes, with an ideology bent on uniting the Mediterranean.

JEFF KING: Now, tell us statistically, in terms of demography and percentages, where are we now in Europe with different countries? Where are we going in twenty, thirty, or fifty years?

Well, it is difficult to speak about demography because it is a hidden secret. No state wants to give the real numbers of their immigrants, so we don't know. Moreover, illegal immigrants cannot be counted.

However, the biggest problem is not demographic, but cultural, social and theological. For instance, the Universal Declaration on Human Rights is not the same as the Islamic Human Rights Declaration, which conforms to Sharia rulings that are incompatible with our laws. Besides, we do not accept the Islamic conception of history that professes that Islam existed from the beginning of humanity and was the religion of Adam and Eve, the biblical kings, and the prophets, including Jesus. This proclaims that Judaism and Christianity are falsifications of the first and true religion, which is Islam. This amounts to denying the anteriority, history and genuine identity of the two biblical religions, which are accused of stealing Islamic history by being only its falsification. Biblical history, in its Qur'anic version is attributed to Muslims. Since the discrepancies between the Bible and the Qur'anic version are extremely important, Muslims accuse Jews and Christians of falsifying their Islamic Scriptures.

We also do not share the opinion that jihad was, and is, a wonderful and liberating process because it suppresses the evilness spread by infidels. As jihad is carried out in obedience to Allah's order, it has no defect, no evil and cannot be criticized. In fact, our historical visions are totally different, even opposed.

JEFF KING: Is the lack of integration with Islamic societies in Europe tied into the welfare system of Europe in any way?

No. The lace of integration results from contradictory values, mores, traditions, and cultures. Muslims do not want to integrate in an infidel society whose laws oppose the Sharia. You cannot transplant millions of people to a totally different culture and expect them to give up the cultural framework that has molded their society for thirteen centuries.

JEFF KING: How about the welfare society?

Unfortunately, in the Muslim countries (except for very rich ones) there is no welfare. So, in Europe, you have all the medicine needs covered by the people who live in Europe. Also, the schools are paid for and often immigrants receive money from the state. So this is very important.

JEFF KING: It's drawing people like a magnet is what you're saying.

Yes, yes. And with that, the idea to take revenge on the West, and to conquest the West.

JEFF KING: In regards to demographics, you talked about France. What about other countries?

Well, in England, it is the same situation as it is in Holland, Denmark, Sweden, and Belgium. Immigration continues one way or another. Neither the European states nor the European Union want to stop it for fear of Islamist reprisals. Prominent Dutch politician Geert Wilders said he will stop immigration…

JEFF KING: Sure, and look what's happened to him…

He is targeted by the Islamists and forced to live protected by bodyguards around the clock.

JEFF KING: He stood up and said, "Look, this is a massive problem culturally. Wake up, this is where we are going." Now, what was done to Geert Wilders in retaliation by the government?

The Islamists are not the only enemies he has. His own government wants to condemn him by applying the Sharia-inspired law punishing any criticism of Islam. He is a victim of a defamation war while, in fact, he defends European values of freedom of opinion and speech with great courage.

JEFF KING: They're not only condemning Geert Wilders, they've brought charges against him under hate speech laws for his free speech—for basically telling the truth. And, at the same time, his political power is rising. So, those with different views are trying to use the state to shut him down, to constrict his speech, etc. It's fascinating. It's a real wrestling match.

This policy was mandated by the European Union, for its member-states, because of constant pressure by the OIC, which represents 56 Muslim states. The OIC succeeded in requiring that the UN Council on Human Rights request the UN member-states to sanction severely what the OIC considers to be defamation of religion—here, Islam and Islamophobia. There is a big gap between the wishes of the European population and the policy of the European Union.

European people, fearing loss of control over their own future, try to fight the EU drift toward totalitarianism or fascism supported by a culture of political correctness that prevents free speech. The problem is not only Islam, but, rather, the OIC's grip on the EU has shown a basic fault mechanism within it and its failure to uphold the fundamental values of European democracies. The wave of legal attacks concerning Islamophobia against those who reject politically correct doctrine points to a grave fracture between the people and their leaders.

It is worth noting that the blasphemy law disguised in Europe as Islamophobia, is one of the most important laws of dhimmitude, which even appears in the poll tax contract between the Muslim conqueror and the vanquished dhimmi. It affirms that dhimmis must: a) neither attack nor deform the Holy Book [Qur'an], b) neither accuse the Prophet of falsehood nor quote him with contempt, c) nor speak of the Muslim faith in order to denigrate or question it, d) nor entice a Muslim from his faith. Carrying out one of these acts nullifies the protection treaty and mandates death. The binding together of theology, jurisdiction and policy in Islam makes any criticism of law or policy an attack on religion.

JEFF KING: Yes, there are certain things that are definitely off limits. You'll be shouted down if you bring them up.

Yes, we live in a state of denial.

JEFF KING: So what does Europe look like in two to three decades with the rise of Islamic immigration? What does the culture look like and how will it change?

Well, we already have Sharia laws in England. We also have the blasphemy law that forbids the criticism of Islam. If we add the fear of terrorism, we can understand the reluctance of the European governments to let the people discuss these problems freely. I want to make clear that, for me, criticism of an ideology or a policy based on facts and historical evidences is different from racism and defamation that feed only on prejudices and hatred.

Although there are many bright Muslim women, fully emancipated from traditional behavior, the majority conform to the Sharia rulings concerning them. Multiculturalism has allowed polygamy, segregation of women, honor killings, and importation of a culture based on a set of beliefs opposed to Western culture and values and shared by millions of immigrants. Since the OIC proclaims itself to be the protector of the rights of Muslim immigrants in Europe, it will constantly interfere in European domestic affairs. Moreover, the OIC's proclaimed strategy is to root the universal Ummah[21]. That is, the whole Muslim population in the Qur'an and Sunnah. Hence, the tendency will be a stronger radicalization of some milieus, while others will probably refuse this foreign control.

If this situation continues, it's clear that the Judeo-Christian civilization will vanish through the processes I have described in my books. Muslim governments do not recognize the evilness of jihad and dhimmitude, rather they promote them and pursue the same old goals. Hence, the war against non-Muslims, the inhumanity of dhimmitude, and the violence of jihad, none of this has ever been recognized. So, things cannot change.

JEFF KING: How is the history of the dhimmis concealed?

It is erased from textbooks and history. It is denied for fear of irritating Muslim states and Muslim immigrants, teachers, professors and students. Authors who speak about it are boycotted and defamed by Western dhimmi intellectuals and media who accommodate Muslim prejudices.

This denial indicates a refusal of self-criticism because relationships with non-Muslims are not based on equality. In Muslim law, the infidel testimony is not accepted because Islam is always right and superior to infidelity. The lex talionis [law of retaliation] applies only between Muslims. Moreover, jihad is a sacred principle based on Qur'anic interpretation, which infidels cannot criticize.

Look at Turkey. Turkey denies the genocide it committed against the Armenians, Greeks, and Syriac Christians. And it was not even this government; it was done under the Young Turks. Not only are the

---

[21] See pg. 346.

Turks forbidden from recognizing it, but so are European and other states. There is no apology and there is no change.

Europe has adopted the Islamic view of history, stating that jihad and dhimmitude were tolerant. This terrible mistake denies and dehumanizes the whole history of millions of people treated as chattel or slaves. If Europe had taught dhimmitude in its schools and universities, Muslim immigrants would have learned self-criticism, accountability and the equality of human beings.

JEFF KING: You said there is Sharia in England. It's not like England is ruled by Sharia but it's been introduced. Where else does it exist in Europe?

In England, Sharia law regarding the family has entered into the legal English code. Throughout Europe, multiculturalism has spread unofficial Islamic rules, like the various forms of discrimination of women and the rigid separation of sexes in health care and school swimming lessons. In some schools, certain subjects are forbidden, like the Holocaust, because of Muslim protests. Teachers are accused of giving a European Christian perspective to history and must adapt to Muslim requests aimed at promoting the Islamic civilization's superiority over the European. Jews cannot attend many public schools because of Muslim aggressiveness toward them.

JEFF KING: The radicalism is growing in Europe, obviously. What should policymakers be doing to tackle the situation?

Well, it is very difficult because this is a complex problem. The Palestinization of European culture, society, and policy has totally modified its Judeo-Christian values and democratic foundations. It has brought Europe to support jihadist and Islamic ideology against the root of Christian spirituality and history, triggering an identity fracture. The freedom of speech and opinion is contested. The basis and criterion of historical knowledge are replaced by political short-term assertions imposed by the OIC.

Many things could be done on several levels, but the first step is to acknowledge the situation that is denied by the politicians.

JEFF KING: What are the implications of Turkey joining the European Union?

Well, if Turkey joins the European Union it will be the end of Europe. First of all, Turkey is becoming more and more an Islamist country with its government. Turkey refuses to recognize the black pages of its own history, which means it will continue. Turkey also wants to open its borders with the Asiatic Turkish Republic from Central Asia to China, because the Turks came from this region and they invaded Byzantium and then Europe. This is their origin. So, this Turkish-speaking Turkish Republic that was under Soviet Union domination is now independent. And, it wants to develop relations with those republics that speak Turkish, and also with the Turks in Caucasia and in the Chechens. Turkey is looking toward Asia, and is becoming a very powerful empire, which is very, very strongly rooted in Islamic culture, in the Qur'an, and in the Sharia and the Sunnah.

Turkey is, in fact, rising, in a way, to what the Ottoman caliphate was. And in fact, now, there is a lot of talk about restoring the caliphate, and Turkey sees itself as a leader of the modern, new, universal caliphate in the twenty-first century, which is the subject of my newest book, *Globalization, Europe, and the Coming Universal Caliphate*.

JEFF KING: How many years do you think it is before Islam becomes the religion of the majority of the population of Europe?

If everything continues like this, it will be probably decades.

ISLAM IN THE WEST

Chapter Eleven:

The European Journalist

Islamaphobi—it's a bogus word. It's only been around for about ten years. At best, it's an exceedingly imprecise word. At worst, simply nonsense. It's absurd. Phobias are irrational things. It's irrational to be claustrophobic because small spaces don't kill you. It's not irrational to be fearful of Islam in some of its guises. It's eminently rational to be scared of jihadis, for instance, just as it's eminently rational to be scared of madmen with guns.

Douglas Murray

Douglas Murray is a bestselling author and award-winning journalist based in London. He has written for numerous publications, including *The Telegraph, Spectator, Wall Street Journal,* and *Sunday Times.* Douglas Murray lectures and debates widely across Europe and the United States about the danger of radical Islam. He has appeared on major TV channels, including: ABC News, BBC, Fox News, Al Jazeera, and many other global media networks.

Douglas Murray is a graduate of Oxford University and the Director of the Centre for Social Cohesion, the first think-tank in the UK to specialize in studying radicalization and extremism within Britain.

I wanted to include Douglas Murray for two reasons. For one, he heads up an organization that deals with social cohesion, which is a huge topic in regards to Islam and Europe. Secondly, though, I felt I had to include him because he is a very clear thinker who can articulate the difficult issues of dealing with Islam from within a democracy. He deals with this thorny subject of religious human rights simply and clearly where others cannot.

Books by Douglas Murray:
- *Bosie: A Biography of Lord Alfred Douglas*
- *Neoconservatism: Why We Need It*
- *Towards a Grand Strategy for an Uncertain World: Renewing Transatlantic Partnership*
- *Victims of Intimidation: Freedom of Speech within Europe's Muslim Communities*

JEFF KING: You are the director of the Centre for Social Cohesion. Can you tell me what the CFSC is focused on and how did you get into this work?

Well, we focus on extremism in the UK, which has been a growing issue in recent years and, particularly, we focus on Islamic radicalization, which is an issue that Britain is at the very forefront of.

Gosh, where to begin? I noticed that a large number of lies were being told, and I have a low tolerance for lies. I don't like them being told in public life, or, indeed, even in private life. I think that people tell a great number of lies about this subject because it is expedient politically, or otherwise, for them to do so.

JEFF KING: You have a background as a journalist, so I'm sure that intolerance for half-truths or outright lies is built into you. I suspect it drives you crazy and makes you want to get to the bottom of an issue and shout the truth.

Yes, quite.

JEFF KING: You've spoken of three "Islams." Tell me about that. What are the three "Islams?"

Well, Islam [type] one is the scriptures, the foundation, the Qur'an, the Hadith, and the advice from Muhammad. Islam [type] two is the way in which these are interpreted through the Sharia and the [historical] interpretation over the course of 1,400 years. How Muslims make sense of the legal and spiritual challenges put forward in these texts. Islam [type] three is how Muslims behave now.

I think this is helpful because Islam is such a wide thing, such a big thing, and we really have to know which one we're talking about, because when we're making a criticism of the Qur'an, for instance, people have to see that we are making a criticism of an historical document without necessarily attacking any Muslim. You have to separate, you have to explain, and in some way separate people and ideas and get back to the important thing, which is the individual. I find it a useful way to do this.

JEFF KING: I find that many Westerners become indignant if you raise difficult issues or questions when discussing Islam because they consider frank discussion of Islam not to be politically correct, and they associate these questions with an attitude of bigotry or hatred. Is that also your read, and how do you get past that?

That's very much the situation; people tend to look at issues and read them in the light of their past experiences. For instance, to fight once again the same war that they have fought before. Britons are only now learning that they shouldn't behave in Iraq as they did in Northern Ireland. In Northern Ireland, they were learning that they shouldn't do as they did in Malaysia. It's very common in warfare and it's very common in general human experience that people go in with a set of [pre-existing] ideas. Western European and American society—particularly in recent decade—have developed a tendency to see everything through the prisms of certain ideas, the most obvious example of which is seeing everything through the prism of racism.

JEFF KING: I think racism is a concern more in the United States, whereas the Europeans would be dealing with fears of Nazism, which includes but transcends racism.

Yes, one of the oddities of the post Second World War period is the attempt to partly alleviate, as it were, German guilt. The whole continent—indeed, the whole world—has to be shown to be as capable of doing what the Germans did. It's a very common motif on the left: "we could all have done that," and then it goes very simply into, "we all did that." It's very interesting, you often hear people saying that in debates. Somebody always says about the West,

"Well look at the Nazis," as though the Nazis *represented* the West, rather than [the group the West] fought against. Effectively, these were all guilt motifs.

Obviously, American and European societies have been racist in the past, as has every society in human history. And that's regrettable, but there is a particular desire to find the West guilty from the start and to see history through this prism. And, into that general messy [orientation] comes this business of Islam, and some people, as a result, have decided that this is another manifestation of the same. This causes, and will continue to cause, huge problems for everyone in this area, because it doesn't matter what your skin color is, it doesn't matter what you believe. There are now a certain number of people who believe that any criticism of Islam, even of Islamic fundamentalism, is a sign of bigotry and racism.

JEFF KING: Is there some way you get past that in debates and diffuse the issue so people can see that we just want to deal with the issues—that we want to deal with Islam as we deal with any other issue? When we talk about Christianity in the West, it's fair game. You can criticize, you can ask any question, and no one gets shocked or indignant. Why is it different with Islam, and how do you get people past that?

Well, there are things that people want to be, which are not, and things that people hope for [and are not]. A lot of people base their opinions on hope. They hope that there's not a problem with religion. They hope that there aren't bad people out there. They hope that they'll live forever, and a whole set of other things. But, just because you hope something's going to be the case, doesn't mean it is the case. We must explain again and again that there is a difference between hatred of people because of the color of their skin versus a variety of things that can be said about ideas and beliefs.

You also have to constantly remind people that it's not an accident that this new sensitivity is being brought up. It's no accident that the

Organization of the Islamic Conference (OIC) at the UN consistently attempts to introduce Islamic hate speech laws, because they know that this is how they can protect their religion from any criticism.

There are other parallels, too. Scientologists, for instance, have increasingly resorted to legal intimidation—as well as other kinds—to try to stop their cult from being criticized. It's what any totalitarian would want to do. The first thing you do is decide what can and cannot be said, because if you decide what can and cannot be said, then down the road you can decide what people can think, what knowledge they're able to have access to.

JEFF KING: That's a fantastic summary. Now, for the uninitiated, explain what these hate-speech laws are that the OIC is trying to promote in the UN, and what would be the outcome if they were put into law?

This is being attempted at national levels and supra-national levels. The goal is that truth is no defense, because if Islam has been offended then a crime has been committed. Under this idea, it would be a hate crime to draw a cartoon—or, not even necessarily a cartoon, any drawing—it would be a crime to do a drawing of someone who you then said was a drawing of Muhammad. That would be a crime because it would be deemed, allegedly, to be offensive to Muslims. Of course, it would only be offensive to the small number who wish to be offended, and they would tell everyone else to be offended as well. But, the point is, that it would be a crime. It would be a crime to say that you thought the Qur'an was made up, because it would be offensive, potentially, to some Muslims.

This is the most obvious, totalitarian attempt to decide what can and cannot be said, and what is so insidious about this is that the truth is not a defense. It doesn't matter if what you are saying is true; it's whether or not anyone can claim to have been offended, and *anyone* could! If I had enough people who agreed with me on a matter, I could say that I wanted to force through laws so that nobody could criticize me. Now, we know from scholars that this is how dictatorships behave, and the idea that democracies should be subjected to this kind of stuff is just extraordinary!

JEFF KING: All right. Let's go back to the big picture questions. I'm going to put forth an argument that's going to be very familiar to you. Many say that every religion has its crazies and it's no different with Islam. They say there's no danger associated with this; it's just these few fundamentalists causing the violence. What's your reaction to that?

Well, all religions have things in common. They are, in my opinion, man-made and can be interpreted differently by different people and used by people to their own ends. That's not a surprise, and it has been like that throughout history. But, having said that, nobody should mistake what is happening at the moment for business as usual in this regard. We are in a very, very, strange position globally now, which is probably best put like this: if you said to somebody, "Christianity is only a religion of peace, it preaches and teaches only peacefulness," sure as anything, you would have people popping up saying, "What about the crusades? What about this? What about that? What about that Florida pastor wanting to burn a Qur'an? Isn't that symptomatic of Christianity?"

If you said Judaism is a religion of peace, people would say, "What about the Old Testament? It's got terribly bloodthirsty bits in it. You know, look at what Israel's done," and so on. All I would say is, if they are going to deal with Christianity and Judaism that way, then, when dealing with Islam, you can't say that any evil thing done by a Muslim does not represent Islam. There is a strange contradiction that has gone on here, which goes something like the following: Every Christian, every Jew is responsible for anything that any Christian or any Jew has ever done. There are American Christians who are expected to be apologetic for the crusades, which was something that America had no part in, so far as I know!

And this is crucial, that every Christian and every Jew be held responsible for the crimes of Judaism and Christianity and, yet, no Muslim is held responsible even for their own actions. This is infantilizing more than a billion people who, when some among them behave badly, should be held to account for that. They should not be let off the hook, and it should not be decided that they cannot be criticized.

This shows, by the way, the quite extraordinary self-absorption and, I would say, pathological narcissism of the West at the moment. The left-wing Western trend in democracy, which is that—even without knowing anything—people decide that, effectively, they are the people who are responsible. You see countless examples of this: another group, another person, another country behaves badly, and instead of saying, "Why are they doing that?" you say, "What did *we* do?" And maybe, you know, just maybe, it's not about you. Maybe it's not about us. Maybe it's not something we did. In other words, it's an extraordinary sort of inverted colonial mindset in which you export only your self-pity.

JEFF KING: That's well articulated. Now, let me ask you a more direct question. Is there something wrong with Islam? Why is there so much pathology? Does it go back to the fundamentals, and if so what is the problem?

The problem, I would say, is that there are a set of theological issues that need to be gotten past which are very hard—and I don't underestimate how hard they are to get past—but they do need to be addressed at the very least.

If a Christian wants to go back to Christian scriptures and look at the sayings of Jesus, they find that with the exception of just one verse, it's all love thy neighbor stuff, which is fine. It isn't going to cause any trouble. That's very important and, what's more, Christianity, for a couple of centuries at least, now, has adapted itself to being read critically as a religion.

JEFF KING: Explain that.

German higher criticism in particular took a very, very long time to sink in as it were, but it allowed Christians for the first time, *en masse*, to read about and think about their religious origins and about the founders of their religion, not as simply divine but as historical figures. And this process was very painful for Christians to go through, and all sorts of implications come from it.

Islam has not yet gone through this period of critical inquiry. The Bible was picked apart in the nineteenth century. I suppose a lot of people have the idea that the Bible was given by God to King James or something. So, the discovery that books were chopped, that Apocrypha were left lying around, and that it was a collaborative and editorial process is something which is now accepted.

Now, the Qur'an and Hadith [the Islamic scriptures] have never really been subjected to the same process. Let me give you an example: Majdi says somewhere that one of the proofs of the perfection of the Qur'an is that, wherever you go in the world, the Qur'an is the same. Except, that it's not; there are different Qur'ans in different countries. Indeed, there are different lengths in some cases. Now, there is nothing that should be deemed offensive in simply pointing out that a period of critical inquiry would be helpful and, indeed, legitimate in this, as in anything else. A few years ago, the television channel in Britain, Channel 4, was going to do a program about these very, very old Qur'ans that were found in Yemen, and the program was cancelled. They didn't make it in the end because they realized—shock, horror—that these Qur'ans differed from the modern version. This threw up questions which a British television company in the twenty-first century didn't want to have to address. This gives you some idea of the extraordinary fear that people have about asking the most basic questions and making the most basic critical inquiries in relation to Islam.

JEFF KING: Let's talk about something else you touched on. You kind of went into a compare and contrast...

Oh yes, on Jesus and Muhammad?

JEFF KING: Yes, delve into that.

Now, that's a very important one because Muhammad, as an historical figure, was, of course, a warlord who spread the religion he began by violence. Now, of course, that doesn't mean that throughout all of history all Muslims have been forced to believe, but this is certainly the beginning of the religion. This sort of violent conquest is a considerable issue that at least needs to be addressed and discussed openly, which it's not at the moment. There is a problem here, because if Muhammad is the perfect human being—and what's more, the messenger of God—then what he does should be a good example. Yet, actually, a lot of what he did was a very bad example. Now, I mean there are all sorts of ways one can get around it and, you know, a lot of people say, quite rightly, that, "Just because he did that doesn't mean I have to do that, and I can make compromises," and all this sort of thing which people do all the time with faith. But, it can't be ignored, I think.

I suppose what I'm trying to say here is that the reason why it has to be addressed is that one of the fatal mistakes that has been made in recent years, particularly among Western political leaders (and Tony Blair is a very good example of this, as is George Bush) is to consistently say Islam is a religion of peace, and that what the extremists say and do is just a grotesque misreading of an otherwise peaceful religion. What I'm saying is that the extremists and others have an interpretation of their faith, which is not the right one, necessarily, and is not necessarily even a majority one. But, it is a *plausible* interpretation of their scriptures and the teachings and the precedents they have.

In that case, the argument has to be had within Islam about how to veer away from that. But it cannot be avoided by simply saying, "You cannot discuss it," or by avoiding any debate or even analysis or inquiry around this area.

JEFF KING: OK, tell us about Muhammad. Who was Muhammad? Is it charitable to call him a warlord? Talk about who he was and what was encoded in the Qur'an and Hadith and how that connects with the picture we see out there today.

Well, it's very hard to sum up, although there have been some very fine attempts to do so. A noted Persian scholar, Ali Dashti, did it in his book *Twenty-three Years: A Study of the Prophetic Career of Muhammad.* This book was published anonymously in the mid-twentieth century, and it caused a huge stir. But, there have been attempts. In the historical analysis, it sums up like this: [Muhammed] was a tradesman. He was also illiterate, which is very interesting, and that is claimed by some people to be proof that a miracle occurred.

JEFF KING: That he wrote the Qur'an was a miracle because he was illiterate?

Yes, but what would seem to me to be the most obvious explanation for what happened would be that certain oral traditions were going around the Arabian Peninsula at that time, in the mid-seventh century. And what's interesting about it is that the Qur'an, as a document, does not come out of nowhere. For Christians and Jews who read it, and anyone who's read the Christian or Jewish scriptures, they will recognize the gist of quite a lot of the Qur'an.

JEFF KING: Many Islamic scholars will even say, "Look this was pulled from myths, this from the Bible, and this from different places but it was then changed and corrupted," et cetera.

The most likely explanation, I think, is that Muhammad—a very remarkable, very determined, very intelligent man—had heard stories around campfires of what had happened in the previous centuries, millennia before he existed. He heard the stories of Eden; he heard the Jewish Torah, effectively, in oral versions. He heard talk of a historical figure called Jesus, whose divinity was claimed by a growing sect of people. So, in other words, the dramatic personae of the Qur'an are all familiar figures if you were wandering around as a tradesman, speaking to people in that part of the world at that time. Now, I suppose, then, you have to ask the question of why he did what he did, what drove him out. And I would say that it is useful to use C.S. Lewis' famous description of Christ, that he's either mad, bad, or God.

So, Muhammad was either mad or he was bad or he was indeed hearing the voice of the Archangel Gabriel dictating this to him. Now, of these three possibilities, I think, as an atheist and rationalist, that it's exceedingly unlikely that an Archangel arrived in the middle of the Arabian Desert in the middle of the seventh century and dictated a plagiarized version of the Old and New Testaments to a wandering tradesman. So, we're left with the other two explanations, the first of which is that he was mad. This, obviously, has been discussed covertly for some time. It's possible that he was epileptic. It's possible that he was otherwise unwell, and that he thought he heard voices when no such voices came. The third possibility would be that he made the whole thing up in order to advance himself and his claims and his ambitions to be a leader of men. I think that those are the only three possible explanations. Muslims, obviously, believe the first of them; and, of the other two, people have to decide for themselves.

JEFF KING: You called Muhammed a warlord and if you look in the Qur'an and Hadith, you see he's responsible for the deaths of many, either directly or by ordering others to kill. He enslaved many victims and he had his way with captured females, and so on. It goes back to the lord, liar, lunatic argument that you were

addressing. He's either mad, bad, or god. The problem is that his life and acts were encoded into holy books and we would say that is the source of the pathology associated with radical Islam that you see out there. The fundamentalists would say, "Look, this is encoded in our books. We have to obey whether we like it or not. This is from God." That is our argument. Do you agree with that position?

Yes. But the problem is not simply what he did; it is whether he should, therefore, be an example. But, it is very hard for organized Islam to get around this, to avoid the fact that Muhammad himself was a very bad man who did very bad things. And it obviously isn't impossible—I know many people who manage to do it—but it is difficult to hold in one's head the fact that this man was chosen by God and also that he was so very bad.

JEFF KING: It's interesting because if you talk to ex-Muslims, whether they've converted to Christianity or they've become atheists, they will say over and over that the mass of Muslims don't truly know who Muhammad was. They were taught that he was like Jesus; he was the perfect human being, he was loving and merciful. But the majority of them don't speak Arabic and/or don't study. Once they do start studying, their eyes open and they say, "My goodness, I had no idea who this individual was." And then there is a real fork in the road, because they either have to reject Islam or they have to buy in and say, whether I like it or not, this is who God sent and this is what God wants.

That's one of the issues, and there's a very interesting thing across religion. Of course, you know the story of the daughters of Lot, who get their father drunk and then essentially rape him in his sleep in order to have children. This is something that most Christians and Jews are not aware of. It's a very uncomfortable episode. People, generally speaking, are taught a faith, which they have their own version of, and that's mediated through the churches or particular branches of religion and so on. And the same thing happened in

Islam. And so, it's perfectly possible to be Christian for your whole life and not know this story, and to be quite shocked when you discover it. Then, they encounter other bits of Scripture and they think, "Wow, I didn't know it was as bad as that." That people find a way around it is one of the problems that exists in Islam. In a way, it's actually a hopeful thing that people don't know what Muhammad himself did. I mean, there's a Bukari Hadith somewhere in which Muhammad punches Aisha, his youngest child wife.

JEFF KING: Whom he'd married when she was nine.

At six, actually.

JEFF KING: The marriage was consummated at nine; they were married when she was six.

Yes, and, obviously, this is a very shocking thing, particularly if you are told this is a perfect human being. So, there have to be ways people find around it. But the ignorance of people about their own religion is actually quite a good thing. You wouldn't want people behaving like this. But this is a huge, huge complexity, and there is a particular problem, which I don't say is insuperable, but is very considerable, which Islam has, and which Judaism and Christianity do not have.

It comes down to whether or not criticism is allowed. Some Christians, and some very orthodox Jews, believe that the [first five books of the Bible] were dictated by God to Moses, but this is a minority view which has not been believed by very large numbers of these faiths for very many centuries. Generally speaking, as I said earlier, Christians and Jews have accepted the fact that their divine scriptures have a human hand in them. In Christianity, of course, it is particularly obvious in that we know that the firsthand account of Jesus may not even be firsthand. People know that the Gospels are descriptions of what Jesus did, and people know from reading them that they are contradictory in places, and there are all sorts of reasons for this. The human hand is a very important element, because it allows believers to rationalize and explain inconsistency. If Matthew and Mark disagree on something, then one of them just got it wrong.

Now, then, the problem with the Qur'an, which is not insuperable, but it is very, very serious, is that it is believed to be uncreated. And by uncreated, I mean that it was derived directly from God, that there is a deity who gave this book to mankind, transmitted via an Archangel, from God directly to Muhammad. Now, that means that when you are criticizing or ignoring a part of the Qur'an, you are ignoring what God has told you directly. It also means that if you criticize part of it, or say something is a bad idea, you are criticizing an idea that has been transmitted by God. So, this hurdle, I think, at the very least, has to be addressed, and preferably not only addressed, but at some point gotten over.

It is very serious because it causes, among other things, terrible cognitive dissonance because, surely, God does not contradict himself. Now, the way Muhammad got around this was to abrogate, that is to replace earlier verses with later ones, later revelations. If a later revelation contradicted an earlier one, then the later one was more correct because it was fresher. That's a very clever way around it.

There is another thing he did, seen in the so-called Satanic verses, which were decided not to have been the voice of the Archangel Gabriel but that of the devil deliberately misleading him. I mean, it's exceedingly clear. If you read [the Qur'an and Hadith] as a skeptic or a rationalist, if the sayings of Muhammad are in contradiction, he always manages to come up with an explanation for the contradiction, and there are times when it's almost funny, actually. It's clear, particularly with his last phases, that his applications of divine messaging are a lot like a slot machine.

JEFF KING: It's interesting that you see within the Qur'an and Hadith that Muhammad was a person who did not like to be questioned, and when he was questioned on certain things (i.e. contradictory statements) he would get angry. In regards to abrogation, the problem is that he was more violent later in life, and those violent verses abrogate the earlier verses.

Well, that's the point that Salman Rushdie makes very beautifully in his book on the Satanic verses. There is a very moving passage with Salman the Persian, as he calls him, who is taking the dictation from the Muhammad character and reading it back without altering it. Salman says, at one point, of course now he doesn't need me; now he will come with armies. I think any critical reading makes it very clear that the more authoritarian tendencies come later on, as he gained power.

JEFF KING: Can you give us the big picture of Islam in the UK and Islam in Europe? What are the issues, and where are things going?

My feeling is they are going backwards, because people have landed on the wrong terrain. When people do violent things, there are a range of responses, but broadly they fall into two categories. You either ask what it is you did to cause it, or you say you don't care and you won't put up with it. We have collectively done the former, which has had a terrible impact. This approach has effectively appeased the radicalism and accentuated it and accelerated it.

Let me give you one quick example: in the wake of the cartoons affair in 2005, there were death threats and lootings directed against Danes and against their embassies. If, in the wake of that incident, every newspaper in the Western world, and in the free world, generally, had simultaneously published the cartoon, we would all be in a much stronger position. And the reason is not just because our free presses would have asserted their right to be free presses, but also because a lesson would have been learned by the extremists—

that freedom of expression is just as much cherished in democracies as holy books are in other places. But when you capitulate, there is a de facto agreement that certain things cannot be done, cannot be said, cannot be thought, and that's where we are now.

We are actually strangely entrenching the extremists within their faith by repeatedly and consistently entrenching their ideas which are the most literal, the most extreme. The cartoon is a good example. Another one is the Burka, or extreme dress. Instead of arguing that a garment that is intended to cover someone over in a desert situation may not be at all needed or desirable on the streets of London in 2010, the debate was had on religious terms. There is now a very common idea for instance, which was not common at all a few decades ago, that for Muslim women to wear the headscarf is a bare minimum requirement and, of course, it's no such thing. But there is a whole set of things like this in which we've strangely entrenched. Another is, of course, that no criticisms can be made in public of certain historical figures.

JEFF KING: So, can you summarize, where is Islam, and where is it going in Europe?

Well, growing, obviously, and beyond its numbers and influence. This is a critical matter, and certain demands were given into, certain things the West gave up. I would say that one of the oddities of the last ten years has been that, strangely, in the wake of 9/11 and actions by certain terrorists, Western government and societies have responded with effectively the largest actual *dawa* ever made. What has happened is that the debate around Islam and about Islam has become one of the primary, if not the primary, debates of our time. And there are ways in which that debate can be good and helpful, both for Islam and for everyone else, and there are ways in which it can be unhelpful. And I think it is currently happening in an unhelpful way, because it is happening on our opponents' terms.

JEFF KING: You said that in three or four generations Europe is going to change due to the growth of the Islamic population, due to immigration and high birth rates. How is it going to change?

Well, the mass immigration that Britain and, indeed, Europe are experiencing is of a kind unparalleled in human history. There's always been movement between societies, but there's never been movement to this degree, and it was done for all sorts of reasons, such as the rebuilding of Europe after the war, in particular. But it just happened at such a speed, nobody really even realized.

Successive governments of all persuasions failed to realize what the longer-term challenges would be. Among these long-term challenges is the fact that questions have to be asked and answered about, not just the people who are coming into European societies, but also about European societies themselves: what we are, who we are. Because there has been a period of intense self-doubt and self-questioning in European democracy, which I would say has been effectively highlighted by the mass immigration question. Because one of the things about the multicultural model was that everyone celebrated their origin, everyone celebrated their background. So, you have Black history month, you have celebrations, Ramadan and Diwali, and all sorts of other things. And the thing is that, while all this was happening, it was thought bad form to celebrate the foundation which was Western political democracy. As a result, you have this very strange experience of people being told they can only represent and celebrate the other culture and not themselves. It's unsurprising that a culture, which was told this repeatedly, would have something like a nervous breakdown, which I think is what's happening.

JEFF KING: Let's talk about something you said about the reasons for massive immigration. There are several ideas; let me throw up three to you. The reason for massive immigration of Muslims into the UK was that, after World War II, Britain

looked at demographics after the death of so many young men, and looking ahead, they realized that they needed to bring people in to increase the workforce; there's one idea. Another is that it is part of a drive for globalism. Now here's a third one—this is from Bat Ye'or, who said—that the biggest component, the biggest reason for the massive immigration, was that the Western European nations were effectively blackmailed by the 1973 oil embargo and that part of the deal made was to open up their societies. Talk to me about the background to the immigration.

I don't go along with that. It's not Britain's experience. Britain's experienced mass immigration since the 1950s, you know, twenty years before.

JEFF KING: So you would attribute it more to the post World War II reality?

Well, in the late 40s and early 50s, Britain needed cheap labor, and the decision was made by Churchill's last government, when he came back into power after the war. Although some people did warn about the long-term implications, by and large people were of the belief that this would only be beneficial.

Of course, it had many benefits, but it also had many drawbacks, and the idea was that you propped up your workforce by bringing in foreign labor. The problem being, that if you're going to start that model, what is described as a pyramid model of immigration, you're going to have to keep importing more and more people in order for them to support the workforce that is retiring ahead of them. As I'm sure you know, on this scale it means that within fifty years, Britain will have a population of 80–90 million. It's utterly ill thought-through as a model. It's an obvious point to make, but immigrants grow old as well. I'm not entirely sure why people thought about it so little or worked it out so little, but I get the strong impression that the idea was that society would gain the benefit of cheap foreign labor and that those people would go back or not have families? I don't know.

JEFF KING: Let's talk about the phenomena of Muslim ghettos and the subject of integration. Are Muslims integrating into society in Europe?

Some are and some are not, and I think it's a noticeable trend that the latter group is growing; there is a reason for that.

JEFF KING: You're saying there's increasing isolation?

Yes, I think that the new generation of young Muslims in Europe are less integrated than their grandparents' generation. And the reason for that is that demagogues have persuaded them that they should be Muslims first, rather than Europeans. It's very possible to have multiple identities, but the primary identity is an important one. And young Muslims have been whipped for some years now into a situation in which they are expected to identify themselves as Muslims. *"What are your brother Muslims dong worldwide, how are they suffering, what is the rest of the Ummah [the worldwide body of Muslims] going through?"* This is accentuated in very big things and also in very small things, which end up having big results.

In western European countries now there is a significant rise in this sort of thing. The Muslim Council of Britain, which is one of the main groups in Britain, which claims to represent Muslims here, was actually supported by the government in going around to mosques in recent years, telling Muslims—educating them, they said—about Muslim finance. What they see is a government-approved program to go around and explain to Muslims how to be more separate. These are very, very significant things. If you are brought up in society to believe that everything you do should be different from your neighbor, including your banking arrangements, then you simply, bit by bit, have less and less in common.

JEFF KING: In a 2007 *Pew* poll, eighty-one percent of UK Muslims said they were Muslims first and British citizens second and, even in the States, forty-seven percent of US Muslims said they were Muslims first and American citizens second. So talk about these ghettos that have popped up. What do these places look like?

Well, it's another effect of immigration, as in France and elsewhere: people didn't want immigrant neighborhoods on their doorstep. And so, partly through the fault of town planning, and partly through the fault of central government, the phenomenon appeared which we now see very clearly in Britain of ghettoised societies. I should stress that immigrants tend to want to be around people of their background, whom they have connections with. In a lot of cases, it's more homely.

But, in Britain you can now almost live an entirely parallel life from the rest of Britain. The National Health Service spends millions of pounds every year on translation services for people who use the National Health Service and don't speak any English. But, that sort of thing is a phenomenon which I think should have been tackled very early on. There should be very basic requisites, like you can't immigrate into Britain, and you don't become a citizen unless you speak the language. Because unless you speak the language and can communicate, what is it to be here? There's no chance of integration.

JEFF KING: So, looking ahead at the massive ongoing immigration experiment that's going on, how do you think it is going to affect Liberal Democratic rights?

As Muslim communities grow in number, and if they continue to identify primarily as Muslim, they will become a voting bloc which democratic parties and politicians will pander to, to try to give them what they think they want. It's already being done. Tony Blair, who had all sorts of good things going for him as a Prime Minister, had a number of bad things as well. And one of them was that he was persuaded to try to institute a "Hate Speech-Hate Crime Law" that would have made it an offence to offend Islam. And this was a deal that Blair had done in order to try to claw back some support from Muslim voters after the enormously disenfranchising, disenchanting, Iraq war. So you already see a fraction of it. That's how democracies work: politicians telling people what they think they want to hear. But, on this topic, there are some very troubling issues down the road.

JEFF KING: For the uninitiated, describe what Sharia law is and talk about why it's dangerous, especially in the context of Western democracies.

Well, Sharia law is very, very complex, and not agreed on by anyone. But broadly speaking, it is a body of law and teachings that derives from the lessons, life, and writings of Muhammad. There are all sorts of schools of Sharia, and they have a lot of disagreements with one another, but there are certain trends that one can say they have in common. And this comes back to the issue that Islam is both a belief system and a legal system.

JEFF KING: It's a political system, it's a religious system, it's all-encompassing.

Exactly, and Sharia is the legal bit that's been practiced for more than a millennium now, and it is making a comeback now in a very surprising way in Britain and other countries. The terrible irony of this is, of course, that very many Muslims came to Britain and America precisely to escape Sharia, and now we see Muslims in Britain expected to adopt it. Very, very troubling!

JEFF KING: Why is it dangerous to Western democracy?

Well, Sharia law is based on what Muhammad said he heard, and although some of that was moderately progressive for seventh-century Arabia, it's not progressive in twenty-first century Britain or anywhere else. In a whole range of ways, Sharia is backward stuff. Particularly, Sharia law's attitude towards women. This is a problem, and one that has very palpable, very demonstrable results. An example is a set of arbitration tribunals in Britain, the Muslim arbitration tribunals, or MAT. These are Sharia courts which operate in Britain now, under the arbitration rule, which have, sadly, started to tread beyond the realm of the arbitration laws and into the realm of family law. They are exceeding their remit, but they haven't yet been slapped back for this.

JEFF KING: And you would naturally think these tribunals would gravitate beyond arbitration because, again, Islam is not just a religion; it's a political system, etc. It's all encompassing, so it's naturally going to expand, and there are plenty of radicals who are using it as a strategy to radicalize and separate the cultures in societies. Do you agree?

Yes, absolutely. It's also part of what I referred to earlier, the Maududi [Sharia finance] mistake. I think that anything which is meant to separate Muslims from everyone else in society is hugely destructive. The idea that Muslims need their own court, even for family arrangements, is a problem. There's also a directional issue. That is, once you allow the Sharia court to begin and to flourish, you have to ask whether it will remain voluntary for many people for long. That is, they may not volunteer for this; they may actually do it because they feel they have to go about things that way.

And there's a second directional point which has to be made, which is that the people calling for these courts are in no case the progressive Muslims. In no cases! They are people who will tell you if you ask them, as I have done, that, yes, they do actually want the stoning of adulterers; yes, the chopping off of the hands of thieves; and so on. And that has to be borne in mind; there is no such thing as a progressive or moderate Sharia court.

JEFF KING: Incredible! You touched on how it would be especially hurtful for women. Tell us about your experience with Muslim women in the UK, especially in regards to the application of Sharia.

Well, there was a very troubling example a few years ago in the MATs [Muslim Arbitration Tribunals] here, in which some Muslims were discovered boasting that they had six cases of spousal abuse dealt with by the Sharia court, not by the police. That's a very disgraceful thing. Second, was the case of a Muslim man in the North of England, who died without a will, and his estate was divided according to Sharia, i.e., the sons inherited twice the inheritance of the daughters, because that's what is in the Qur'an. This is very important, as indeed is the issue of domestic violence, because the status of women in Sharia is that they have half the worth of men. Not just in inheriting estates, but indeed as witnesses. In other words, the testimony of a woman is not as important as that of a man. Now, there are very serious questions that have to be asked once you tolerate even an ounce of that.

JEFF KING: Right, incredible ramifications.

Yes, it definitely can't be justice in the way that we understand it.

JEFF KING: Douglas, in 2009, you were awarded the Douglas-Home Memorial Trust Award for an essay on Sharia, and you spoke about Sheikh Suhaib Hasan and Anjem Choudary, [whom I've interviewed] and their push to impose Islamic laws in the UK. Who are the guys who are pushing for Sharia law, and what kinds of statements are they making?

Well, yes, I interviewed them both for this piece. Sheikh Suhaib Hasan is very, very clear about what he wants. He says that he would like to stone adulterers and chop off the hands of thieves because he said that when he lived in Saudi Arabia he never saw any adultery. I suspect he didn't look quite hard enough, or at all, but anyhow, that's his viewpoint. To say it's medieval is to flatter him. He is one of the people in the UK who is a strong advocate of Sharia courts here, so they say it's very important to know the direction people like him would take us in. Choudary claims to have been involved with this for some years. He calls himself a Sharia court judge, but as far as we can ascertain, he has no courtroom; he seems to only have a van, and issues judgments from the back of it—a drive-by judgment.

He's a very troubling figure because he's partly ridiculous and what he says is so absurd. So absurd that I can't take him seriously. On the other hand, unfortunately, a lot of people do. One in every six or seven Islamists convicted of terror-related offenses in the UK in recent years has been a member of his group. This is very troubling, and he is perfectly open about this as well. He's an advocate for full Sharia, as some would like to say; he's not after any half-measures. He also believes this ludicrous idea, which is so laughable one hardly knows where to start, that under Sharia bad things just don't happen. I think he once claimed, in the debate I had with him, that only three thefts had happened during the whole last caliphate. I don't know where he gets this s___ from, but there you have it.

JEFF KING: According to a recent survey of Muslims in the UK, thirty-seven percent of young Muslims ages sixteen to twenty-four preferred Sharia, compared with only seventeen percent of people over fifty-five. This kind of goes back to an earlier statement you made; a lot of these people left these societies because of Sharia law, but why are the young Muslims so attracted to it?

Yes, this is exactly the point. It is notable in a number of surveys being done. This is the case among the young, and there is a desire for more of this. One has to speculate about why that is. One possible explanation is that they have never lived through Sharia themselves and there are certain totalitarian ideas which are only appealing to people who have never had to suffer under them. People who have suffered under communism very rarely want it back. You only find that kind of idiocy in universities in the West, among privileged academics who've never, never spent a day having to suffer under communism.

JEFF KING: It's great as a theory but the practical application is not so pleasant.

Yes, it's like the lunatic, lone, teenage neo-Nazi sitting in his mum's basement; it's fantasy stuff, and it's the same with Sharia. My own feeling is it's the way in which confused young people try to make sense of the world. If it weren't this, it'd be something else.

JEFF KING: When you look around the world, and you say, "Look it's ... it's not a perfect place at all, it needs to be changed." People grasp at answers and so there are people who offer theories as solutions. Sharia would be one of them. It's very easy to say, "This Sharia, [it] is the answer."

Yes. Young Muslims growing up in Britain or Western Europe, are not sure where they belong and they've never been told they need to integrate into the culture. Like everyone else, they don't like some of what they see in society, but along comes an apparent panacea, an apparent answer, and they go for it. I think it's a terrible fantasy to think that this can deliver anything, let alone justice.

JEFF KING: What approach should the British government take towards Islam?

I think they should view it as a private matter for individuals who, if they wish to believe, can believe it, just like you can believe anything else. But, it must get no special rights, no special privileges, no special protection, and indeed far from it; it should be subjected to the full force of freedom that is expected to be applied to everything else.

JEFF KING: Sure, Christians shouldn't have special rights, nor should Jews, Mormons, or anybody else; we're all citizens with

equal rights and equal protections. You've spoken about UK universities and how they're being used to recruit Islamic radicals. Can you elaborate on that?

Yes. We've done several reports on this, but there have been a number of cases of very high-profile terrorists who've come from British universities. The murderer of Daniel Pearl [*The Wall Street Journal* reporter] was a graduate from the London School of Economics, as were the 2003 Tel Aviv bombers.

JEFF KING: Daniel Pearl's murderer was a graduate of the London School of Economics?

Yes, and the person who tried to bring down the airline in Detroit on Christmas Day last year [2009] had just left University College London. The reason is that they come to university in Britain where certain metropolitan areas are hot spots of radicalism, of extremism, an environment where extreme radical preachers appear on a weekly basis. In light of that, it's understandable that they come under the impression that this is normal. It gives them a swamp in which to swim. It is something which I think university authorities should be made to think twice about.

JEFF KING: But there are people in the system, actively recruiting on the university campuses?

Yes, I believe so.

JEFF KING: Two more questions. You've said it's five minutes to midnight in Britain's battle against radicalism. What do you mean by that?

Well, I mean that unless it's turned around quite soon, it can't be turned around at all because our institutions of state are being so corrupted—our legal and university systems, all sorts of things. If you don't deal with it now, you'll eventually discover that you don't have the wherewithal to do it. You won't have the tools anymore.

Although the time when we know we've lost might be some time away, the beginning of the period of losing will come quite soon.

JEFF KING: One last question. Many people, after reading this, would say you're an Islamaphobe. Are you?

There's no such thing. So, no. It's a bogus word. It's only been around for about ten years. At best, it's an exceedingly imprecise word. At worst, simply nonsense. It's absurd for a whole set of reasons. One is that phobias are irrational things. It's irrational to be claustrophobic because small spaces don't kill you. It's not irrational to be fearful of Islam in some of its guises. It's eminently rational to be scared of jihadis, for instance, just as it's eminently rational to be scared of madmen with guns.

It's not phobic. But more than that, the canard of *Islamaphobia* is a deliberate invention to make criticism of anything to do with Islam illegal or impermissible or out of the purview of decent society, and I think it's one of the things which needs fighting most. I think it's part of the game I described earlier. That is, if anything that offends any individual Muslim at any one time can be described as Islamaphobic, then the debate is lost, and we might as well just pack up and go home, because the discussion we had earlier about the historical nature of Muhammad would be deemed Islamaphobic.

If something that is true can be dismissed as a manifestation of a phobia then we are in trouble. I think that *Islamaphobia* is a word that has been deliberately invented in order to stop Islam, even radical Islam, from being able to be criticized in any way. I think it is a totalitarian idea, a deeply oppressive use of the language, and it must be resisted. And any time anyone uses the word *Islamaphobia*, they should be laughed at.

Chapter Twelve:

The American Jihad Expert

"The Islamic terrorist threat in the United States is one of the most important issues we face...We now face distinct possibilities of mass civilian murder the likes of which have not been seen since World War II."

Steven Emerson testifying
before the Senate Judiciary Committee three years prior to 9/11.

"Al-Qaeda is... planning new attacks on the US...[It has] learned, for example, how to destroy large buildings.. Al-Qaeda and other terrorist groups ...have silently declared war on the US; in turn, we must fight them as we would in a war."

Written a few months prior to 9/11, on May 31, 2001

Steven Emerson

Steven Emerson is a journalist, award-winning documentary producer and author who has written extensively about Islam and national security. He was labeled an American Cassandra for his public warnings about Osama bin Laden and Islamic terrorism prior to 9/11. This included testifying before the American Congress six times on this issue. He currently is the Executive Director of the Investigative Project on Terrorism headquartered in Washington, D.C.

Books and Documentaries by Steven Emerson:

- *Jihad in America* (a documentary) won the 1994 George Polk Award for best Television Documentary, and top prize for best investigative reporting from Investigative Reporters and Editors.
- *The American House of Saud: The Secret Petrodollar Connection*
- *Secret Warriors: Inside the Covert Military Operations of the Reagan Era*
- *The Fall of Pan Am 103: Inside the Lockerbie Investigation*
- *Terrorist: The Inside Story of the Highest-Ranking Iraqi Terrorist Ever to Defect to the West*
- *The Worldwide Jihad movement: Militant Islam targets the West (Policy forum)*
- *American Jihad: The Terrorists Living Among Us*
- *Jihad Incorporated: A Guide to Militant Islam in the US*
- *Al-Qaeda in Europe: The New Battleground of International Jihad*

JEFF KING: Tell us about your involvement with the work of exposing radical Islamists. How did you get involved in this work? Have you faced personal threats for your work?

I started getting interested in this subject while I was a correspondent for CNN in 1992. I was sent by CNN to Oklahoma City on December 24, to cover a slowly unfolding news story.

The next day, Christmas Day, I had nothing to do so I drove my rented car to downtown Oklahoma City in an effort to find an open fast food restaurant. When I passed the Oklahoma City Convention Center, I saw hundreds of people flowing from the Center dressed in Middle Eastern clothing: long robes for the men and head scarves for the women. My initial reaction was that there must be a film being made and these are the "extras." So I parked my car and walked into the Convention Center.

There was no film being made. Rather, to my everlasting surprise, I had stumbled into a meeting of the Muslim Arab Youth Association [known as MAYA]. I later found out that a relative of Osama bin Laden was involved in running this group at the time. What I witnessed was absolutely shocking to me. On the floor of the convention center, there were scores of tables, all hawking their militant Islamic groups and giving out literature in support of Islamic terrorist groups. There was a table for Hamas, which went by the name of the Islamic Association for Palestine and was based in Texas. There was another table for the Islamic Jihad. And still another table for the precursor to al-Qaeda, Makdat al-Kidmat, a group that recruited Muslims in the US in the 1980s to fight the jihad against the Russians in Afghanistan. When the Russians withdrew in the late 1980s, this group trained its ire at the United States. And now they had offices all over the US, but the major one was in Brooklyn, operated by the Blind Sheik, where jihadists were recruited to carry out attacks against the United States or sent on different jihad missions around the world.

Later that evening, there was a special program called "Palestine Night." Inside were about 3,000 attendees. The speakers were the head of Hamas, who called for killing Jews, and a leader of the Muslim Brotherhood, who declared a war by Islam against the West. These were all leaders I had seen on television or read about in newspapers. To see them on American soil issuing declarations of terrorist violence was absolutely shocking to me. At the end of the program, I went two floors below where there was a bank of public telephones. I tried to reach a senior FBI counter-terrorism official to ask him if the FBI was aware of what was then taking place in Oklahoma City. But, because it was Christmas, the FBI official was not in the office. So, I called the FBI switchboard and asked them to patch me through to the home of the FBI official as I had urgent information to impart to him. When I reached this FBI official at home, I asked him if he knew about this Islamic terrorist conference being held in Oklahoma City. He responded by telling me he knew of no such conference and then asked if I was smoking something. I later found out that there were local FBI reports about this conference, but it never got to FBI headquarters.

After collecting hundreds of propaganda pamphlets, audio tapes and books published by these groups, I could easily discern the fact that all these terrorist entities had offices throughout the US. When I went back to D.C., I strongly suggested to my bosses at CNN that we do a story on this amazing conference. But, when my editors sought confirmation of what I relayed to them, they went to FBI headquarters to see if my information would be corroborated by FBI officials. But the FBI officials said they had no such information, and therefore my editors said I could not put such a story on the air since they didn't believe me. It was a very frustrating experience. Two months later, the first bombing of the World Trade Center (WTC) in lower Manhattan occurred on February 26, 1993.

Within days, the FBI had caught some of the perpetrators who turned out to be radical Muslims living in the New York/New Jersey area.

Their leader was the Blind Sheik. Then, when Islamic fundamentalists entered our lexicon, CNN asked me to do reporting on the bombing (which killed seven civilians and wounded nearly a thousand), especially on the roots of that bombing. Having been already made aware of Islamic terrorists operating on American soil some two months earlier, I had a head start on all the other network and newspaper reporters doing the same investigation.

In April 1993, CNN asked me to do a one-hour special on the roots of that WTC bombing. I came back to them with a proposal to investigate the Islamic terrorist groups already operating on American soil under the radar screen. CNN had something else in mind: they wanted me to go to Afghanistan to report on the "blowback," the process in which the Islamic jihadists we had supported against the Russians now turned their hatred on the US. I told CNN that the "blowback" story was indeed important to report, but the larger and totally unknown development, to which I had singular info about, was the establishment on American soil front offices for nearly all Islamic terrorist groups in the world. I waited for a green light from my editors but never got one. Finally, one month later, I pulled a friendly editor aside and asked him why I did not get the green light to do my proposed documentary. The answer was a shocker: CNN felt that the story I wanted to do was "too politically sensitive." I found it quite strange for a news organization to invoke [political sensibility] on one of the biggest stories in the last twenty-five years.

Well, hell hath no fury like a journalist scorned! I quit my position at CNN and was determined to make an independent documentary. I received seed money from the President of the Corporation for Public Broadcasting, Dick Carlson, an amazingly courageous public television executive, which allowed me to go to Peshawar in the Northwestern Frontier Province of Pakistan, where many of the world's jihadists had made their home.

I was taken in by the family of worldwide jihad leader Abdullah Azzam, who was killed in a bomb blast in Peshawar in 1989. Azzam was the mentor, I later discovered, to Osama bin Laden. The Azzam family was very generous and gracious in accepting me as a guest. And, as such, they protected me and also introduced me to other mujahideen[22] in Peshawar. Although I did not know it at the time, these mujahideen were actual members of the newly-founded al-Qaeda terrorist group. An Arab journalist offered to take me to Afghanistan to meet bin Laden, whose name I had heard of vaguely. I spent two weeks in a run-down hotel in Jallabad waiting to meet bin Laden, but he never arrived. And I was totally miserable living in a hotel without heat or hot water, with locally-produced bottled water that was full of parasites, and a bed that seemed to have been slept in by a thousand earlier guests.

I left to return to Peshawar where the holy warriors gave me many VHS tapes. When I returned to the US to watch these tapes, I found out something startling: These were tapes of jihad conferences held in the United States, from Oklahoma City to Tucson to Chicago to Boston to Tampa. I realized then I had my story. I raised additional funds from several foundations and produced and reported a documentary called *Jihad in America* that aired on PBS in November 1994. While the film gained several prestigious journalism prizes, it was attacked by Muslim groups who denied there was any Islamic terrorist presence in the US and dismissed in the politically correct mainstream media who said that all I found were videos of fiery rhetoric by jihadists living here but no evidence that they intended us any harm. I am sure that if I had done a documentary on the KKK, it would have been lauded by the media.

After the film aired, I realized that I had collected primary intelligence on terrorist groups operating here. And, soon enough,

---

[22] See pg. 344.

law enforcement officials came knocking on my door to find out what I had because they did not. There were the infrequent media calls trying to find out what was the real agenda of these benign-sounding groups.

In 1995, I created the Investigative Project on Terrorism, a nonprofit group that was dedicated to combating and exposing the threat of radical Islam on American soil. I have to admit that between 1995 and the attacks on 9/11, I was scarcely given much attention until I testified before Congress some half a dozen times, including being the first Congressional witness to warn of the dangerous threat posed by Osama bin Laden. It was also during that time that I found out through the FBI and the State Department security services that I was the object of an assassination plot by jihadists from South Africa who had infiltrated the US under a South African-issued fatwa that I was to be killed. Within a week of being informed of this plot, I moved from my condo on Connecticut Avenue in D.C. to a rented apartment where the owner allowed me to fill in a lease form under a different name. I still live there now.

After 9/11, I was then lauded by the media as a modern day "Cassandra," a nice compliment, but one I did not deserve. All I was doing was investigative work that other journalists should have been doing. My organization subsequently grew to some twenty staffers today. We have a popular website [www.investigativeproject.org] where we post investigative articles, government documents, and background reports on various Muslim Brotherhood front groups masquerading as "civil rights groups" with the witting and unwitting assistance of the mainstream media. We also work with law enforcement agencies, both federal and local, in providing intelligence on what these supposed "moderate" groups are really up to.

JEFF KING: Who was Muhammad? What was he like? Why is this question so important in understanding fundamentalist Islam and Islamic terrorist efforts?

Steven passed on this question.

JEFF KING: What is the Muslim Brotherhood? What is their connection with Islamic radical groups?

The MB was founded in Egypt in 1920 by a man named Hassan al-Banna. His actions were a reaction to the secularization policies of western colonial empires in the Muslim world. Banna sought a return to the "fundamentals of Islam," i.e., a return to the periods during which previous Islamic empires enforced totalitarian versions of Islamic rule. To al-Banna, the new organization that would form a popular movement to overthrow westernized Islamic countries would be called the Muslim Brotherhood. Its principles can be encapsulated in several easily digestible demands: 1) Death to the infidels, 2) Dying for Allah was the supreme commitment that Muslims could make, 3) Instilling the Sharia was mandatory, 4) Toppling all non-Islamist regimes to make this Islamic radical regime, and 5) Ultimately, taking over the world to impose Islam. The movement began to grown in Egypt and other countries. Although Banna was executed in 1948 by Egyptian government forces, his legacy lived on and expanded around the Islamic world, then the Western world. In 1963, Muslim Brotherhood leaders moved to the United States and immediately established the Muslim Student Association at the University of Champlain in Urbana, Michigan. New adherents to the MB continued to come to America until the MSA gave birth to the National Association of Islamic Trusts, a Saudi-funded holding company that owned the deeds to some 80% of all mosques in the US. Then, the Islamic Society of North America was founded in 1981 as an umbrella organization for all MB groups. Ultimately, the entire spectrum of MB legacy groups were founded, including front organizations for Hamas, the Islamic Jihad, the MB, and nearly every other radical Islamic group in the world. Of course, none of these

MB groups had the word Muslim Brotherhood in their names. They were designed to mislead the American public and American law enforcement by calling themselves by benign-sounding names.

JEFF KING: What are the major Islamic radical groups in the world?

There are several sets of Islamic radical groups in the world. Those who were derived from the Muslim Brotherhood, including al-Qaeda, Hamas, Islamic Jihad, Islamic Salvation Army, Lakshar al-Tayba, Armed Islamic Group, al-Gama'a al-Islamiya [from Egypt], and, ultimately, Al Ittihad al-Islami and al-Shabaab from Somalia, as well as more than forty other not-so-well-known, but equally vicious, Islamic terrorist groups. The aforementioned groups are all Sunni groups. From the Shiite side, those Islamic terrorist groups included Hizbollah, as well as Hizbollah chapters in all the Persian Gulf countries. Of course, the Iranian regime itself is a de facto terrorist group.

In the West, many of these groups established front organizations or charitable fronts to infiltrate American society and falsely portray themselves as "moderate" or as "civil rights" groups. In the United States, the MB led to the creation of MSA chapters on colleges across the US, the Islamic Society of North America, the Islamic Association for Palestine, the Council on American Islamic Relations, the International Institute of Islamic Thought, the Islamic Committee for Palestine, and more than twenty others.

JEFF KING: Is all this talk of Islamic radicalism just fear mongering or is it substantial? Talk about what radicals were planning in Canada.

Islamic radicalism is a real and growingly threatening movement across the US and Canada. In the last nine years, both countries have experienced more than 90 Islamic terrorist plots that were, fortunately, interdicted by law enforcement and intelligence agencies of both countries. Some have succeeded, like the killing of thirteen people at Fort Hood in 2009 by military psychiatrist Nidal Hassan. In Canada, officials stopped a major plot by a dozen Islamic radicals to blow up Canadian government buildings, including the Parliament and also planned to kidnap the Canadian Prime Minister and decapitate him. Included in this plot were American jihadists who planned to blow up iconic buildings in D.C.

JEFF KING: What data do we have on the spread of radical Islamists' theology/worldview to Western Muslims? What percentage or number of American Muslim individuals in the United States might be willing to participate in a terrorist act?

There are, unfortunately, no reliable or accurate polling data on the attitudes of American Muslims, although there is better data on European Muslims. Despite polls by *Pew* and *Gallup* of American Muslims, the data they produce is intrinsically faulty. For example, in claiming that a vast majority of Muslims condemn "terrorism," there is no effort made to determine how American Muslims define terrorism. For example, do they consider Hamas and Hizbollah to be terrorist groups? Do they consider "martyrdom operations" against US troops and Israelis to be terrorism? Do they support MB leaders like Yousef al-Qardawi [the spiritual head of the MB who has issued numerous fatwas to kill Americans and Jews] as "moderate" leaders? Even absent these aforementioned questions, a *Pew* poll a few years back showed that a third of all US Muslims between the ages of eighteen to twenty-nine admitted to supporting "suicide operations," which means to me that if a third openly admitted it, there must be double that amount that truly support it but would not admit it. In Great Britain and France, the polling of their Muslims have actually produced more honest results, which includes, for example, the fact that Muslim majorities in those countries aspire to make their governments to be "Islamic governments" where the draconian Islamic laws encapsulated in the Sharia should be implemented.

These answers however do not tell us how many would participate in a terrorist act. My own informed speculation suggests that a relatively small percentage of US Muslims would actually be prepared to participate in a terrorist attack–as low as three to five percent of the US Muslim population (which is estimated to be anywhere from two to five million). The larger number of radicalized Muslims in the US, perhaps as high as twenty to twenty-five percent of their population here, would not be prepared to carry out an act of terrorism by themselves. But, they could be considered what I call "cultural jihadists"–unwilling to pull the pin on a hand grenade but provide moral support to those who do. These cultural jihadists propagate the view that the United States and the West are engaged in a "war against Islam," a false but incendiary conspiratorial belief that believes in a narrative that the US, Christians and Jews, have embarked on a secret conspiracy to subjugate Islam. This view, of course, comes from the Islamist supremacist view that views Islam as the only authentic religion that is supposed to rule the world. And, anyone who is perceived as standing in the way of this religiously-mandated goal must be part of a conspiracy to wage war against Islam. By the way, this conspiratorial view of the West is the number one motivating factor in inducing Muslims to carry out violent jihad. Most dangerously, it is a view propagated by so-called Islamic "civil rights" groups who are in reality Muslim Brotherhood-derived groups: CAIR, MPAC, ISNA, MAS, ICNA, and other radical Islamic front groups who have shockingly been made legitimate by the mainstream media and federal and local law enforcement. To its everlasting credit, the FBI severed its relationship with CAIR in late 2008 on the grounds that it was a Hamas front group.

JEFF KING: Do fundamentalist Muslims in the US tend to be immigrants or converts?

They tend to be both.

JEFF KING: Many Muslim groups argue that American Muslims are well integrated, unlike, for example, Muslims in

UK. Is that true? If not, what evidence do you have to support your position?

It is true that US Muslims tend to be more integrated than Muslims in the UK and France. But the failure of that integration in Europe derives much more from the refusal of European Muslims to integrate than from the State's alleged racism. Muslim American populations have achieved neither the percentages of overall populations as they have done in Europe, nor have American Muslim populations achieved the same density as they have in various cities in Europe. Nevertheless, the number of attempted terrorist attacks in the US by American-based Muslims, even though they are more integrated here, does not seem to have lowered the number of would-be Muslim attacks here.

JEFF KING: What are the goals of the radical groups?

The goals of radical Islamic groups are twofold. One is violent jihad, an effort to commit violence and cause death and casualties [as part of a campaign to avenge the "conspiracy against Islam"] and to show the United States or other Western countries that even though these countries have massive defense budgets, the jihadist can still cause pain. In the jihadist's eyes, this pain will result in Western countries changing their foreign policies and also cause these countries to stop dealing with non-Islamist ruled countries and, instead, start legitimizing these jihadist movements so that they can take over.

The other goal of the radical groups is the "stealth jihad"–the effort to infiltrate and sabotage Western governments from within. A critical MB document, that was prepared in 1991 by a US Muslim Brotherhood leader, but only found by the FBI in 2006, was labeled the "civilizational-jihad" document. It spells out very clearly the goal of the MB and their derived groups to infiltrate American institutions, like the media, law enforcement, Congress, Hollywood, and publishing houses.

Looking back at what has been achieved since 1991 until late 2010, I would say that radical Islamic groups have managed to successfully penetrate the mainstream media (through witting ideological collaborators, and through journalists who have been trained by MB groups and have then been hired by organizations like the *NY Times*, *LA Times*, and the *Associated Press*), Hollywood (where Islamic groups have successfully caused major studios to drop any Islamic terrorist protagonist), in law enforcement, in Congress, etc.

JEFF KING: What role do the Saudi's play in growing and funding radicalism in the US and around the world?

The Saudis, ruled by puritanical Wahhabist religious dogma, have had a long tradition, going back decades, of funding radical mosques, Islamic terrorist "charitable" front groups, and the MB groups carrying out "stealth jihad," and even of being able to buy significant chunks of the American media. In the past few years, however, Saudi Arabia has significantly stopped this direct funding, but has left it up to radical Islamic Saudi "charities" such as the World Assembly of Muslim Youth and the Muslim World League, the al-Haramain "charity," and the International Islamic Relief Association, to name just a few militant charities which continue the funding of radical institutions in the West, as well as directly fund terrorist groups like Hamas. This has given the government of Saudi Arabia "plausible deniability" in claiming that the regime no longer directly funds radical or terrorist groups.

JEFF KING: Tell us about mosques in the US which are controlled by radical Muslims. How widespread is this phenomenon?

Hard to say exactly, but based on the fact that the Saudi-funded National Association of Islamic Trust (NAIT) controls the land deeds of about 70% of American mosques, it would be a fair conjecture to claim that 70% of American Mosques are controlled by the radicals, since any mosque owned by NAIT has traditionally been given the right by Saudi Arabia to help select the imams at those mosques.

It should also be said there exists a growing, albeit small, number of genuinely moderate Islamic leaders and Islamic mosques in the US who have courageously spoken out against radical Islam, against the Muslim Brotherhood, against Wahhabism and against the notions of either violent or stealth jihad.

These amazingly courageous leaders and mosques deserve our support and ought to be recognized and invited to US governmental forums. If there is ever going to be a genuine reformation in Islam, it will have to come from within. These authentic moderates, who have taken their lives into their hands every time they speak up, need to be empowered by the USG, not the radical MB groups that the US government now supports.

Moderate Islam is the only answer to radical Islam. And while the moderates have only minute amounts of funding and do not get called upon by the US media for their views, we should insist that our own government stop their dangerous recognition of stealthy radical groups and, instead, delegitimize these radical groups by stopping inviting them to White House events, by stopping DHS and other federal agencies from propping them up, by complaining to the mainstream media that they are dangerously promoting jihadist groups by giving them prestigious venues, and by telling major donors to universities across the country to immediately stop giving to universities where their faculty in Middle East Studies programs and politics departments continue to indoctrinate their students in "hate-America" ideology, where radical jihadist professors have found permanent refuge and where many of the more than 600 Muslim Student Association chapters continue to flourish by advancing a hate ideology against the US.

THE HISTORY OF

ISLAMIC

EXPANSION

Chapter Thirteen:

The Professor

Jihad is, and has always been, extolled as the noble, traditional and violent form of martyrdom. The ultimate goal is to submit the entire globe to Islam and to Islamic law. [In regards to the jihad campaigns against India] you're talking about conquests that go until the arrival of the Europeans into the seventeenth and eighteenth centuries. I've worked with a demographer from the University of Chicago and their best estimate is that approximately eighty million Hindus were killed during those centuries. Historians Will and Ariel Durant gave a summary statement that they consider the conquests of India to be the bloodiest in human history. These were very, very devastating conquests. There was also mass enslavement. I would say the whole issue of slavery under Islam was another one of these eye-opening things for me, as far as its duration and its extent. There's no other civilization that has enslaved as many people as Islamic civilization.

Andrew Bostom

Dr Andrew Bostom is an associate professor of medicine at Brown University. He is the author of *The Legacy of Jihad: Islamic Holy War and the Fate of Non-Muslims* and *The Legacy of Islamic Anti-Semitism: From Sacred Texts to Solemn History*. To learn more about Dr. Bostom and his work you can go to www.andrewbostom.org.

Books by Andrew Bostom:
- *The Legacy of Jihad*
- *The Legacy of Islamic Anti-Semitism*

JEFF KING: What motivated a medical doctor to start writing books about Islam?

It was a result of 9/11. I grew up in New York and my wife and I did all of our education, through medical school, in New York City. We still have some family there and many close friends who either lived in the area near the World Trade Center or worked in Manhattan. It was a very harrowing day, trying to account for everybody we knew there. I stopped in a bookstore and grabbed a couple of books on Islam. One of them was by Karen Armstrong. Well past midnight that night, I was reading the book and I said to my wife, "This [the material in the book] just sounds patently ridiculous. It just doesn't jive." That made me curious as to what really was the story and one thing led to another. As an academic, I have access to the incredible resources of the Brown University library system. I wound up meeting some independent scholars who were very generous and provided some good mentoring.

JEFF KING: How did you get into the publishing world?

I started out by writing essays. Ibn Warraq [an apostate atheist Muslim author] lived with us for a few weeks while in the process of obtaining permanent residency and he liked my essays. He encouraged me to go ahead with a book. I said the only way I would write one was if he wrote a foreword. He was a great encouragement to me. That's really what got it started.

JEFF KING: Was it about ten years after Muhammad had come to the belief that he was a prophet that he became more violent in his teachings and writings, along with his personal example?

[The violence] begins when he goes to Medina and becomes a political leader and engages in all the kinds of human things that we would associate with politics, both good and bad. In terms of assassinations and rather murderous [jihad] campaigns, there are many, many things about concubines, slavery, taking Aisha as a bride when she's six years old and still playing with dolls, and consummating the marriage when she's nine.

All these things are told by the foundational texts and are now deemed "Islamophobic" if they're mentioned by non-Muslims. Even if secular Muslims or liberal Muslims try to talk honestly about these things in the hope of pointing out that some of this material needs to be ignored or dismissed, they, too, are called Islamophobes.

JEFF KING: After Muhammad came up with the doctrine of jihad, what happened in terms of the number of his followers or his popularity?

There's probably nothing unique about this phenomenon historically, particularly amongst the Arabs. They were successful, they were daring, and his following grew. They were raiders, so pillaging and plundering became sacralized and part of the whole institution of jihad.

JEFF KING: What is Islamic jihad and when did this start? What is the background of it?

There's really only one historically relevant meaning of jihad. The root appears in the Qur'an about forty times in different grammatical forms. It comes from the root "striving," but it really was used in the Qur'an as "fighting." Out of the forty usages, thirty-six refer directly to fighting. There are only three or four verses out of the forty where you really get the sense of it being a personal struggle which could be interpreted in a spiritual way. In fact, Sura Chapter 9 has been aptly termed an entire chapter of war proclamations. There are also Qur'anic commentaries that make very, very clear that these so-called jihad verses are in fact referring to actual war against the infidels to subdue them.

The ultimate goal of jihad, whether it's by clear-cut physical violence or just having non-Muslim populations submit peacefully, is the spread of Islamic law and Islamic rule. The goal is to force non-Muslim populations to live under Islamic law. It's further elaborated in what are called the Hadith. These are, in a very crude sense, analogous to the Gospels because they are the words, deeds, and even physical gestures of Muhammad as recorded by his earliest pious companions, the first Muslims.

There are six canonical collections that are held most important by Muslims, and two that are particularly important: a collection by Sahih al-Bukhari and a collection by Sahih Muslim. These two have entire chapters, again, devoted to jihad as warfare. There are also the earliest pious Muslim biographies of Muhammad, the so-called *Sira*, the first one being by ibn Ishaq, and others by people like al-Tabari and ibn S'ad. Here, we see a tremendous amount of biographical material devoted to Muhammad's actual war-like campaigns against the pagans, against the Jews, and against the Christians. The most recent treatment of Muhammad modeling jihad is by Yusuf al-Qaradawi. He gave a sermon called "The Prophet Muhammad as a Jihad Model" around 2001 that reiterates the fact that Muhammad is a prototype jihadist, certainly by the time he gets into his Medinan period, the last decade of his life.

JEFF KING: What are the main goals of jihad?

The ultimate goal is to impose Islamic law, whether in its most nascent form as expressed in the Qur'an and by Muhammad, or in the more formalized way it came to be expressed in terms of the jurists, etc. The goal of jihad is to create an Islamic society that should ultimately include the whole globe. The jurists evolved this concept of Dar al-Harb vs. Dar al-Islam. Dar al-Islam were the lands that were already Islamized and were under Islamic rule; the Dar al-Harb, or the zone of war, were the contested areas. The reason they were contested is that they weren't yet under Islamic rule.

JEFF KING: What about Sufism? Sufis hold the view that jihad is more of a struggle within oneself. What's your opinion on that?

Al-Ghazali is considered the greatest Sufi. He was the one who actually saved Sufism. Sufism was possibly going to be exterminated because it was too mystical for mainstream Islam, and he reintegrated Sufism into mainstream Islam. Ghazali said something about the jihad that had real consequences because he inspired these kinds of campaigns during his lifetime. He said, "One must go on jihad at least once a year and may use a catapult against them [non-Muslims] when they are in a fortress, even if among them are women and children, when they set fire to them or drown them. If a person of the *Ahl al-Kitab* [the people of the book, typically Jews and Christians] is enslaved, his marriage is automatically revoked. One may cut down their trees. One must destroy their useless books. Jihadists may take his booty wherever they decide, and they may steal as much food as they need."

The fundamentalists will always point out the verse that supposedly says, "Muhammad said on returning from the campaign that it [the battle] was the lesser jihad and the greater jihad is this internal personal struggle." There is no such Hadith in any of the canonical collections. The fundamentalists know this. In fact, the opposite is true. It comes from the Sahih Muslim, which states very plainly that the first order of jihad is fighting, and then there's jihad of the mouth (propaganda), and then they say jihad of the heart is acceptable, but it's the *lowest* form of jihad.

JEFF KING: You had already mentioned that Muhammad personally participated in jihad. What would you cite in the Qur'an to support that?

I think this is spelled out extensively in the *Hadith* and, more particularly, in the *Sira*. Ibn Sa'd's *Sira* is the campaigns of Muhammad. Those are the most clear-cut examples, and also ibn

Ishaq's *Sira*. The *Sira* gives very, very detailed descriptions of the campaigns that Muhammad waged against the indigenous peoples of the Arabian Peninsula—mostly pagans, Jews and Christians.

JEFF KING: Any big campaigns that come to your mind that he participated in?

The more infamous ones would be against the Jews of Medina. Another example is used as the cover art on my book. It is about the massacre of the Qurayza [Jews], one of the Medinan tribes who were subdued. The males were beheaded and the women and children were enslaved. This was in the period of Muhammad's development where he was an unabashed conqueror.

JEFF KING: Tell us about the explosion of jihad after Muhammad's death. Where did Islam go? Where did they start subjugating and conquering?

They burst forth into what's historical Palestine. So, all the lands that we now know as historical Palestine—Gaza, Israel within the green line, Judaea, Samaria, Syria, Jordan—those were the initial lands conquered. Egypt and Iraq would be subsequent. The extent of the areas conquered within a decade was actually quite remarkable. I have some maps in my book that actually lay it out century by century so you can see that within a century of his death in 632 conquests are going as far west as modern Spain and Portugal, and Pakistan-Sindh. They also went into central Asia with, at least, attacks, if not full conquests, as far as Dagestan in what's now one of the former Soviet Republics. It was a very extensive area. That's just the first hundred years of Arab-Muslim jihad conquests.

There were waves afterwards. Perhaps the more prominent would include the Seljuk and, later, the Ottoman Turks who wound up Islamizing all of the Balkans, extending their conquests up into Hungary, Tatars who conquered into southern Poland and large parts of Russia, and another group of Islamized Turko-Mongols who conquered Hindu Afghanistan and then spread from Hindu Afghanistan throughout the Indian subcontinent. Now, there was some spread of Islam to places like Indonesia which appears to have occurred by trade and proselytization, although even there you do see hotbeds of more violent jihad and jihad piracy.

JEFF KING: Why were people converting to Islam? Were they so enamored with Muhammad and his doctrines?

The Arabs and Turks were great warriors and were very formidable. They were brutal conquerors, consistent with the eras in which they lived. This is very well chronicled, by both the Muslims who were conquering and the people being conquered. We have two parallel series of chronicles. One is the triumphal chronicles of the Muslim historians, saying that jihad is great and here's what we did and here's the number of infidels slaughtered and enslaved and the villages sacked and booty taken, etc. Then, you get these very poignant chronicles of the suffering of the non-Muslim victims of these campaigns, and often the two narratives, for historical purposes, fit together quite neatly.

JEFF KING: Some apologists or moderate Islamists would say that Islam doesn't call for support of the sword to force others to change their religion, and they would cite Qur'an 2:256 [there shall be no compulsion in religion]. What are your thoughts on that?

Rudy Paret is a great German Qur'anic scholar, one of the best in the twentieth century. He wrote a whole essay about Qur'an 2:256 and, even without getting into the notion of abrogation (which is critically important and the only way to make sense out of the Qur'an in the end), he pointed out that if you take an approach of looking at jihad vs. Qur'an 2:256, how could they exist simultaneously? He said that he wasn't so sure that this was a statement of any form of tolerance or compassion. He feels that Qur'an 2:256 is a straightforward statement of resignation that no matter what a Muslim does he can't guarantee that a person is going to practice Islam, whether it's an infidel that he wants to forcibly convert or not. The act of practicing Islam, of being a real Muslim, is a matter of the heart, not something that can be forced. This is not a statement of tolerance if you also have a verse like 9:5, which says that the pagans ought to be slaughtered if they don't convert. He says there's nothing to support 2:256, on that ground alone, as a voice of moderation.

JEFF KING: These teachings of jihad, are they in the Qur'an, the Hadith, the Sira?

I think the Qur'an is pretty straightforward. In the Qur'anic commentaries, you get a real window into how the best theologians, jurists, etc., have interpreted these sources for a millennium now. The Hadith can be a little strange and confusing at times, but many of them are really straightforward. As I mentioned, there are entire chapters dedicated to jihad in the Hadith that go into much more detail than you would get in the occasionally more elusive verses in the Qur'an.

JEFF KING: It's in the Qur'an, it's in the Hadith, it's in the Sira. Then, if you go to the commentaries, you see it there. You're saying, "You see the continuity?"

I might add that there are four schools of Sunni Islamic law that have survived, and while they have differences over many other issues that may pertain to religious practice and piety, when it comes to the issue of jihad against the infidels they are remarkably consistent.

JEFF KING: Muhammad's career started peacefully, became violent and ended violently. Because of different verses in the Qur'an that are conflicting, they came up with a system called abrogation so that the later verses, which are all violent, abrogate, or supersede, the earlier verses. Correct?

I think that's a perfectly reasonable way to look at the Qur'anic narrative. An Ottoman jurist, the leading sheikh for the Ottoman Empire, wrote his own work on jihad in which he says, "Jihad is *fard al-kifaya.*" That is, one must begin the fight against the enemy even when he, the enemy, may not have taken the initiative to fight. The reason is because the prophet (Muhammad), early on, allowed believers to defend themselves. Later, however, he ordered them to take the initiative at certain times of the year, such as at the end of the *Haram*[23] month, saying, "Kill the idolaters wherever you find them" (Qur'an 9:5). He finally ordered fighting without limitations, at all times and in all places, and then he cites Qur'an 9:29, "Fight those who do not believe in Allah or the Last Day, or acknowledge that Islam is the religion of Truth, even if they are Jews or Christians, until they submit to slavery to you willingly and feel themselves subdued."

JEFF KING: Let's bring our microscope onto one of the areas that Islam conquered. Let's talk about the campaign against the Hindus. How many centuries did these campaigns cover?

You're talking about conquests that go literally all through until the arrival of the Europeans into the seventeenth and eighteenth centuries. I've worked with a demographer from the University of Chicago and their best estimate is that approximately eighty million Hindus were killed during those centuries. Historians Will and Ariel Durant gave a summary statement that they consider the conquests of India to be the bloodiest in human history.

You've got this Sunni Arab wave, which is very early on in the eighth century, and then you're getting Islamized Turkic peoples who wound up conquering Hindu Afghanistan, and then that becomes the staging ground for the more extensive conquest of the

---

[23] See pg. 343.

Indian subcontinent. The devastation to the Hindu populations, in terms of written chronicles, is quite extensive, but there are a few that have survived. It's the flipside, the Muslims' narrative that tends to support the triumphal narratives.

JEFF KING: Most Westerners have no idea what happened in terms of Islam trying to subjugate the Hindu peoples. What happened there?

The first forays were actually by the Arabs, and they managed to get at least a foothold, temporarily, in the Sindh province. But the more permanent conquest that was made was eventually Hindu Afghanistan. The Islamized Hindu Afghanistan became an area where enormous forays were directed against the rest of the Indian subcontinent. The most infamous of these Muslim raiders was Mahmud of Ghazni. Ghazni was responsible for about twenty campaigns that ravaged Northern India. Massive, massive, massive casualties were inflicted along with mass enslavement and destruction, but he had assembled a whole court that was very well-versed in the jihad. He was a pious Muslim jihadist. The permanent presence of Islam in what we know as India doesn't take place until a subsequent ruler, and then you see a period of conquest that comprises something called the Delhi Sultanate, which goes up until the beginning of the sixteenth century. These were very, very devastating conquests. There was also mass enslavement. I would say the whole issue of slavery under Islam was another one of these eye-opening things for me, as far as its duration and its extent. There's no other civilization that has enslaved as many people as Islamic civilization.

JEFF KING: Tell us more about some of the atrocities committed by Muslim conquerors.

There is no civilization which has engaged as extensively in the hideous trade of manufacture of eunuchs to serve in the harems as the Muslim civilization. Now, the Chinese created this human gelding procedure of creating eunuchs, but they didn't go outside the Chinese population. They didn't raid other civilizations and make eunuchs out of them. Only Islam, as far as I know, has done this. It's absolutely horrific to read some of the chronicles, and as a physician, it's just mindboggling to think of the horrible suffering and the 90% plus mortality rate in sub-Saharan Africa due to this human gelding procedure. We're talking about sub-Saharan African people, so the eunuch procedure was directed against black populations. When it began, the populations that were being ravaged were in Europe and Asia, but eventually it evolved to being almost purely an enterprise where the eunuchs are being procured from black populations in Africa.

JEFF KING: How did the Muslim rulers treat their Hindu subjects?

The Hindu chronicles and Muslim chronicles verify that the Muslim tax collector could demand that the Hindu open their mouth for the Muslim tax collector to spit into as a form of humiliation. The point is for the Hindu to be humiliated because they are a living example of religious error.

JEFF KING: Let me ask you this: killings and violence have been part of Islam's legacy, but Christianity has had its own ugliness. Look at the Crusades, the Inquisition, etc. How do you respond to the argument that Islam is unfairly targeted?

The major Islamic teaching institutions, down to the local schools throughout the Islamic world, are still teaching jihad war today. It has never been renounced. I find that this civilization is uniquely devoid of mea culpa. That's the huge difference between Christianity and Islam. Christianity has always had a very, very vigorous, self-critical strain. To this date, in Islam, there has been no critical re-assessment of the suffering that jihad has caused. It is a constant, endless rationalization without any sort of self-critical examination other than a few truly brave and independent voices. There is nothing on an institutional level, nothing remotely like a Vatican II. This is what's needed.

JEFF KING: You could argue that the odious parts of history associated with Christianity are an aberration in terms of the core teachings of Christianity.

They go against the doctrine. What is different about Christianity is that there has been a discussion. It hasn't been simply excused as a distortion of the doctrine, case closed. How can any of these institutions change if they're not even willing to recognize the deleterious effects that they've had?

JEFF KING: Culturally, within Islam, questioning is absolutely not allowed. Muhammad would not allow anyone to question him. He would get furious and he would strike out at those who questioned or mocked him. That's still going on today.

The only way to move forward is to renounce these things, and they refuse to do that. They refuse to acknowledge that they've occurred, and that's why I think it's up to the non-Muslim world to say "enough."

JEFF KING: There's a common perception among many that every religion has its crazies, and jihad is only carried out by a few radical, violent Muslims. How do you deal with that?

It's time to put those things to rest. They're self-deluding; they give a false sense of security. Jihad is, and has always been, extolled as the noble, traditional and violent form of martyrdom. But it has always also been about propaganda; it's been jihad by money. Again, the ultimate goal is to submit the entire globe to Islam and to Islamic law.

The Organization of the Islamic Conference came up with its own declaration called the Cairo Declaration, or the Universal Declaration of Human Rights in Islam, which states very plainly that the Sharia,

Islamic law, supersedes all so-called man-made rights constructs. They have now begun, particularly in light of the Muhammad cartoons episode, to try and impose their version of blasphemy law internationally. I would call this another version of jihad.

JEFF KING: More subtle, more savvy, as you said, but still jihad.

The most straightforward and clear way to formulate jihad is to use all the means available to impose Islamic law. I would say that the very existence of an organization like the OIC (Organization of the Islamic Conference), which is committed to a human rights construct (which is anathema), and the Universal Declaration of Human Rights is proof positive of the global nature of jihad.

JEFF KING: The argument's true that most Muslims don't pick up arms, but what we want to get at is the mindset of the average Muslim.

I think Samuel Huntington's analysis, *The Clash of Civilizations*, was brilliant. Parts of that book never get discussed adequately. He has hard, tabular data in there which shows that, even in accounting for the cataclysms of World War I, World War II and the Cold War, Muslim nations in that period were disproportionately likely to settle disputes by warfare.

There is also polling data from 2007 that was face-to-face interviews—roughly a thousand participants per country—in Morocco, Egypt, Pakistan, and Indonesia. Two questions in this survey jump out and show you the staggering extent of this problem. Sixty-five percent answered affirmative to wanting "strict" application of Sharia law. Sixty-five percent answered affirmative to the creation or the re-creation of a transnational caliphate. You're getting a very consistent two-thirds answering affirmative to both questions. You also have to look at the question. The question was "strict" application. By the time we get to "strict," most people would interpret that as meaning mutilating punishments and things like that. The word "strict," to me, conjures up the worst of the worst.

There was also a local poll more recently in terms of these questions, and forty percent of British university Muslims wanted England to be a Sharia state. You could say, "Well, we know the universities have had a radicalized local population, maybe there's a lot more moderate people," but then you've got to say, "These are supposed to be the intellectuals and the fire power of the next generation." That's not good.

JEFF KING: What's the relationship between suicide bombing and jihad?

You have to flesh out the difference between suicide and martyrdom. That's really the way to understand this. Death as a result of a jihad martyrdom operation is the noblest undertaking of all. It has Qur'anic sanction, Qur'an 9:111, and even more specifically, in the Hadith, Sahih al-Bukhari, Volume 4, Book 52, Number 4. It says, *"By him in whose hand my life is! I would love to be martyred in Allah's cause, and then get resurrected, and then get martyred, and then get resurrected again, and then get martyred, and then get resurrected again, and then get martyred."* You can't get much more explicit than that.

JEFF KING: You've said that 9/11 was a jihad attack. What leads you to that conclusion?

First of all, it's classic in the way it's described by the perpetrators who celebrated it as a jihad attack. The notion of conquest of a non-Muslim power like the United States, and attacking in this fashion, is very consistent with the whole history of jihad. The idea is to sow such terror that the infidel will long for peace and submit. September 11, 2001, was perfectly consistent with that idea. What's very interesting is that when you see some of the protests against al-Qaeda from Muslim institutions, etc., you have to peel away the layers. There was this famous meeting in Amman, Jordan, where they come out with these generic denunciations of "terrorism," but then 550 of these luminaries signed on this Amman agreement where they said that any Muslim who believes in one of the validated schools of Islamic law cannot be excommunicated. Well, that would include Osama bin Laden. What I think is going on here is that [al-Qaeda] and the Organization of the Islamic Conference share a goal in terms of global Islamization and having the world under Sharia law. They just don't agree on tactics.

The Muslim Brotherhood has come up with a much savvier, slower, more patient method. What is the goal of that? The imposition of Islamic law. So, while Muslim institutions and governments can protest against al-Qaeda, it's really a question of tactics. If you're going to commit an act of mass murder like this, and cause a violent reaction from a powerful nation like the United States, it's counterproductive. It's a tactical mistake. On the other hand, from al-Qaeda's point of view: no, no, no, it's a triumphal attack that instills terror in the infidel, and that's what we're supposed to be doing according to classical jihad. So these are debates really about tactics, but not goals.

My feeling on this is that we need to separate ourselves from these societies. We need to become, on a very concrete level, energy independent. You look at Iraq and Afghanistan and the incredible sacrifice and the incredible restraint with which our troops have operated in those countries, and other than a small minority of people, there's not even gratitude for having liberated them from Saddam Hussein or from the Taliban.

Friends of mine who formed Former Muslims United came up with this *brilliant* thing. It's called the Freedom Pledge. It was sent to the fifty main Muslim organizations in this country (about a hundred and fifty individuals), and it simply says that you will pledge to guarantee our safety and our freedom to be agnostic, or to practice our new faith, without threat, and without any form of coercion. Out of a hundred and fifty individuals representing fifty organizations, how many people do you think have signed that pledge? It's ten months old now.

JEFF KING: Do tell.

Two. That's less than two percent who are willing to guarantee freedom of conscience to their former co-religiants.

Chapter Fourteen:

The Historian of Jihad

I then entered into meticulous study of the Qur'an, Hadith and Sira [Muhammad's biographies] for the first time. These foundational texts of Islam read, as I've said, like "a manifesto of open-ended war against non-Muslims for converting them or for subjugating them into horribly degraded dhimmi [second-class] subjects."

"The exact estimates [of how many died over the centuries in India from Islamic jihad and rule] are very difficult to make because the casualties in every campaign were not properly recorded. From the available documents, one historian estimated the number killed to be in the range of 60 to 80 million."

(Due to his many death threats,
Mr. Khan declined to provide a picture)

M.A. Khan

Most Westerners have no idea that Islam expanded primarily by the sword and through the death of millions. The scale of murder and enslavement is truly mindboggling. Yet, due to political correctness, government strategy and the fear of radicals, the media won't tell you the truth. Unless you study it on your own, you will assume that it expanded organically, as have all the other religions. Islam, though, is not just a religion. It is a religious/cultural/political/military system.

M. A. Khan was born into a Muslim family but has left Islam and is now an atheist. After finishing his graduate studies in India, he moved overseas to further his education. He holds an M.Sc. and an M.A. degree and worked in the field of science for a decade. He has also done extensive research on Islam, namely on the Qur'an and Hadith, as well as on Islamic history.

M. A. Khan's book, *Islamic Jihad: A Legacy of Forced Conversion, Imperialism and Slavery* is a meticulously researched masterpiece on the subject of the history of jihad that is a must-read for anyone interested in this topic. It is for that reason that I wanted to include him as one of our interviewed experts.

Books by M. A. Khan:
- *Islamic Jihad, A Legacy of Forced Conversion, Imperialism and Slavery*

JEFF KING: Tell us about your background as a Muslim and how and why you left the religion.

I grew up in the countryside in a conservative Islamic environment, but my family was rather liberal and progressively minded. More than anything else, my parents wanted my siblings and me to excel in studies. I grew up as a Muslim, but never followed Islam diligently.

Sometimes, I would pray five times a day for a few weeks, then drop out. Parts of Islam, such as regular praying and fasting didn't become part of my life because they just didn't appeal to my inner instinct. By the time I graduated from university, I had become convinced that praying five times a day was a waste of time. If I was to be rewarded, I wanted to be rewarded for working hard, being intelligent, and doing good to others.

Apart from this, I still felt, as do all Muslims, proud to be part of Islam; proud to be a Muslim. Islam's high moral ethics, especially in sexual behavior, in contrast to the West's, was something which strongly appealed to me. The West, with their past colonial rule in the Muslim world, and their ongoing enmity towards Islam, [unconditional support for Israel and interference in Muslim countries], really angered me. These are common sentiments amongst Muslims everywhere. So, when the 9/11 attacks happened, I felt a sense of justification for it; it was a revenge against America's support for Israel, etc.

Following 9/11, as militancy flourished all over the Muslim world, including my home country, I started becoming disillusioned with Islam. During this time, many of my innocent countrymen were killed by militants. Militants used Islam's sacred texts to boldly justify these horrendous events, while critics blamed the same texts for spiraling violence all over the world. At this point, I had not read the Qur'an and Hadith. However, I slowly gained an interest in checking references associated with anti-Islamic arguments. In almost all cases, the accusations made sense. I then entered into meticulous study of the Qur'an, Hadith and Sira [Muhammad's biographies] for the first time. These foundational texts of Islam read, as I've said, like "a manifesto of open-ended war against non-Muslims for converting them or for subjugating them into horribly degraded dhimmi subjects."

All my life, non-Muslim classmates were among my best friends. Non-Muslim teachers were not only my best teachers, but were also great influences in shaping my career. Yet, Islam told me to hate them, even to kill them, just because they were Hindu. I began to experience a gradual movement away from Islam. Some years after the 9/11 attacks, I realized I wasn't a Muslim anymore. I consider myself an atheist now. Liberal humanism suits me as a good way to look at and live life.

JEFF KING: Tell us about your book on Islam. What things do you deal with in the book?

Islamic Jihad: A Legacy of Forced Conversion, Imperialism and Slavery, deals with jihad in Islam. More specifically, it discusses how, and under what circumstances, Allah gradually revealed the doctrine of jihad. It reveals how Muhammad implemented jihad and set it as an ideal which Muslims would replicate until the end of the world.

It also deals with three major integral parts or aspects of jihad: 1) Forced conversion of infidels to Islam, 2) Expansion of Islam through violent attacks of non-Muslims lands. Islam is by nature imperialistic and colonial. 3) Slavery. I was shocked to discover slavery was the biggest industry in the Muslim world before the European colonial age.

JEFF KING: What threats have you faced for speaking against Islam?

Death threats on quite a few occasions! But, thanks to my not criticizing Islam in my real name, I am still alive. Yet, there's always a fear that I will be exposed and receive my due punishment as many other critics of Islam have.

JEFF KING: Who was Muhammad in your opinion?

I am inclined to accept what is generally told about Muhammad. He grew up as an ordinary, illiterate, and neglected orphan in Mecca. His contact with Jews and Christians made him inclined toward monotheism, the idea of one true God. He had become afraid of punishment after death as preached by these faiths and, from this, he grew to hate idol-worship in his hometown.

Prodded and pushed by his wealthy wife and her Christian cousin Warraqa, he started his prophetic mission to preach a monotheistic faith among the people of his hometown, Mecca (c. 610 CE). He presented himself as a prophet for the Meccans, like the Israelites had Moses and the Romans had Jesus: *"[the Qur'an] is the Truth from thy Lord, that you may admonish a people [i.e., Meccans, Arabs] to whom no warner has come before thee: in order that they may receive guidance"* (Qur'an 32:3).

His aim was to abolish idol-worship from Mecca, from the Ka'ba, and establish a monotheistic faith like Judaism/Christianity among the Meccans and his Arab brethren. However, when he was unable to convince people to join his faith he was determined to succeed and persevered as situations demanded. When in difficulty, he continued to press on, maintaining composure, and even staying quiet. When his power increased from having more followers, he made the best use of their muscle to achieve his objective—to exterminate opponents and critics, and to destroy rival faiths that were within his power and reach.

JEFF KING: How did Muhammad deal with Jews and Christians?

Initially, Muhammad wanted his new monotheistic faith to be one alongside earlier ones, namely Judaism, Christianity and Sabianism. Qur'an 5:69 says, *"Those who believe [in the Qur'an], those who follow the Jewish [scriptures], and the Sabians and the Christians, any who believe in Allah and the Last Day, and work righteousness, on them shall be no fear, nor shall they grieve."*

But he failed to convince the Meccan idolaters to embrace his faith and had to take up arms to [implement Islam]. His hold grew among the idolaters, starting from Medina, where they joined his faith in large numbers. This made him not only an overlord, but also enriched him with huge wealth obtained from plundering raids and attacks. He became inclined towards winning the Jews and Christians to his faith so that he could become the absolute overlord of the region, and to enrich himself further in power and wealth.

In order to do this, he started coaxing and exhorting the Jews and Christians with "revealed" verses to embrace Islam. He started telling the Christians and Jews that Islam was sent by the same God as theirs; he was only affirming their faiths with new and accurate additions. He told them that he was the prophet whose coming was mentioned in the Gospel and the Torah. In Jewish-dominated Medina, he adopted many of their religious customs like circumcision, fasting, prohibition of pig meat consumption, and turning toward Jerusalem while praying.

These were all a well-thought-out ploy to impress the Jews and Christians to join his new religion, but Muhammad got caught in his own game by the learned rabbis and priests of the Jews and Christians. In his folly, he claimed that his scriptures affirmed the Jewish and Christian scriptures. But in his [Qur'an] verses, he said things that were inaccurate in relation to Judaism and Christianity.

Moreover, he had, in agreement with the Bible, already revealed his own verses that said only the descendants of Abraham through Isaac and Jacob would enjoy the right of prophethood. But Muhammad, an Arab and alleged descendant of Ishmael, was out of that genealogy and could not claim prophethood as promised in the Bible. The Jewish rabbis in Medina exposed his folly by pointing to his inaccuracies and contradictions.

So Muhammad, in trying to convert the Jews and Christians to his faith, fared even worse than his attempt with the polytheists of Arabia. The polytheists had no familiarity with the Bible/Torah and, therefore, had no inkling of the inaccuracies and follies in his verses. The Jews and Christians, however, could clearly see them, and were eager to point them out. Thus, the Jews and Christians became a grave threat to his doctrine, because they exposed Muhammad's lies and could bring down his whole mission. He was particularly worried about, and angered by, the Jews of Medina, who lived in proximity to him.

Thereafter, he showed consistency in dealing with both peoples— polytheists, Jews/Christians. He was already wielding the sword at the polytheists to make them embrace Islam. The same came to apply to the Jews and Christians for their rejection of his invitation to embrace Islam. The Jews were the worst threat to his entire mission, so Muhammad resolved to exterminate them root and branch. After defeating a Jewish tribe known as the Banu Qainuqa, he began making preparations to slaughter them all and began attacking them all.

After defeating the Banu Qurayza (another Jewish tribe in Medina) in battle, he slaughtered all the grown-up men, and took their women and children captive. The Banu Qurayza Jewish tribe vanished. He applied similar measures upon the Jews of Banu Mustaliq (627) and those of Banu Nadir (628), who, having been forced out of Medina by Muhammad four years earlier, had resettled in Khaybar.

Muhammad's dealings with Christians varied from that of the polytheists and the Jews. This was because there were no organized Christian communities within Muhammad's proximity. Because of this, he did not have similar encounters with Christians.

Once he became capable of defeating strong Jewish communities like that of Khaybar, he started sending missives to foreign sovereigns. Some of these were Christians, such as in Egypt, Oman, Himyar, Syria and one to Emperor Heraclius of Byzantium, then the most powerful leader in the world. These letters demanded that they embrace Islam, although the language differed depending on the power of the addressed sovereign.

When the ruler was weak, he demanded their submission to Islam and to himself as the leader and prophet of God. If they did not relent, he threatened to attack them to prove his claim.

Letters to powerful leaders like Heraclius would also demand submission to Islam and recognition of Muhammad as a prophet, but, initially, the only penalty for ignoring the letter was that they would be guilty of misguiding their people.

After some time, when he felt powerful enough, he started sending forces to attack Christian territories like Himyar, Oman, Nejran, and Muta in Syria, as well as others. Those areas were forced to both embrace Islam and to pay tithes.

JEFF KING: You said that "Islam is a horrible and shameful ideology, unfit for the civilized world." That is a really strong statement that many people would recoil from. Can you explain yourself?

The reason is all too obvious. Indeed, most Muslims and Islamic countries don't practice and follow what Islam's divine texts and Sharia law explicitly demand of them. Where these laws *are* practiced with some measure of strictness, say in Saudi Arabia or Afghanistan under the Taliban, the situation is disturbing.

Apart from the most pious and radical, most Muslims would agree it's disturbing. This is because, through their study and observation, their conscience has been influenced by civilized ethics of the modern world that surrounds them. A civilized conscience demands dignity of human beings and human rights to all. It is irrespective of faith, color, or race, as enshrined in the constitution of Western secular democracies. One of the finest documents dealing with the treatment of our fellow human beings is the United Nations Declaration on Human Rights (UNDHR). Most Muslims, and certainly those living as minorities, would agree.

Unfortunately, Islam, the Qur'an, and Sharia Law don't agree to the dignity and equal rights to all. Islam explicitly and unequivocally demands supremacy of Muslims over peoples of other faiths. It pushes subjugation of non-Muslims under the Muslim power as humiliated, discriminated, repressed and exploited subjects. Apart from this, Islam sanctions slavery, including sex-slavery and polygamy. These things are all shameful and incompatible with the civilized conscience, and are in sheer contrast to what the UNDHR demands for all individual human beings. The truth is, most Muslims find those sanctions of Islam shameful, and they make desperate, but futile, attempts to prove that those are not sanctioned in Islam, that they are a perversion of Islam. But my book makes it crystal-clear that these ideologies are "divine," "eternal," institutions of Islam. They are sanctioned explicitly, unequivocally and repeatedly by Allah in the Qur'an, and even more explicitly practiced by Prophet Muhammad as the ideal life for Muslims to emulate until end of the world.

JEFF KING: You also said Islam is actually "a manifesto of open-ended war against non-Muslims for converting them or for subjugating them into horribly degraded dhimmi subjects." Please tell us why you said that.

Commands of the Qur'an and examples set by Muhammad in accordance with the same make that clear. Qur'an 2:193 and 8:39 clearly say that Muslims must fight until faith in Allah, Islam, becomes the only faith everywhere, amongst every people on earth. These verses, therefore, explicitly declare an open-ended war or fight against non-Muslims until all other faith systems, be it idolatry, Judaism or Christianity, are abolished and Islam is accepted everywhere on the globe. Moreover, Qur'an 9:1-5 commands Muslims to fight and kill the polytheists wherever they are found; they must embrace Islam or be killed. Qur'an 9:29 demands that the Jews and Christians, if they refuse to acknowledge Allah and Islam, must be fought until they are subjugated into humiliated and exploited subjects, so-called *dhimmis* of Islam. Islam is, thus, clearly a manifesto of open-ended war upon non-Muslims for abolishing their faiths, to exterminate the polytheists or force them to Islam, and to subjugate the Jews and Christians into pliant, humiliated, and exploited subjects.

JEFF KING: Why do Muslims insist that Islam is a religion of peace in the face of clear evidence showing the connection between violence/war and Islam? Why, if they are pushed too hard on this point, do they threaten to kill people who argue with them?

I was a Muslim. Muslims are a people of twisted logic, which others cannot understand. They are, all and sundry, most eager to emphasize that "Islam is a religion of peace," despite the fact that Islam's sacred text says otherwise. The reality of the Muslim world also says otherwise. Muslim countries/communities are everywhere relatively more violent and less peaceful, compared to their non-Muslim neighbors. Look at how they make a mockery of their own claim to Islam being peaceful. If someone says, as the Pope suggested a few years ago, that Islam is *not* a religion of peace, how they react to defend their most prized claim about Islam. They immediately unfurl violence and threaten to kill the offender, thereby reaffirming and giving credence to, what they sought to protest.

JEFF KING: Islam's holy books describe Muhammad killing many people and ordering many more to be killed, marrying and having sex with a nine year old girl, and many other things. Why then, do Muslims react with such anger when it is suggested Muhammad was violent, et cetera?

An overwhelming majority of Muslims don't know that Muhammad killed so many people and without any justification! They are only told that it was Muhammad and his followers who were cruelly and unjustifiably persecuted by the polytheists of Mecca and the Jews of Medina. They believe the polytheists and Jews caused the wars. What happened in those wars is not told to nor known by them. Most Muslims know even less than this.

Their mind is also groomed from childhood to view whatever Muhammad did with a divine aura in an unquestioning manner. They all know and agree that Muhammad married Aisha when she was six and had sex with her when she was only nine. This is outright pedophilia. But, since it was done by Muhammad, their prophet and an example of an ideal human being for all time, they can't just put the pedophilia angle into it.

Thus, while they will be very eager to condemn pedophilia, especially when a white man is caught, say, in Bangkok for sexually abusing little girls, they just can't apply the same to Muhammad and to what happens in their own surroundings. They will point their finger at Western immorality. They will eagerly point fingers at white men caught here and there for buying sex from underage girls but when, in their own neighborhood, an elderly Muslim man, often a cleric, takes a poor, underage girl as wife, they will just ignore it; it's part of their culture. It would even probably be deemed as a laudable gesture of kindness toward the helpless poor girl. That's the mentality of Muslims. Murder and pedophilia by Muhammad doesn't, and can't, exist in the Muslim mind. And, when such references are made, how do they react? With violence, with which they are groomed as being their religious and cultural ethos and norms in their societies and communities.

JEFF KING: You cited Qur'an 9/111 in which dying as a martyr is indicated to be the only sure way to paradise. How is this fueling violence by Muslims?

Verse 9:111 says: *"Allah hath purchased of the believers their persons and their goods; for theirs [in return] is the garden [of Paradise]: they fight in His cause, and slay and are slain: a promise binding on Him in truth, through the Law, the Gospel..."*

This is one of the last verses revealed by Allah to Muhammad. So, you can say it contained Allah or Islam's final decree on the matter in question. And it says Allah has purchased the Muslim's life. A Muslim's life is not their own anymore. Their lives belong to Allah; they are Allah's purchased slaves. So, what must they do to receive their master Allah's grace and blessings? Namely, a place in the Islamic Paradise? The verse clearly defines that *"they [must] fight in His cause, and slay and be slain."* It is the ultimate, the most prized, dream of every Muslim, the motivation for her/his every action in earthly life. *"They [must] fight in His cause, and slay and be slain."*

To pious Muslims (whom we call fanatics, radicals, fundamentalists or bigots), assuring a seat in Allah's Paradise is worth whatever price. What that means is clearly defined by Allah himself in his sacred verses. Muslim clerics, especially terrorist recruiters, widely use this verse to inspire them to engage in jihad. It is the inspiration that fuels the growing violence among Muslims, especially among jihadi groups. Its importance can't be underestimated. All jihadi fighters know, and are inspired by, the fact that their attacks against the infidels and deviant Muslims are a fight in Allah's cause, i.e., jihad. If they die in it, that will be the best death, which will ensure them a place in Paradise.

JEFF KING: You discussed slavery in Islam extensively in your book. Can you elaborate on this subject?

I was shocked to discover that the Qur'an clearly and repeatedly sanctioned slavery, including sex-slavery. It sanctions waging of wars and enslaving the women and children of the defeated. These slaves could be sold and the women could be used for sex by their Muslim masters, alongside his permitted four wives. The prophet Muhammad, in accordance with those Qur'anic sanctions, did exactly that. He practiced and expanded slavery in Arabia. After slaughtering the Jewish men of Banu Quraiza, Mustaliq and Khaybar (Nadir tribes) en masse, he drove away their women and children as slaves. He also made the prettiest and noblest of the young, captive girls his personal sex slaves: Rayhana of Banu Quraiza, Juwairiya of Banu Mustaliq and Safiya of Banu Nadir (at Khaybar).

Muslims, my former self included, hate the West, firstly for their imperial rule in the Muslim world, and secondly for their role in transatlantic slavery. Muslims believe slavery is completely absent in and alien to Islam. What could be more shocking and embarrassing to discover than the fact that Islam created one of the most extensive slavery industries in history? Islamic slavery overwhelmingly outweighed the practice of the slavery in any other nation or culture at the time of its practice. Muslim slavery was also especially cruel and dehumanizing. Namely, sex slavery, the use of young good-looking boys for sodomy (ghilman), and the most extensive castration of male slaves, particularly of black slaves.

Even in the much-condemned transatlantic slavery by European-traders, Muslims had their own decisive role. It was Muslims who captured and reared those slaves in Africa and elsewhere. It was only from Muslims that European traders purchased slaves and shipped them to both North and South America.

The practice would have likely continued to be a large industry in the Muslim world even today if European colonialism had not banned slavery and made efforts to suppress the slave trade. It is still being practiced in one form or another in some Muslim countries, including Mauritania and Saudi Arabia. Worst of all, it is being revived by Muslims in countries like Sudan.

JEFF KING: Talk about Islam's genocide of other cultures.

Islam, as Muslims proudly and universally claim, is a "Complete Code of Life." It is a guide to Muslim life that contains prescriptions and proscriptions of sacred nature for every action and every situation human beings may find themselves in. It extends its reach into morality, social conduct, governance, economics and other areas of life. Islam, in principle, is a social, cultural, ethical and political system in itself; it's a blueprint of a complete civilization.

Also, as its central doctrine, Islam came to view anything existing before it or outside its specific codes as *jahiliyah*, the fruits of ignorance. Ideas in the social, cultural, political, and scientific arenas fall into this group. These things must be avoided, rejected, and replaced by the Arab Islamic equivalent.

Thus, when Muslim invaders brought Islam from Arabia to the vast parts of the world through conquest, one of their central aims was to destroy the vestiges of jahiliyah achievements or traits that existed in those lands and replace them with the Islamic code of civilization. To that end, they have destroyed libraries, from Alexandria to India, and religious institutions, including churches, synagogues, monasteries, and temples of the conquered peoples. Muhammad himself started it by destroying temples, synagogues and churches in Arabia, the prime example being the idolatrous temples of Ka'aba of the pagan Arabs, which he turned into Islam's most sacred mosque, as it is till today.

In India, even at the end of the seventeenth century, a zealous Sunni proselytizer, Emperor Aurangzeb, destroyed thousands of Hindu temples. In fact, he destroyed over 200 in 1679 alone. Look at the Syrians, Palestinians, Egyptians, and Algerians! They were not Arabs before the Arab-Islamic occupation in the seventh century, but today they see themselves as pure and proud Arabs. This speaks volumes about the extent and ferocity of Islam's incursion upon the culture and heritage of its conquered peoples. Similar Arab-Islamization of the culture and civilization of the Muslim world elsewhere is going on at increasing speed.

JEFF KING: Tell us about the Pact of Umar that was to be ideally imposed by Muslim rulers upon their conquered subjects. How did this pact come into being? What does it contain?

The Pact of Umar is an agreement of terms that was dictated to the defeated Christians of Syria by the second caliph Umar [some attribute it to Caliph Umar II, r. 717-720]. It was chosen by later Muslim rulers as the ideal blueprint for the treatment of *dhimmi* subjects in a Muslim state. Famous eighth-century *Hanafi* jurist Abu Yusuf wrote that it would 'stand till the day of resurrection.'

It contains a series of prescriptions, proscriptions, and impositions that Christians must abide by to secure their life and right to live in Muslim lands. It demands a complete and humiliating subjugation of the *dhimmis* to Muslim rule. It forces them to pay discriminatory taxes as a symbol of their lowly status, and suffer many other degrading and dehumanizing socio-political disabilities. It accords perfectly with the Qur'anic verse 9:29 that commands Muslims to fight the Jews and Christians to subjugate them "*until they pay the tribute readily, being brought low.*" A few clauses of the Pact are given below:

- You shall not refuse to do anything we demand of you.

- You shall not display in any Muslim town the crosses, nor parade your idolatry, nor build a church or place of assembly for your prayer, nor beat the Nakus [church bell], nor use your idolatrous language about Jesus, the son of Mary (i.e., Jesus is the son of God), to any Muslim.

- You shall wear a cloth belt [zunnar] above all your clothes [as a distinguishing mark], which must not be hidden.

- You shall use peculiar saddles and manners of riding and make your kalansuwas [cap] different from those of the Muslims by a mark you put on them.

- You shall not take the crest of the road, nor the chief seat in the assemblies when Muslims are present.

JEFF KING: Some argue that Islam is egalitarian and treats all equally. But you have a different opinion on that. Give us your reasons for opposing such a claim?

All major scholars of Islam, from Jawaharlal Nehru to Bernard Lewis, think that Islam is egalitarian. *It doesn't make any distinction between Arabs and non-Arabs, between Blacks and Whites; all people are equal before Allah.* Of course, this assertion is made in reference to the community of Muslims only. All scholars agree that Islam has been extremely hateful, degrading and repressive toward non-Muslims. Slavery is affirmed and reaffirmed by Allah in the Qur'an. How can the term "egalitarianism," at all, be attached to such a horrendous faith?

Towards 80% of the world's population, Islam is obviously discriminatory, humiliating and dehumanizing. Consider it within the context of Islam. Islam subjugates its women. The lordship of men over women is all too obvious, even today. A Muslim woman is worse off than a male slave, who can buy his freedom or be freed by his master. For Muslim women, there is no escape from the clutches of men. When Islam eternally subjugates half of its own members, how can one call it an egalitarian faith?

Interestingly, the same scholars regret that the egalitarianism that Islam truly preaches was never realized, even within Islamic society, which remained class-bound and discriminatory. *Arab Muslims remained the masters and rulers; non-Arab Muslims second-class citizens, slave-like subjects.*

This is indeed what the Islamic scripture, and the Islamic god, wanted. I have mentioned above that Allah had revealed Islam exclusively for the Arabs to whom no prophet or warner had come. And who are these Arabs in the eyes of Allah? *"Ye are the best of peoples, evolved for mankind, enjoining what is right, forbidding what is wrong, and believing in Allah"* (Qur'an 3:110). Allah is clearly a racist overlord who places the Arab race above all other races. Prophet Muhammad had also said that Allah had chosen his tribe, the Quraish[24], as the best tribe of all. Only the Quraish have the authority to rule.

Allah is also anti-black. He asserts that on the Day of Judgment, the blessed will have their face shine white, while the faces of sinners will be blackened; they will become like black people. This means that Allah had less liking for blacks. Indeed, the blacks of Africa have suffered the worst treatment at the hands of Muslim invaders amongst the races they had conquered. They turned "Black" Africa into a slave-hunting and breeding ground very early and it continues to this day in many countries. Moreover, the black slaves destined for the Muslim world suffered the most extensive castration.

---

[24] See pg. 344.

In summary, it is obvious that those scholars who assert that Islam brought the idea of egalitarianism to mankind, are obviously ignorant of Islam's classical texts.

JEFF KING: You argued that Islam is imperialistic. How is that? How did Islam expand?

Well, that's all too obvious. What did Muhammad do to advance his prophetic mission? Unsuccessful in Mecca, he moved to Medina as a refugee in 622. In order to make a living, he took to raiding caravans, specifically targeting groups belonging to Meccans. As he started to become successful, the polytheists of Medina began to join his raids out of greed. After his invitation for the Jews to embrace Islam was rejected, he started attacking them, one tribe after another, with the intention of evicting or exterminating them all. This made it possible for him to take possession of their land.

Having come as a refugee, he thus established an Islamic state in Medina. From there, he continued expanding the borders of that state by subjugating one non-Muslim community after another. Sometimes, this subjugation was accomplished by force; other times, only the threat of violence was enough.

He captured all the major power centers in the Arab Peninsula, including Mecca, Khaybar, Taif, Hawazin, and others. He established an expansionist Islamic state in the Arab Peninsula. He had already sent letters to powerful foreign sovereigns, including the rulers of Persia and Byzantium, demanding that they embrace Islam and accept him as their prophet and overlord. In an attempt to expand the reach of Islam beyond the Arab Peninsula, he sent or led campaigns to Palestine, and to Muta and Tabuk toward Syria. This expansionist campaign of Islam continued after his death, reaching the far corners of the world, as we all know.

Now, one may think that Muhammad's political activities were separate from his religious mission, that Islam itself is only a religious and spiritual domain which had nothing to do with Muhammad's political ambition. That assumption is absolutely false. In fact, Muhammad's every political move and expansionist campaign was directed or commanded by Allah with revealed verses. Allah claims that He Himself is the absolute owner and sovereign of the Universe. And out of all his possessions, he has bestowed ownership of the earth upon Muslims. So Allah says in the Qur'an: "*[Allah] hath made you [His] agents, inheritors of the earth*" (6:165), and that He "*has promised to...make them rulers in the earth*" (24:55).

So, with the coming of Islam, Muslims became the true owners and rulers of the whole world. All countries not under Muslim rule were thus illegal possessions. Islam requires that all Muslims fight until Islam is the only religion in the world. Therefore, Islam is clearly a blueprint for establishing a global imperial Islamic state under Arab-Muslim rule. This mode of globalization was started by Muhammad and continued by later Muslims, and it remains today an ongoing pursuit. When Muhammad started acquiring the lands of non-Muslim communities, from the "illegal occupiers," attacking them one after another, it was actually Allah Himself executing the whole operation. It was Allah helping Muhammad acquire those lands bit by bit, and the Qur'an says so in these two verses:

- Do they [the infidels] not see that We [Allah] are bringing destruction upon their land by curtailing it of its sides?" (Qur'an 13:41).

- See they [the infidels] not that We [Allah] gradually reduce the land [in their control] from its outlying borders?" (Qur'an 21:44)

This should make it clear that Islam, at its heart, is a political ideology with an ambitious, expansionist dream—a dream of establishing an imperial Islamic state encompassing the entire globe, and ruled by the Arab Muslims. Obviously, Allah's dream remains still unfulfilled, but it's not the end of time yet.

JEFF KING: What has jihad meant throughout history, from its inception to today?

Jihad, in the language of the Qur'an, is striving or, more dominantly, fighting, "in the cause of Allah," which obviously means, "for the expansion Islam," eventually upon all peoples of all places in the world. The meaning of jihad as "fighting in Allah's cause" is all too obvious—waging wars to expand Islam. There is peaceful jihad and violent jihad.

When Muhammad was weak at the beginning, namely during the first twelve to thirteen years of his prophetic mission in Mecca, his jihad to propagate Islam was of a persuasive, peaceful nature, simply because he had no power then. When he moved to Medina, he found security, refuge, and protection. There, the numbers of his followers grew rapidly, as did his muscle. This was, in large part, due to the ready acceptance of Islam by the polytheists of Medina.

It was at this time that he went on the offensive, raiding and plundering trade caravans, and attacking and looting non-Muslim communities. The persuasive form of jihad had been thrown out the window; violent raids and wars became the modus operandi for Islam. In the process, Muhammad attacked the Jewish communities of Medina and elsewhere and exiled them, as he did in Banu Qainuqa, and Nadir, or exterminated them outright, as in Banu Quraiza and Mustaliq—by slaughtering all the adult males and enslaving the women and children. This latter *modus operandi* was responsible for the success of Muhammad's jihad in Allah's cause, for the success of Islam, and for what Islam is today.

JEFF KING: You said that, "Violent jihad is the heart of Islam; without it, Islam would most likely have died a natural death in the seventh century." Elaborate on what you mean by that.

The early years of his mission were a failure; he accumulated only about 250–350 disciples combined from Mecca and Medina. He had no power, no Islamic state. But during the next ten years in Medina, through the violent mode of jihad, Muhammad brought all of Arabia under Islam's feet with the help of tens of thousands of Muslims. He put a powerful, expansionist Islamic state firmly in place. Had Muhammad continued in the old persuasive manner of jihad during the entire period of his prophetic mission, he probably would have left behind 500 disciples, or certainly no more than 1,000–a small, powerless community of Muslims without a state of their own, which would have withered away soon after his death.

The fact is, Muhammad left behind an absolutist and powerful Islamic state. As news circulated that Muhammad was lying on his deathbed, many of the Bedouin tribes of the Arabian Peninsula renounced their allegiance to the Islamic state of Medina. They had been forced into Islam, and they believed that with Muhammad's demise the threat of Islam would be gone. With much difficulty, these revolts were put down by the first caliph, Abu Bakr. The insurrection was bloody and became known in the Islamic annals as the *Ridda Wars* (Arabic for "Wars of Apostasy").

So the validity of the above statement is all too obvious. Islam has spread, since its beginning, through violent jihad. It has survived and it stands today because of violent jihad.

JEFF KING: You have written about the jihad against the Indian subcontinent. Most Westerners know absolutely nothing about this part of history. Can you lay out a brief history of this multi-century campaign and how it played out?

Between 712 and 715, Islam made a successful and lasting encroachment into Sindh and Multan (in today's Pakistan), but stopped at the bank of the river Sindh. From the 990s to the 1020s AD, Sultan Mahmud of Ghazni, having consolidated power in Afghanistan and Pakistan, crossed over Sindh and made seventeen devastating expeditions into northwest India, establishing the power of Islam in Punjab.

In the 1190s AD, Afghan Sultan Muhammad Ghauri came to India. Having consolidated power over previously Muslim-conquered lands, he pushed further toward Ajmer and Delhi, eventually establishing the Islamic seat of power in the heart of India, namely the Sultanate of Delhi. From there, Islam continued to expand throughout the rest of India over the next 500 years.

After the establishment of the Sultanate of Delhi in 1206, Islam witnessed significant expansion under Sultan Alauddin Khilji (r. 1296–1316), reaching Southern India. Sultan Muhammad Shah Tughlaq (r. 1325–51) continued the push, but it was under the rather tolerant Mughal Emperor Akbar the Great (r. 1556–1605) that Islam established its strongest hold over the most expansive parts of India.

The only remaining non-Muslim territory was a small region in the extreme south. Next, Akbar's great-grandson Aurangzeb (r. 1658–1707), a zealous Sunni proselytizer, tried further expansion, but wasn't successful. While he tried to expand and consolidate in the South, his power fell apart in the North. Islam's hold on power was faltering, and a few decades later the mercenaries of the British East India Company started consolidating their power. They had moved into India in 1600, and began gaining control in Bengal in 1757.

JEFF KING: How violent was it?

Let me first point out that the mildest school of Islamic Law, the Hanafi School, was implemented in India. It elevated the polytheists of India (Hindus, Buddhists, and Jains) to the category of *dhimmi* subjects like the Jews and Christians. This was in spite of the fact that all schools of Islamic law demanded that non-Muslims be given the choice of death or conversion, as Muhammad had done. This shows that the invaders and rulers who came to India were milder in their treatment of the Indian infidels.

Regardless, the conquest was extremely violent. Muhammad Kasim (712–15), the first success story of the Islamic invasion of India, slaughtered all males of weapon-bearing age and enslaved their women and children. The violence of Sultan Mahmud's seventeen expeditions was extremely harsh. He killed large numbers of men, enslaved their women and children, and forced the remaining people to accept Islam. Indians received similar treatment during the campaigns of Muhammad Ghuari. Even after Muslim power was established in Delhi in 1206, Muslim rulers kept themselves busy with new incursions, either to put down revolts or to capture new territories. In all those campaigns, a similar *modus operandi* was applied: kill every man who carries a weapon in his hands, and enslave all the women and children. Only under emperor Akbar was the slaughter of captive soldiers prohibited. Still, when Akbar faced serious resistance, he would slaughter all the captives out of anger. This happened in Chittor in 1568. After he took the fort, following a long and difficult siege, he ordered the mass slaughter of the 30,000 defeated peasants who had fought on the side of the Rajput defenders.

JEFF KING: How many died over the centuries? How were Hindu women and children treated? How many went into slavery? What about the places of worship of non-Muslims?

The exact estimates are very difficult to make because the casualties in every campaign were not properly recorded. From the available documents, one historian estimated the number killed to be in the range of sixty to eighty million.

As concerns the treatment of women, the young ones were generally captured and used as slaves. They were used both as sex slaves and for household chores. The number of the enslaved was much larger than those killed. For example, the rough estimate of those killed by Muhammad Kasim (712–15) would not exceed 50,000, but he enslaved around 300,000 women and children. Similarly, Sultan Mahmud returned to Ghazni from his campaign to India in 1001-02 with 500,000 enslaved women and children. The number he had killed in that campaign was undoubtedly lower.

Places of worship were generally destroyed without exception. The priests of the temples, whether Hindu, Buddhist, or Jain, were targeted for slaughter as well.

JEFF KING: What were the methods used by Muslims to convert Hindus and other non-Muslims to Islam? How did Muslims deal with people who refused to convert to Islam?

Muhammad Kasim's mentor, Hajjaj, the governor of Iraq, sent him toward India with the instruction to kill anyone who would not embrace Islam. Kasim, after establishing himself in Sindh, found that Indian infidels were adamant in refusing Islam. They would rather die than convert. He was faced with too many infidels in densely populated Sindh who needed to be killed. He began to show them mercy on the condition that they pay higher taxes. When Hajjaj got wind of this leniency, he wrote to Kasim in anger, reprimanding him for breaking Allah's sacred command to kill all polytheists if they reject Islam. He threatened Kasim with charges of disobedience if he continued in this manner.

After that, Kasim started putting to the sword all those who refused to embrace Islam. But, it was too difficult a task to kill such a great multitude of resolute infidels. It also seemed to Kasim that killing them gained him nothing. Instead, he found it more useful to leave them alive and impose higher taxes upon them, which was the proposal made to him by the Hindus. He wrote back to Hajjaj in this regard. Hajjaj sent back a letter approving this practice. He called the Hindus a "protected people," once they had accepted submission and agreed to pay taxes, as was allowed for Jews and Christians in Islam. That's how India's Hindus, Buddhists, and Jains became elevated to the level of *dhimmi* subjects, which was later incorporated into the Hanafi Law, albeit in violation of Allah's command in the Qur'an.

Nonetheless, many later invaders, like zealously pious Sultan Mahmud and Taimur Long, among others, were not so lenient. Non-Muslims were forced to embrace Islam or death. The measures applied in conversion varied in different times and places, but Sufis in Kashmir, coming from the Middle East, prodded the rulers to treat Hindus harshly.

Similarly in Bengal, the young Hindu prince Sultan Jalaluddin (1414-1431) converted to Islam after his father was defeated by Muslim invaders. After he was placed on the throne, Jalaluddin gave infidels the choice of the Qur'an or death. More people converted to Islam in Bengal during his seventeen-year rule than during the next 300 years.

The most common incentive would be the implementation of crushing discriminatory taxes, which impoverished Hindus terribly. They had to beg at the doors of Muslims and even sell their wives and children in slave markets to pay the taxes imposed. Muslim tax collectors often drove away the children of tax-defaulting infidels to sell them as slaves. Many infidels, hundreds of thousands of them, unable to bear the exploitation and oppression of their Muslim rulers, took refuge in the jungle to live among wild animals. Of course, they could easily have escaped from these extreme, degrading difficulties by embracing Islam, as this compulsion did force a substantial number of Indians to do.

In my reading, enslavement was the most common method of conversion. I have mentioned the scale on which Muhammad Kasim and Sultan Mahmud took women and children as captives. With rare exceptions, such as under tolerant rulers like Emperor Akbar (1556–1605) and Sultan Zainul Abedin of Kashmir (r. 1423–1474), such enslavement remained a common feature in almost all Muslim campaigns in India. The captives, without exception, became Muslim. Moreover, the captive women, the major component in the enslaved lot, became tools for producing Muslim children for their Muslim masters, inflating the Muslim population in India.

JEFF KING: You challenge the widely held belief that Sufi Muslims expanded peacefully in India. What are your counter-arguments?

That paradigm has gained heavy currency among scholars of Islam, whether Muslim or non-Muslim. But my study of Indian historical documents reveals that the most famous Sufis of India were ideologically hateful of non-Islamic faiths. Their attitude toward Hindus reflected this sentiment so they didn't have the kind of outlook that would allow them to interact with Hindus in a respectful and humane manner or persuade them to embrace Islam.

Moreover, even the most-famously tolerant Sufis of India, such as Khajwa Moinuddin Chisti, Nizamuddin Auliya, and Shah Jalal, had come there from the Middle East to take part in the jihad to kill the infidels. Historically, most Sufi saints of the Middle Ages were generally *Ghazis*[25]. That is, they participated in jihad and killed infidels.

Khajwa Moinuddin Chisti fought alongside Muhammad Ghauri to defeat Prithviraj Chauhan in Ajmer (1192–93). Nizamuddin Auliya fought in a jihad led by Nasiruddin Qibacha in Multan, and Shah Jalal fought in a jihad expedition as well against King Guar Govinda of Bengal. It is said that these Sufi saints and their disciples played the crucial role in defeating the infidels in those wars.

Apart from this, Indian historical documents are rich in references to conversion in large numbers, which was generally achieved through violent or coercive means. There are no instances mentioned in which a Sufi saint converted a large number of non-Muslims to Islam through *peaceful* means. There are records of involvement of Sufi masters in large-scale conversions, namely in Kashmir and Gujarat.

---

[25] See pg. 340.

But, in all of those instances, the Sufis were found to have prodded and inspired their Muslim rulers to unleash barbarism against the infidels to force them into Islam. In this context, we can also add the example of Sultan Jalaluddin of Bengal who, after being converted and groomed by a famous Sufi, gave the infidels the choice of Islam or death. As already mentioned, this resulted in a huge number of conversions in his seventeen-year reign, which was not achieved again during the next 300 years.

Solid research of historical data reveals only this pattern of Sufis' role in conversion. Any assertion to the contrary is just fantasy, and is not historically supported.

JEFF KING: What threat does the growth in the Islamic population of the West pose?

It is rare that anyone who feels he is a Muslim would be able to subscribe to Western values. No matter how liberally-minded he or she might be, Western liberties, especially in sexual matters and freedom enjoyed by women, would be difficult to accept. Even a Muslim who thinks the West is much better than Muslim countries also feels inside that with restrictions on its liberty and sexual immorality, the West would become perfect. Now, with the radical and average Muslims, who are the overwhelming majority, one can easily get a sense of how Muslims will deal with those abhorrent, immoral Western values. They will have to increase in numbers in the West before this happens, but with high breeding rates, they will eventually gain the numbers to do what they wish. Moreover, since each and every Muslim finds Western culture abhorrent and immoral, their hatred of Western values tends to bring them closer to their faith. They become much more pious and follow religious prescriptions and proscriptions much more closely than when they were in their home countries. Their children's faith also becomes a degree more radical than that of their parents' generation. This trend is clearly visible in the West. So, with the second, third, and subsequent generations of Muslims, the threat to Western liberty becomes greater. If Muslims achieve the numbers they need, which they will, liberty will go; and without liberty, Western society will be dead.

JEFF KING: What is the goal of Muslims in the West? To Islamize it? What strategies are they using to achieve their goal?

Muslims are very a power-conscious people. Seeking dominance— Muslim dominance—is in their blood. The Qur'an outlines a blueprint for them to gain control of the whole world and establish Islamic rule. Consciously or subconsciously, even the most non-practicing Muslims believe that Islam, being the best and only true religion, will rule the world someday. Anywhere in the world, they will collectively work to that end. It is all too visible everywhere and no less conspicuously in the West. Today, Muslims in the West are demanding small concessions here and there, and as their numbers grow, they will demand more and more compromises and changes in Western society, culture, and governance to suit their Islamic outlook on life. Islamization has already begun; it will only gain strength with every passing year and decade. It may be possible that, within four or five decades, certain countries of Europe, such as the Netherlands and the UK, may become more Islamic and radical than Bangladesh, Indonesia, and Malaysia are today.

JEFF KING: What do you think should be done to tackle the danger of Islamism?

The only and lasting cure for Islam's threat to humanity is to expose Islam for what it is. The majority of Muslims are ignorant of the basic texts of Islam: the Qur'an, Hadith, and Sira (Muhammad's life story). They are mainly told that Islam is the last and the best monotheistic religion of God, and that, being the best religion, it will become the only religion on earth eventually. With this impression of their religion and their ignorance of Islam's real foundation, they just fiddle along as the radical few run the show. Under that state of affairs, Islam will become even more dangerous than it is today.

But if ordinary Muslims closely read those fundamental texts of Islam, it will become crystal-clear to them how fraudulently Muhammad founded this religion. They will see that he set up the doctrine in order to achieve his lust for power, wealth, and sex, and they will realize how horrible a person he was. Once they have knowledge of the inner workings of how Muhammad did it all, most of them would leave Islam. In this enlightenment lies the ultimate, lasting solution to Islam, the scourge of humanity.

In order to achieve that, those who have been enlightened to the true face of Islam must be active in pointing to the flaws in Islam's foundation. Both ex-Muslims and non-Muslims must force Muslims to take a close look at Islam's sacred texts. With the increased criticism of Islam in the days following 9/11, many Muslims have started to examine those canonical Islamic texts, and are duly leaving Islam. The community of ex-Muslims is silently growing at an ever-increasing pace, but I am unconvinced that this is happening at the rate needed to save progressive civilization from destruction by Islam. Unless there is a substantial change in the attitude toward Islam among both Muslims and non-Muslims over the next two to three decades, we may be done for. Islam may be the final winner in this battle for civilization.

Conclusion

You now know the truth about fundamentalist Islam. These truths aren't secrets hidden from public view, passed on from generation to generation through membership in a secret society.

Rather, fundamentalist Islam is very open about its beginnings and teachings. Islam's own holy books, the Qur'an and Hadith, tell us about Muhammad, his actions and personality, the tactics he used to spread Islam, and how Muslims are instructed to treat those who do not share their faith.

History tells us how Muhammad's successors consistently used warfare and slavery to advance Islam beyond the Arabian Peninsula. Experience tells us how Muhammad's most ardent and faithful followers interpret their faith today. The actions of today's Islamic fundamentalists dovetail perfectly with Muhammad and early Islam because their lives are dedicated to being faithful to Muhammad's life-example and his teachings.

Of course, most Muslims, especially in the West, are not radical Islamists. But the people who I interviewed for this volume (including fundamentalist Anjem Choudary) warn that most Muslims don't know what Islam actually demands of them. To put it bluntly, we live in peace with the Muslims around us because *they are unaware of, or unwilling to follow, the intolerance and violence demanded by their faith's most basic scriptures and Muhammad's example and commands.*

When speaking candidly, Muslim leaders do not disagree with this analysis. Many Muslim leaders will tell Westerners what the latter want to hear. But Islamic fundamentalists tell the faithful something very different: Islam is at war with those who refuse to submit.

For a long time, none of this seemed to matter very much. After all, Islam appeared to be far away. The Middle East was a slightly exotic place and most of us had never met a Muslim.

But all that has changed.

September 11 demonstrated that Muslims from the Middle East and elsewhere could bring war to America and, today, the US seems to be permanently at war in the Middle East. Immigration is bringing more Muslims to the US and especially to Europe, and suddenly we are hearing calls to allow the enforcement of Shariah law in the West. For ten years, Muslim governments have been going to the United Nations demanding laws and penalties against those who defame Islam. That is, they have been actively pushing for laws that would criminalize criticism of Islam.

The bottom line is that Islam needs to be *confronted as a religion and as a political system.* Islam's greatest need is for a great reformation to balance out its birth from a warrior culture and find a way to fit into modernity.

Presently, the West seems to be collectively closing its eyes, wringing its hands, and repeating the mantra, *"Islam is a religion of peace. Islam is a religion of peace."* Personally, I hope that most Muslims will agree with the mantra and reject the massive, decades long, and highly effective push to radicalize the world's Muslims by the Saudis and other Gulf Muslims. I'm all for trying to create a divide between the moderates and the radicals, but the West's efforts to do this are a bit like a man at the beach trying to turn back the tide with a bucket.

We must be more open about the founder of Islam and the violence encoded into the Qur'an and Hadith. Most people are not violent and don't want to follow violent people or systems. When confronted with the more distasteful elements of Islam they will leave it or they will force change from within Islam. They will push to reform Islam and bring it into modernity.

Westerners must learn more about Islam and the challenges which it poses. This isn't just a job for people in Washington. This is a job for you, your neighbors and your friends. Think independently and do more research about Muhammad, the Qur'an, and Hadith. You've just read from fourteen different leaders on Islam. Read more!

Many people, including Islamic fundamentalists, are trying to shut down discourse in regards to Islam. They intimidate, beat and kill those within Islam that disagree too strenuously or ask more questions than they are comfortable with. Open debate and questioning within fundamentalist Islam is not allowed.

Incredibly, you can see the same thing in the West! Many resort to name-calling of those who bring up unpleasant and inconvenient criticisms of Islam. Don't be cowed by those who say that anybody who criticizes Islam is a bigot or a racist! In fact, you should be very suspicious when this happens.

This clearly shuts down debate and open discussion. Ask them what other topics are there that we should not talk about in a democracy founded on free speech. Why is open discourse and independent thinking being so restricted on this issue? Why are people in a democracy siding with violent fundamentalists to shut down open debate?

The whole picture makes me think of a quote from a famous preacher of the 1800s: "The house is being robbed, its very walls are being digged down, but the good people who are in bed are too fond of the warmth, and too much afraid of getting broken heads, to go downstairs and meet the burglars; they are even half vexed that a certain noisy fellow will spring his rattle, or cry, 'Thieves!'"

The way forward is to bring Islam into modernity. Without open discussion, debate, and discourse we won't get there. My hope is that you will rouse yourself from your bed and listen to one noisy fellow.

I say the discussion on Islam must be uncensored!

Lessons & Takeaways

I've given you a lot of information from a great cross-section of sources, but I hope that you've been able to see the common elements in the mix. Here's my own list of "takeaways" that I drew from the process of interviewing these experts (as well as others). I hope that these and your own observations will help clear away some of the noise and debris and help speed your journey through the maze of understanding fundamentalist Islam.

1. **Don't hate.** The reason I gave this book the title I did is because the information the general public receives regarding Islam is truly censored. There are several reasons for this (fear comes readily to mind in the case of the media) but one of them could be altruistic.

   That is, the main danger of exposing Islam and Muhammad is that many people will respond with hate towards Muslims. Unfortunately, as human beings, we are tribal to the core and always ready, willing, and able to attack those who are different from us. In revealing the information in this book, I can only hope that my readers will not respond in that manner. That is absolutely not my intent.

   I am the president of an organization that helps victims of religious persecution, and I have seen too much hate and narrow-mindedness and the aftermath of the same. I've seen enough violence perpetrated on those with a different worldview or religion to last a lifetime. My core desire is to cut through the lies and confusion about Islam and bring an understanding of what Islam is, and to face the unpleasant truths about Islam, and yet to respond with mercy to the followers of Islam.

2. **Islam as a religion should be subject to criticism just like Buddhism, Christianity, Hinduism and Judaism.** Islam is not a race; it is a religion (and a political system – see #7). It is not racist to evaluate and discuss its shortcomings, even though many Muslims react violently in response. Such behavior must not be accommodated and enabled. Just as it is fair to discuss black marks on Christianity (or its denominations), such as the Crusades or pedophilic priests, it is fair to discuss Islam's shortcomings.

3. **Christianity, beginning in the 1800s, has gone through a period of intense scrutiny and challenge from outsiders.** Christianity did not welcome this scrutiny but it has led to the acknowledgement that it's acceptable for outsiders to question and challenge articles of faith. Islam's greatest need is modernization or reformation. A key to that happening is to encourage open discussion and to create an environment of self-criticism.

Europeans and Americans live in cultures that value diversity, tolerance, and equality. Americans came through a national struggle for civil rights for African Americans, while Western Europeans lived through the Nazi horror. Both of these watershed events gave us a well-earned sensitivity towards bigotry and hatred. While this sensitivity is inherently a good thing, it seems to have morphed into a political correctness that has left us effectively gagged on discussing questions of evil when associated with religion or perceived to be associated with a people group.

Criticism of Islam is not racism or bigotry. It is sheer silliness for anyone to throw that epithet around in response to open discussion of Islam.

In their effort to shield Islam from criticism, Muslim countries have introduced a resolution at the United Nations every year since 1999. The resolution, titled "Combating Defamation of Religions," effectively bans criticism of Islam but it's not binding on nations. They have introduced and passed the resolution ten years from 1999 to 2010 because they have attempted to take it to the next level and make it binding on nations. If they succeed with their effort, it will be the beginning of the end of the concept of freedom of religion and freedom of expression as we know it. 2011 was the first year it was defeated due to Western nations' opposition.

4. **Muhammad is completely different from other historical religious leaders.** While Islam is a religion like Buddhism, Christianity, or Judaism, its leader was nothing like Buddha, Jesus, Moses, Lao Tzu, or Gandhi. Far from being a peacemaker, he was a warlord in every sense of the word. This is not blasphemy or libel. In fact, our understanding of who Muhammad was comes from Islam's own holy books (The Qur'an, Hadiths, and Sira), not from books critical of Islam.

5. **Radical Islam is fundamentalist Islam.** Al-Qaeda, the Taliban, the Muslim Brotherhood, Wahhabi Islam, Hamas, al-Shabaab, etc. are all Islamic fundamentalist movements. Rather than being fringe groups who have twisted their own holy books, these groups are all striving for strict adherence to Muhammad's teachings and lifestyle as revealed in the Qur'an, Hadith, and Sira.

6. **Most Muslims in the West aren't interested in taking up arms, but a significant percentage has radical views.** Surveys of Muslims in many countries over the last few years produce data that is both reassuring and alarming. The bottom line is that, as you would expect, most Muslims in the West aren't ready to take up arms for the cause. At the same time, many have quite radical views and there seems to

be a clear worry among Muslims in the West about a trend of increased radicalization. When you combine these last two points with my point in #5 about the role of the Saudis and their massive multi-decade effort to radicalize the world's Muslims, it produces a worrisome picture.

In 2006, *Pew Research* conducted two landmark surveys of Western Muslims:

http://pewglobal.org/2006/06/22/the-great-divide-how-westerners-and-muslims-view-each-other/

http://pewglobal.org/2006/07/06/muslims-in-europe-economic-worries-top-concerns-about-religious-and-cultural-identity/).

There was a fairly high percentage of Muslims who found there was a struggle between being a devout Muslim and living in a modern society. This is somewhat of a Rorschach question, but when compared with other data, I tend to see this as a condemnation of modern secular society by Muslims—a gauge of dissatisfaction with the societies they live in, but you can take that conclusion with a very large grain of salt.

Sense of Muslim Identity Among Muslims *(2006 Pew Research Poll)*			
Country	Percentage of Muslims that see a "fairly strong" to "strong" sense of Muslim identity in the country	Percentage of Muslims that see sense of Muslim identity among youth growing	Muslims that see a struggle in their country between moderates and fundamentalists
France	75%	58%	56%
Great Britain	72%	77%	58%
Spain	64%	46%	21%
Germany	46%	54%	49%

Other points of concern were the percentage of Muslims who want to remain distinct from society, as well as the high numbers who put their Muslim identity ahead of their nationality. Putting God ahead of country is not disturbing in itself, and is even laudable, depending on what God is telling you to do via your scriptures and your theological leaders.

This next chart of data was alarming because of the high number of Muslims that reported that there was a struggle under way between the moderates and fundamentalists in addition to the growing Muslim identity among youth. Again, combine this with lesson #5 and you should be concerned.

Religious Identity According to Nation (2006 Pew Research Poll)				
Country	Muslims that see a conflict between being a devout Muslim and living in a modern society	Percentage of Muslims that want to remain distinct from society	Percentage of Muslims that see themselves as Muslims first (as opposed to being a Brit or German)	Percentage of Christians that see themselves as Christians first
Great Britain	47%	35%	81%	24%
Spain	25%	27%	69%	14%
Germany	36%	52%	66%	33%
France	28%	21%	46%	14%
Nigeria			53%	53%
Pakistan			87%	
Turkey			51%	
Egypt			59%	
Nigeria			71%	53%

The most alarming finding by far was in regards to Muslim citizens' views on suicide bombing. You can see in the next table the percentage of Muslims in various countries who said they support suicide bombing: often, sometimes, or rarely. In other words, the percentage of Muslims who fully support, or at least don't rule out, the most violent, heinous, and indefensible tool of radical Islam: the killing and dismemberment of innocent men, women, and children. Please keep in mind that strangers called these people on the phone and asked them about something that can get them targeted by the security services. How many didn't answer honestly? We'll never know, but the percentage of honest answers were chilling enough.

When you start doing the math in terms of how many Muslims there are in each country who support suicide bombing, it is even more alarming. This number in each country is the pool that radicals are fishing from and trying to grow.

Suicide Bombing Support (2006 Pew Research Poll)			
Country	Percentage of Muslims that said they support suicide bombing (often/sometimes/rarely)	Number of Muslims in each country*	Number with radical views
Germany	13%	4,026,000	523,380
Great Britain	24%	1,647,000	395,280
Spain	25%	650,000	162,500
France	35%	3,554,000	1,243,900
Egypt	53%	78,513,000	41,612,000
Jordan	57%	6,202,000	806,000
Nigeria	69%	78,056,000	18,733

*Muslim population data came from 2009 *Pew* poll "Mapping the Global Muslim Population."

There was another alarming poll in 2006 by the *Sunday Telegraph/ICM* that attracted widespread notice because it found that 40% of British Muslims wanted Sharia law. Some common parts of Sharia are:

- females receive half that of males in inheritance

- men may divorce women by the triple talaq (repeating a phrase three times)
- drinkers and gamblers are to be whipped
- physical abuse of women is condoned since it is approved in the Qur'an and Hadith
- thieves have their hands cut off
- homosexuals could be executed
- unmarried fornicators could be whipped
- adulterers are to be executed (typically just the women).

You can argue that in the West if we had Sharia it might or might not include this law, but the point is that 40% of British Muslims are in favor of Sharia and all of the above are common laws/punishments under Sharia in various countries.

In the same survey, 20% of respondents felt sympathy with the "feelings and motives" of the suicide bombers. Again, how many others, who have sympathy for terrorists and radical ideas, did not answer a stranger's questions because they felt as if they were under suspicion in their culture?

Another 2006 UK poll of 1,000 British males found that 23% of British Muslims said the London Tube bombings were justified. That's 370,000 Muslims who said the murder of fifty-six and the wounding of 700+ innocents was justified!

A 2007 survey of American Muslims seems to bear out the experience of most Americans. That is that US Muslims are more mainstream and integrated than Muslim immigrant populations in other Western countries.

http://pewresearch.org/assets/pdf/muslim-americans.pdf

Still, there are worrisome answers. For instance, 61% of US Muslims polled were worried about the rise of Islamic extremism in the US. They know their culture, their youth, and the influences on them and 61% said they were worried radical Islam is growing in the United States.

When asked the question, "Is suicide bombing justified," *Pew* chose to assemble the data in a different way than they have in the past so it's hard to know just how much of an issue it is. Previously they gave three choices (1. Often/Sometimes, 2. Rarely, and 3. Never). In the 2007 survey they combined the answers for "rarely" and "never" justified.

This is a departure from the past where they combined "rarely" with "sometimes." It basically renders the question useless and has to make you wonder. After all, "sometimes" and "rarely" are essentially different grades of "yes." To combine a partial "yes" answer with a definitively negative answer makes me wonder what is going on.

Finally, 60% of respondents said Arabs either didn't carry out the 9/11 attacks or they didn't know who did.

7. **Jihad: The world of Islam vs. the world of war.** Muhammad and fundamentalist Islam divide the world into "us" and "them." There are Muslims, and then there are *kafirs* (a derogatory name for non-Muslims). That isn't too different from many religions or from basic human nature, but the fact is that Islam divides the world into what it calls the World of Islam (*Dar al-Islam*), areas that have been conquered by Islam, and the World of War (*Dar al-Harb*), parts of the world not yet dominated by Islam or Islamic law.

Jihad is the tool that Islam has used historically to expand Islam into areas that were not subjugated by Islam already. Jihad, as a term in the Qur'an and Hadith overwhelmingly means violent attack. Many apologists and others will attempt to say jihad means "inner-struggle." That is, growing Islam inside one's self. Do the research. This is at best a joke. At worst, it is intentional deception.

Islam exists today, overwhelmingly, because of Muhammad's doctrine of jihad. Without jihad, Islam would have died in obscurity. After more than a decade of preaching, Muhammad had only about 150 adherents. It was at this point that Muhammad introduced the doctrine of jihad. He said that Allah directed him and his followers to violently attack, kill, and plunder non-Muslims and subjugate them.

Muhammad personally participated in more than twenty-five of these attacks. Tribes and nations that submitted to Islam and became his followers could live. If they resisted, and they were infidels, then the men were killed and the women and children sold as slaves. If the conquered were "people of the book" (Jews and Christians), then they weren't forced to convert but were subjected to humiliating lives as third-class citizens within Islamic lands. For centuries after Muhammad's death, various Caliphs used his same methods to subjugate vast tracts of land resulting in the deaths of up to 80 million in India alone.

8. **Islam is more than a religion. It's a religious/political system.** The introduction of jihad caused the number of people following Muhammad to explode and represents Islam's transition from a garden variety religion into a new politico-religious hybrid. Islamic law (or Sharia) was established with all kinds of regulations to give guidance as

to how to rule those within the confines of Islam and how to deal with those peoples not yet conquered. There has been no Reformation or Vatican II in Islam. In other words, there has been no acknowledgement that the political and theological realms are separate and that jihad is illegitimate.

9. **It's not cherry picking. It's abrogation.** There are many conflicting verses within the Qur'an and Hadith, which often leads to confusion on issues like violence and jihad. You will find one verse advocating kindness to people of other faiths and another one urging that they be oppressed and killed. Therefore, anytime a critic of Islam brings up one of these verses they are accused of "cherry picking" violent verses. "After all, the Bible, has many violent verses" will accompany the charge of cherry picking.

    Muslim scholars have dealt with these contradictory verses for over a thousand years through the doctrine of "abrogation." That is, Muhammad's later sayings supersede or "abrogate" earlier ones. This might seem unexceptional to Christians, who believe that the New Testament supersedes the covenant established by the Old Testament. However, in the case of Muhammad, his sayings tend to grow more violent over time. Early in his life he had little power and thus emphasized tolerance. Over time he grew in military might and was able to impose his will on others. Thus, in general, Muhammad's violent instructions usually overrule his more peaceful utterances.

10. **Taqiyya–All is fair in the world of war.** Sharia law stipulates that it is *halal* (approved/legal) to use lying and deception with your enemies during war. Muhammad and later Caliphs involved in military escapades extensively used deception as a strategy to defeat their enemies. Because Islam considers itself at war with all those who are not yet

under Sharia law, many leading Muslims who follow the most intolerant form of Islamic theology employ this principle in dealing with the Western public. They will cite peaceful verses (abrogated verses) to Western audiences, while preaching the hateful verses in Arabic back in their own countries.

A good place to start your research into this topic is: The Middle East Research Institute (MEMRI). MEMRI has collected a lot of video evidence of top Muslims camouflaging their true intentions when speaking in the US or Europe (go to www.memri.org).

11. **The role of Saudi Arabia.** Saudi Arabia plays a malignant role throughout the Muslim world and beyond. Spurred by the massive influx of petro dollars, starting roughly forty years ago, the Saudi government has spent more than $100 billion building radical mosques and madrassas (Islamic boarding schools), paying the salaries of Islamic clerics, and indoctrinating imams and students alike in Wahhabi Islam. The most fundamental strain of Islamic interpretation, Wahhabism, demands strict observance of and adherence to the teachings of Muhammad as presented in the Qur'an and Hadith. These teachings are commonly used to justify violence, especially against non-Muslims. In this way, the Saudi investment has paid off in hatred, bloodshed, violence, and the recent rise in Islamic terrorism. In the US, many experts are warning that up to 70% of US mosques are funded and controlled by Saudi/Wahhabi Islamists.

12. **Islam is a religion of peace.** The ultimate strategic answer to Islamic radicalism is the rise of more moderate and tolerant interpretations of Islam. *"Islam is a religion of peace"* is a tool in the strategy to marginalize Islamic fundamentalists. The downside to this strategy is that it has

led to the strangulation of open debate, which is vital to bring about the modernization of Islam that is so desperately needed. Without discussing Islam's shortcomings and weaknesses, there is less impetus for change.

While the West should look for policies that will encourage an intra-Islamic transformation, that process will have to be led and adopted by Muslims. While I applaud efforts to build up the moderates and shame the radicals, these efforts, in light of the massive, long term radicalization program by the Saudis, feel very insignificant in comparison to the overwhelming efforts of the Saudis.

13. **Islam is the persecutor—not the persecuted**. Saudi and other wealthy Gulf Arabs have funded a massive propaganda campaign in the UN and Western countries via certain groups that portrays Islam as a victim. This campaign has paid off in terms of public perception that Islam has been unfairly picked on.

The truth is that fundamentalist Islam is responsible for a never-ending series of extremely violent attacks around the world. Far from being a victim, Islam, in keeping with the nature of its founder and in keeping with its history, is a violent aggressor.

If you would like to research this you can start by going to: http://www.thereligionofpeace.com/index.html#Attacks. This website keeps an ongoing, up-to-date, list of Islamic attacks against other Muslims and people of other faiths. The scale of attacks is truly mindboggling.

Two US government resources you can access are from the State Department and the US Commission on International Religious Freedom. These reports are not as detailed or extensive and have to run through the political correctness gauntlet of the US government. Still, they are excellent as authoritative sources.

State Dept. Report: http://www.state.gov/g/drl/rls/irf/ .

US Commission on International Religious Freedom Reports: http://www.uscirf.gov/reports-and-briefs/annual-report.html

Glossary #1

Terms

A:

Abrogation: The doctrine that the latter verses of the holy book supersede the earlier verses.

Ahl al-Kitab (people of the Book): The term is specific to Christians, Sabians, and Jews. Because these groups follow the God of Abraham, they are allowed tolerance by the Qur'an.

Allah: Most commonly used name for God in Islam. Its roots stem from *al* (the) and *ilah* (Deity). The word was used in pre-Islamic Arabia in association with one of many gods, and referred to the deity of creation in pagan Mecca.

B-F:

Banu Qurayza/Banu Qainuqa: At the time of Muhammad, there were three main Jewish tribes in Medina. These are two of the tribes. After defeating the **Banu Qurayza,** Muhammad slaughtered all the adult male inhabitants.

Caliphate: The first government of the Islamic nation. It is a republic system that links Islam's political principles.

Corvee: Usually unpaid labor that is imposed upon individuals of lower class. The individual is not owned outright, but is used occasionally for mandatory work.

Dar al-Harb: "Domain of War." This is a term used to describe a country not under Islamic law. It can be assumed there is hostility between these territories and Islamic states, as the areas that have peace agreements may be referred to as dar al-ahd or dar al-sulh.

Dar al-Islam: World of Islam. Areas that have been conquered by Islam.

Dawa(h): The preaching or proselytizing of Islam.

Dhimmi/Dhimmitude: A dhimmi is a non-Muslim living with restrictions that effectively make him a third-class citizen in Muslim lands. Dhimmis are individuals; dhimmitude is the state they find themselves in.

Dinars: Currency of Middle East and certain North African countries.

Fatah: A military organization of Arab Palestinians that began in the 1950s. Its founder was Yasir Arafat.

Fatwa: An opinion concerning Islamic law in light of religious insight. Fatwa is made by a scholar, and in the case of Shia, it can be binding.

Fedayeen: "Those who sacrifice." Groups not in the military, but who volunteer (militia).

G-I:

Ghazi: "To Raid." It is a term used to refer to those who have fought for Islam, specifically the "Ghazi warriors."

Ghazwa: Having its roots in the word Ghazi, it is used in regards to a battle that Muhammad led.

Hadith: One of the two holy books of Islam. The Hadiths can simply be defined as the "words and deeds of Muhammad" and are viewed as practical guides to a Muslim's life and a "road map" for holy living. Whereas the Qur'an is a confusing jumble of unrelated narratives in an ancient Arabic dialect not understood by the vast majority of the non-Arabic speaking Muslim world, the Hadiths on the contrary are quite readable and comprehensible. In actuality, most Islamic theology comes not from the Qur'an as one might expect, but rather directly from the Hadiths. This includes Sharia, or Islamic law. Islamic countries today which are governed by a strict code of conduct designed by Allah (such as Iran, Saudi Arabia, and Afghanistan under the Taliban) extract their tyrannical ordnances directly from the Hadiths.

Hadiths

There are 6 major authoritative Hadiths

Sunnah: The Hadiths and the Sira from which the Hadiths are drawn.	The Two Most Authoritative Hadiths:		The Remaining Four Authoritative Hadiths:			
	Sahih al-Bukhari Imam Bukhari (died 870), includes 7275 verses	**Sahih Muslim** Muslim b. al-Hajjaj (died 875), includes 9200 verses	**Sunan al-Sughra** al-Nasa'i (died 915)	**Sunan Abu Dawood** Abu Dawood (died 888)	**Jami al-Tirmidhi** al-Tirmidhi (died 892)	**Sunan ibn Majah** Ibn Majah (died 887)

Sira

The Hadiths were drawn from the Sira (biographies) of Muhammad, written by various authors.

Sira 1	Sira 2	Sira 3
Sirat Rasul Allah written by Ibn Ishaq (written 780 150 years after M.'s death). Translated into English by A. Guillaume. Professor of Arabic at the University of London.	Ibn Hisham	Ibn Tabari

Prior to the Sira, the acts of Mohammad were carried forward by the Qussas. A qussa was a professional storyteller who kept the verbal record of history).

Halal: The term refers to something that is permissible by Islamic law.

Haram: The first meaning of haram is an act or deed that is unlawful, or legally forbidden. Secondly, it refers to a sanctuary or holy site, such as a mosque.

Hezbollah: A group of Shiites (or Shias). It is a military and political group from Lebanon.

Imam: The person responsible for leading prayers and services (Sunni). It can also refer to a community's spiritual leader.

Islam: The word Islam means, "Submitting to Allah". It is the religion the follows the Qur'an, and the teachings of the Prophet Mohammad. It is a monotheistic faith following in line after Judaism, and Christianity. It believes that Abraham, Moses, and Jesus were all prophets of God. However, Islam teaches the writings found in Hebrew and Christian literature have been corrupted. Islam follows five pillars of faith:

1. Shahadah: The wholehearted reciting of the basic creed of Islam (there is none worthy of worship except Allah, and Muhammad is his prophet)
2. Salah: The five daily prayers
3. Sawm: Participation of fasting during Ramadan
4. Zakat: Giving of alms
5. Hajj: A mandatory pilgrimage to Mecca for all who can afford the trip

J-L:

Jihad: "To strive." The term can refer to the internal struggle of Muslims to keep their faith or the external struggle to enlarge Muslim territory. The overwhelming use of the term in the Qur'an has to do with external struggle (warfare). A Muslim who perishes in violent jihad is granted a place in heaven.

Jizyah: A tax imposed on non-Muslims living under an Islamic government. The tax allowed them to live under the protection of the state and remain exempt from military service and payment of Zakah (alms)

Kharaj: A land tax placed on lands conquered by Muslims. The tax has no direct ties to the Qur'an, or the hadith.

M-Q:

Madrassa: A Muslim school or academic institution.

Mecca (Makkah, Bakkah): Saudi Arabian city known as the holiest meeting place in Islam.

Medina: The city where Muhammad was buried. It is the second holiest city of Islam.

Mujahideen: Someone who participates in jihad. It is from the same root as jihad.

Muslim: "One who submits to God." The term refers to someone who accepts Islam as truth, and their way of life.

Quraish (Quraysh): The dominant tribe in Mecca at the time Islam was introduced. It is also Muhammad's tribe.

Qur'an (Koran): The Holy book of Islam. Muslims believe it to be the direct words of Allah, orated by Gabriel, to Muhammad between the years of 610 and 632 AD.

R-S:

Ramadan: The ninth month of the Islamic calendar and the month of fasting. During the month of Ramadan, Muslims refrain from eating, drinking, and sexual relations from sun rise, to sun set.

Salah: "Prayer." The five daily prayers are:

1. Fajr; morning prayer
2. Duhr; early afternoon or noon prayer
3. Asr; late afternoon prayer
4. Maghrib; sunset prayer
5. Isha; late evening prayer

Second Intifada: Palestinian and Israeli conflict beginning in 2000.

Sharia (Shariah): The law of Islam.

Shiites (Shia): A group of Muslims who believe the imam must be in the lineage of Muhammad.

Sira/Sirat Rasul Allah: These are the biographies of Muhammad that were used to assemble the Hadith. These biographies are the backbone of Islam, have influenced the creation of Sharia law, and have been helpful in interpreting the Qur'an. The oldest surviving Sira, which is also deemed most reliable, is the Sirat Rasul Allah written by Ibn Ishaq approximately 150 years after Muhammad's death. It is farfetched to believe that anything close to accuracy can be attained generations after the death of the primary source. Yet, even worse, Ishaq's original biography no longer exists, but only now survives in later editions by Ibn Hisham and Ibn Tabari who omitted large segments from the original.

Sunnah: Sunnah are the acts, deeds, and words of Muhammad and encompass the Sira and Hadith (see also "Hadith").

Surah (Sura): A chapter of the Qur'an.

T-Z:

Tafsir: "Interpretation." The term commonly refers to an exegesis of the Qur'an.

Taqiyya (Tauria): The practice of intentionally deceiving others. It is considered halal (legal) within Islam when dealing with enemies. Muhammad and later Caliphs used deception to conquer their enemies and the practice continues today. Many fundamentalists adhere to the traditional Islamic view that the world is divided into: 1) that already conquered by Islam, 2) the rest of the world where Islam is at war. In that viewpoint, it is appropriate to use Taqiyya in dealing with non-Muslims.

Ummah: The community of believers of Islam.

Wahhabi: Fundamentalist religious branch or movement within Islam. This is the most violent and intolerant sect of Islam formed by religious leader Muhammad ibn Abd al-Wahhab in the 1700's. Wahhab and Ibn Saud formed a strategic partnership that to this day lies at the core of the Saudi power structure. It is the most influential sect of Islam due to Saudi/Gulf funding. The Saudi's have admitted to spending more than $100 billion expanding Wahhabi Islam since the major influx of petro dollars in the 1970's. Funds to expand Wahhabbi Islam go to building radical mosques led by radical Wahhabi clerics and madrassas (Islamic boarding schools) around the world. If there is a big shiny new mosque in your town, odds are it is Wahhabi-funded.

Zakat: The giving of alms, almost charity-giving. It is mandatory.

Glossary #2

Islamic Groups

Council on American-Islamic Relations (CAIR)

CAIR is an Islamic advocacy group in Washington DC. They were founded in June 1994, partially in response to the view of Arab and Muslim stereotypes. In the 2007 Holy Land Foundation trial, they were listed as unindicted co-conspirators. After the time of the trial, there were several reports of concern as to CAIR's alleged relationships with terrorist groups. These include alleged ties to Hamas' senior leadership.

Hamas ("Islamic Resistance Movement")

Hamas has participated in dozens of suicide bombings against Israeli civilians since 1993, killing over 500. Iraq, under Saddam Hussein, provided a stipend to families of suicide bombers, but since the Iraqi War, funding comes primarily from Iran, Saudi Arabia, and a large network of Islamic charities. This democratically elected terrorist organization (winning elections in 2006) has issued threats to the West, pledging to defeat Israel and anyone who has ever supported Israel.

Islamic Society of North America (ISNA)

INSA has been described in the media as the largest North American Muslim organization. It was formed in 1982 and is headquartered in Plainfield, Indiana. They are an umbrella group with a large number of affiliations throughout the United States. They hold an annual conference that has the capacity to be the largest single meeting of Muslims in North America.

The group was named in the Holy Land Foundation trial in 2007. They were listed as an unindicted co-conspirator. According to Wikipedia, one journalist's interpretation of the court documents states, "ISNA is an integral part of the [Muslim] Brotherhood's efforts to wage jihad against America through non-violent means." (http://en.wikipedia.org/wiki/Islamic_Society_of_North_America). They have also had allegations that they are a front for the promotion of Wahhabi political, ideological, and theological structure in the United States, as well as having ties to extremists.

The Muslim Brotherhood (TMB, MB, The Society of Muslim Brotherhood)

This organization is the world's largest and oldest Islamic political group. Hasan al-Banna (a twenty-two-year-old schoolteacher) founded the Muslim Brotherhood in 1928 with the objective of creating an Islamic revival after the fall of the Ottoman Empire. He built on the foundation of Wahhabism, and trained his students in the way of jihad. The Muslim Brotherhood sees itself in a titanic struggle between Islam and the rest of the world – from which there will only be one victor.

TMB soon entered politics, began a violent campaign against Israel and committed acts of terrorism inside Egypt. TMB hopes to spread Sharia law to all countries, and fights to achieve that goal. Numerous assassination attempts were carried out, and two were successful, in 1948 and 1981 (when Anwar Sadat was killed). In 1987, TMB founded Hamas, and has given birth to a host of other terrorist organizations and political, theological, and financial entities since then.

North American Islamic Trust (NAIT)

Founded by the Muslim Student Association in 1973, NAIT is the financial arm of that group. Based in Indiana, they are a 501(c)(3) non-profit. They hold titles for mosques, and schools, as well as other estates. They advertise that, "NAIT facilitates the realization of American Muslims' desire for a virtuous and happy life in a Shariah-compliant way" (www.NAIT.net).

The group, as well as one of their board members, was named in the 2007 Holy Land Foundation terrorist trial as an unindicted co-conspirator. This trial dealt with funding going to Hamas.

Organization of the Islamic Conference (OIC)

With three official languages, the OIC is an international organization that represents fifty-seven member states with a permanent delegation to the United Nations. The group was established in 1969 to serve as a collective umbrella to Islamic nations. They act as a voice unifying Islam. They support Palestine becoming an independent nation with Jerusalem as its capital.

The World Muslim League (International Islamic Relief Organization, IIRO)

This group is an international non-governmental organization (NGO) based out of Saudi Arabia. It was formed by royal decree in 1979 under the arm of the Muslim World League. In the US, they have been accused of spreading Islamic militancy around the globe, and have been called a radical Islamic institution. There have also been strong accusations that IIRO has been the front to launder money to Al Qaeda. The group itself is asking the UN to remove its name from its list of groups supporting terrorism.

Resources for Further Study

Dhimmitude:
- *Islam and Dhimmitude: Where Civilizations Collide* by Bat Ye'or
- *The Dhimmi: Jews & Christians Under Islam* by Bat Ye'or
- *The Decline of Eastern Christianity Under Islam: From Jihad to Dhimmitude* by Bat Ye'or

Muhammad:
- *The Life of Muhammad* by Ibn Ishaq and translated by A. Guillaume
- *Muhammad: His Life Based on the Earliest Sources* by Martin Lings
- *The Truth about Muhammad: Founder of the World's Most Intolerant Religion* by Robert Spencer
- *The Quest for the Historical Muhammad* by Ibn Warraq

Jihad:
- *The Legacy of Jihad: Islamic Holy War and the Fate of NonMuslims* by Andrew G., M.D. Bostom
- *Stealth Jihad: How Radical Islam is Subverting America without Guns or Bombs* by Robert Spencer
- *Islam and Terrorism* by Mark A. Gabriel

Qur'an:
- *What the Qur'an Really Says: Language, Text, and Commentary* by Ibn Warraq
- *The Origins of the Qur'an: Classic Essays on Islam's Holy Book* by Ibn Warraq
- *The Complete Infidel's Guide to the Qur'an* by Robert Spencer
- *Secrets of the Qur'an* by Don Richardson

Sharia Law:
- *Reliance of the Traveller: The Classic Manual of Islamic Sacred Law Umdat al-Salik* by Ahmad Ibn Lulu Ibn al-Naqib and Noah Ha Mim Keller

Islam:
- *Why I Am Not a Muslim* by Ibn Warraq

- *The Politically Incorrect Guide to Islam (and the Crusades)* by Robert Spencer
- *Religion of Peace?: Why Christianity Is and Islam Isn't* by Robert Spencer
- *Muslims: Their Religious Beliefs and Practices* by Andrew Rippin

History of Islam:
- *The Middle East: A Brief History of the Past 2,000 Years* by Bernard Lewis

About the Author

Jeff King has been the president of www.persecution.org (International Christian Concern) since 2003.

Persecution.org is a Washington, D.C.-based non-profit 501(c)(3) dedicated to assisting and sustaining international victims of religious persecution through effective Assistance, Awareness, and Advocacy for international victims of persecution.

In regards to advocacy, they work with the US Congress, Senate, State Department, and White House to free prisoners jailed for religious activities and to pressure countries that persecute.

32932623R00202

Made in the USA
Middletown, DE
23 June 2016